Patrick Pearse and the Theatre
Mac Piarais agus an Téatar

PATRICK PEARSE
AND THE THEATRE
Mac Piarais agus an Téatar

Eugene McNulty & Róisín Ní Ghairbhí

EDITORS

FOUR COURTS PRESS

FOUR COURTS PRESS LTD
7 Malpas Street, Dublin 8, Ireland
www.fourcourtspress.ie
and in North America for
Four Courts Press
c/o ISBS, 920 NE 58th Avenue, Suite 300, Portland, OR 97213

A catalogue record for this title
is available from the British Library.

ISBN 978–1-84682–618—4

Printed in England by
CPI Antony Rowe, Chippenham, Wilts.

Contents/*Clár*

Illustrations

Acknowledgments/*Buíochas*

The editors wish to thank Martin Fanning and everyone at Four Courts Press for their dedication to this project and for steering it with such patience and fine judgment. Thank you to Sam Tranum for his good-humoured stewardship of the project in its closing stages. A special mention is due to Brian Crowley, curator of the Pearse Museum, whose generosity of vision and careful curation of Pearse papers and artefacts have helped smooth the path for countless scholars. We thank our colleagues at St Patrick's Campus, Dublin City University, and Mary Immaculate College, Limerick, for their interest and support. The staffs of the National Library of Ireland and of the libraries in our two home institutions have been as helpful and crucial as always. We also wish to register our appreciation to the research committee of St Patrick's College for the strong support offered to this project at various stages of its development.

This book has its origins in a symposium designed to (re)consider Pearse's connections to the theatre in various contexts, and the editors gratefully acknowledge the contributions of all those who attended that event, particularly the speakers, whose passion and intellectual rigour made the symposium such a stimulating and memorable occasion. Many additional insights came from astute audience members and theatre workshop participants. Míle buíochas to Colm Hefferon for guiding the workshop with such care and insight and to Síle Denvir and the Caithréim team for their wonderful musical contribution. Buíochas le Foras na Gaeilge a chuir maoiniú ar fáil chun go ndéanfaí aistriú comhuaineach ar pháipéir Ghaeilge an tsiompóisiam. Is mór againn gur roinn siad linn fís bhunaigh an tsiompóisiam: an dátheangachas agus an éigse a bheith lárnach sa phlé acadúil.

Buíochas leis an Dr Ríona Nic Congáil agus leis an Ollamh Máirín Nic Eoin a roinn arís go fial a sáreolas ar fhoinsí a bhain le tréimhse na hAthbheochana. Buíochas le Liam Ó Paircín as an innéacs a ullmhú agus le Róisín Nic Dhonncha, Breandán Ó Cróinín, Deirdre Nic Mhathúna agus Caitríona Ó Torna as a gcabhair agus leis an Ollamh Mícheál Mac Craith a chuir suim leanúnach sa togra. Ba mhaith le Róisín tacaíocht a muintire agus a cairde a aithint agus aitheantas ar leith a thabhairt do Cheann Roinn na Gaeilge, Máire Ní Neachtain, agus dá comhghleacaithe nua i Roinn na

Gaeilge agus i ranna eile i gColáiste Mhuire gan Smál agus dá hiar-chomhgh-leacaithe i gColáiste Phádraig as a spreagadh intleachtúil agus as a gcairdeas buan. Eugene McNulty would like to give a special mention to his colleagues, old and new, in the recently formed School of English at Dublin City University. It is a privilege to be part of such a brilliant group of scholars and educators. In the end, of course, this book is the culmination of the work of its contributors, and we extend our heartfelt thanks to each of them for their patience and dedicated scholarship.

Introduction: stages of the Rising

EUGENE McNULTY AND RÓISÍN NÍ GHAIRBHÍ

When Pearse summoned Cuchulain to his side.
What stalked through the Post Office? What intellect,
What calculation, number, measurement, replied?
—W.B. Yeats, 'The statues', 1938

In recent years it has become common to describe the Easter Rising in terms derived from the theatrical: as a self-conscious act of political performance in search of a new ('postcolonial') *mise en scène*; as a piece of 'guerrilla theatre' intent on occupying and capturing Dublin's streets (and thus rupturing the political fourth wall); as a symbolic performative act attuned to the conceptual contours of the Christian Easter narrative; as a cathartic show of independence; or, alternatively, as a scene of betrayal when locating the rebellion in the context of those entrenched in the Western Front. Standing centre stage in most of these depictions we find Patrick Pearse, a political activist who understood intimately the mechanics and potential of public performance. As a theatre practitioner and theorist Pearse had long reflected on the relationship between performance and audience, and on the mobilizing effect of drama. Like Pearse, then, the essays in this book are interested in the politicality of performance and the performativity of politics. The present editors' 2013 edition of Pearse's dramatic works, *Patrick Pearse: collected plays/Drámaí an Phiarsaigh*, was envisaged as an initial sourcebook for those interested in Pearse's life and work in theatre.[1] This introduction to the current volume identifies the key contours of Pearse's theatre-work and the various phases of critical studies that have addressed his life and afterlife in theatre. The contributors to this volume, a gathering of scholars from a range of disciplines, seek to reassess Pearse's dramatic work by examining it within further critical contexts, and by posing new questions about its content and impact. The present reassessment takes place against a backdrop of renewed reflection on the cultural and intellectual formations of those who participated in the Rising, and on how these lines of influence informed their wider outlooks on life and politics.

1 Róisín Ní Ghairbhí and Eugene McNulty (eds), *Patrick Pearse: collected plays/Drámaí an Phiarsaigh* (Dublin, 2013).

In 'The statues', Yeats recalls the creative impulse that drove what has now come to be called the 'revolutionary generation'. It could be contended that the impulse of the foundation myth of modern Irish nationalism – synopsized a little egotistically in Yeats' own speculation in another poem as to whether his play *Cathleen Ni Houlihan* had 'sent out certain men the English shot'[2] – engendered a constrictive narrative of Irish cultural history. The trajectory of a cultural nationalism that builds a dizzying momentum and then culminates in a (failed) Rising informed much historiography of the twentieth century. Thus the cultural revival was seen as a prelude to the 'real' story – the fight for freedom (or indeed the failure of the fight for freedom) – and the nuances of that cultural reawakening were often swept away by the compelling metanarrative. More often than not historians discuss Pearse's theatre solely within the context of his radicalization. The fact that the Rising was in simple military terms a failure also served to create the sense of it as coda: the ideas that circulated previous to the Rising were literally shot down. However, that well-worn historiographical path, which prioritized the narrative of men gaining and using guns, has now given way to a more nuanced story, of a revolutionary generation influenced by feminism, socialism, art and literature.

Recent scholarship has drawn renewed attention to the myriad links between networks of creative writers, artists, theorists and activists of the revival.[3] As was the case for many of his contemporaries, culture, society and politics were for Pearse a kind of continuum. If we look to the years before 1916, we find Pearse playing a leading role in the Gaelic League, editing its newspaper (*An Claidheamh Soluis*) from 1903 to 1909, serving on its highly successful publications committee, and helping to recruit members for its branches, as well as audiences and performers for its yearly Oireachtas cultural festival. After a 1905 visit to Belgium and further reflection on current educational approaches, Pearse championed a new bilingual education model that would be child-centred and deeply humane.[4] This led to the founding of his school, Scoil Éanna/St Enda's, in 1908. In terms of his key interests in this period it is of note that Pearse used both newspaper and school as platforms

2 W.B. Yeats, 'The man and the echo', *The collected poems of W.B. Yeats* (London, 2000).   3 Recent examples include R.F. Foster, *Vivid faces: the revolutionary generation in Ireland, 1890–1923* (London, 2014); P.J. Mathews and Declan Kiberd (eds), *Handbook of the Irish revival: an anthology of Irish cultural and political writings, 1891–1921* (Dublin, 2015); and Róisín Ní Ghairbhí, *Willie Pearse*, 16 Lives (Dublin, 2015). The magisterial Beathaisnéis series by Diarmuid Breathnach and Máire Ní Mhurchú, published by An Clóchomhar, gives comprehensive biographical details for hundreds of revival-era personalities. It is now searchable at www.ainm.ie. 4 Patrick Pearse, *The murder machine* (Dublin, 1916).

to discuss and advance a newly energized Irish theatre. Throughout these years of extraordinarily committed cultural endeavour Pearse shared radical ideas in speeches and publications. Through his organizing work with the League and his role on its publications committee, he played an energetic part in bringing marginalized Gaelic culture and its occluded texts to public attention. Given the scope of this ambition, it is unsurprising that Pearse, like many of his contemporaries, should have been attracted to the theatre, with all its potential for representation, shared reflection and motivation. From 1909 to 1916 he was the author and producer of ten original plays and pageants written in Irish and English, ranging from the 1909 production of the pageant *Macghníomhartha Chúchulainn* to the quasi-autobiographical *The singer*, which was completed shortly before the Easter Rising. In between, he would write two miracle plays – *Íosagán* (1910) and *An rí/The king* (1912); and two further pieces that dealt with the politics of rebellion – the short and simple *Owen* (1913) and the more nuanced *The master* (1915); and he would mastermind four dramatic pageants – *An Pháis/The Passion play* (1911), *The defence of the ford* (1913), *The Fianna of Fionn* (1913) and *Fionn: a dramatic spectacle* (1914).[5]

During Pearse's lifetime theatre played a central role in the cultural life of Ireland and passionate debates on the development of a specifically Irish theatre took place in lecture halls, newspaper columns and magazine articles. Since his death, however, the publication of critical studies that deal specifically with Pearse in his role as an Irish dramatist has been sporadic. That said, over the decades there have been a number of important assessments (and reassessments), and it may be useful to chart briefly a representative sample of these here. In the years immediately following 1916 Desmond Ryan republished Pearse's plays in his bilingual series of editions of Pearse's works. Ryan's biographical and historical accounts of Pearse and St Enda's include an important early attempt to assess the significance of Pearse's theatre work.[6] Máire Nic Shiubhlaigh's 1955 account of her memories of a life in theatre, *The splendid years*, includes accounts of her interactions with Patrick Pearse and his brother Willie in their shared theatre world.[7] The primary purpose of Ryan's and Nic Shiubhlaigh's writings was to recall lost friends and their deeds and describe dramatic productions for the historical record. Though they did not set out to provide a comprehensive critical survey of Pearse's theatre writings

5 In addition to these works there is the unfinished play *Eoghan Gabha*, which remained unpublished until 2013. For the script and history of this piece see Ní Ghairbhí and McNulty (eds), *Patrick Pearse: collected plays.*   6 See this volume's bibliography for a list of Desmond Ryan's vital contribution in this area. 7 Máire Nic Shiubhlaigh, *The splendid years* (Dublin, 1955).

and productions, both these contemporary witnesses contribute much that is of interest. Nic Shiubhlaigh provides an important account of the amateur and professional networks that intersected with the Pearse brothers' work in theatre, while Ryan provides relatively detailed first-hand accounts of the actual productions and their preparation.

For a long time (though with notable exceptions) canonical accounts of the emergence of a specifically Irish theatre tended to equate its development with the establishment of the Abbey Theatre. The dramatic works of Pearse as well as those of groups like Inghinidhe na hÉireann were marginalized or even occluded in many such accounts. Although there were sporadic productions on stage and on radio of *Íosagán* and of *The singer* in the decades after the Rising, for much of this time there was little significant criticism of Pearse's dramatic works. Tellingly, Ryan's editions went out of print. But the plays re-entered the public domain in 1979 with Séamas Ó Buachalla's excellent popular editions of Pearse's writings in Irish and English. Since then, while many mainstream accounts of the revival have continued to sideline Pearse's work in theatre, there have been some important exceptions. William Feeney's painstaking survey of the work of the Irish Theatre, for example, included important information on the staging of *The master* and *Íosagán* there.[8] Philip O'Leary's monumental *Prose literature of the Gaelic revival, 1881–1921* provided, inter alia, a forensic account of texts and contexts for the Irish-language theatre movement, and included a detailed discussion of Pearse's plays and their sources.[9]

More recently still, several important works have sought to draw attention to an 'alternative' dramatic revival. The work of scholars such as Mary Trotter and Karen Vandevelde has included an assessment of Pearse's dramatic works as part of a more wide-ranging discussion of neglected strands in Irish theatre history.[10] Other studies have provided important accounts of the wider context. All theatre is, of course, sited within a complex fabric of production and reception, (performance) text and context and interpretation: Elaine Sisson has traced the connections between Pearse's theatre and the Irish art world while Mary Trotter, Catherine Morris and Joan Fitzpatrick

8 William Feeney, *Drama in Hardwicke Street: a history of the Irish Theatre Company* (Rutherford, NJ, 1984).
9 Pádraig Ó Siadhail's *Stair dhrámaíocht na Gaeilge, 1900–1970* (1993) was the first book-length attempt at a history of theatre undertaken in Irish, but it did not include a discussion of Pearse's work, nor did any Pearse plays feature in the millennial celebration of Irish-language plays, *Drámaí an chéid*.   10 Mary Trotter, *Ireland's national theaters: political performance and the origins of the Irish dramatic movement* (Syracuse, NY, 2001); Mary Trotter, *Modern Irish theatre* (Cambridge, MA, 2008); Karen Vandevelde, *The alternative dramatic revival in Ireland* (Dublin, 2005).

Dean have each provided important accounts of the role of pageantry (such as that pioneered by Inghindhe na hÉireann) in the articulation of a nationalist public space. James Moran's *Four Irish rebel plays* (2007) includes an annotated edition of *The master* and a preface that discusses *The master* alongside other nationalist plays of the revolutionary period. Criticism by Máire Ní Fhlathúin and Róisín Ní Ghairbhí has examined Pearse's writings, including his drama, through the lens of postcolonial theory,[11] an approach that is also at play in Trotter's recent work.[12]

In all of this it has become increasingly clear that theatre and performance played key roles in the expression of cultural-nationalist identity in the years before the Rising. The first decade of the century had seen Irish identity being represented in new ways on stage. As cultural nationalism took hold (and notwithstanding the Gaelic League's supposedly apolitical ethos) language parades, fundraising concerts and commemorative marches increasingly encompassed both performative and political aspects. After 1914 the (armed) Irish Volunteers and the Fianna drilled in public and partook in military displays, sometimes alongside performances of plays.[13] The Irish Volunteers had mustered in huge numbers in Dublin city on St Patrick's Day 1916. Notwithstanding Mac Neill's famous notice of cancellation in the *Irish Independent*, the Volunteers' 'parades' and 'manoeuvres' on the streets of Dublin and elsewhere on Easter Monday 1916 would not have seemed untoward to a public used to displays of force by this armed body. James Moran, a contributor to this volume, has previously highlighted the ways in which the Rising was mistaken for an actual piece of street theatre by some Dubliners that Easter weekend. On ambling into Liberty Hall, itself the scene of many theatrical performances, one man thought he had stumbled into preparations for a children's play (Constance Markievicz reputedly set him straight with the words: 'No, this one is for grown-ups'). On Easter Monday Joseph Holloway would likewise spot a hoarding displaying a poster-like 'Proclamation of the Irish Republic' and assume 'he was looking at the announcement for the Theatre of Ireland'.[14] As Moran notes, when 'Holloway saw Pearse's name surrounded by the names of authors and organisers of the

11 Máire Ní Fhlathúin, 'The anti-colonial modernism of Patrick Pearse' in Howard J. Booth and Nigel Rigby (eds), *Modernism and empire* (Manchester, 2000); Róisín Ní Ghairbhí, 'The battle before us now is a battle of words: Pearse and postcolonial theory' in Roisín Higgins and Regina Uí Chollatáin (eds), *The life and after-life of P.H. Pearse* (Dublin, 2009). 12 Trotter, *Modern Irish theatre*. 13 For a discussion of this, with a particular focus on displays alongside theatre productions organised by Pearse, see Ní Ghairbhí, *Willie Pearse*. 14 James Moran, *Staging the Easter Rising: 1916 as theatre* (Cork, 2005), p. 15.

Irish stage' he 'understandably concluded that he was looking at a theatre announcement rather than a revolutionary manifesto'.[15]

This conflation of the theatrical and the political would have struck Pearse as not just appropriate but in fact as entirely natural. Many revival-era plays took place outside of mainstream (and especially commercially driven) theatre. The *tableaux vivants* of Inghinidhe na hÉireann found their way into the public sphere in parades and language processions. Dramatic productions took place in a myriad of alternative spaces: in gardens, in halls associated with voluntary cultural and political groups or as parts of eclectic community festivals like *feiseanna* or the national mustering of Gaelic culture that was the annual Oireachtas. Indeed, a Gaelic term adopted for one of the League's most popular cultural ventures, *aeraíocht*, had the literal meaning of an open-air cultural gathering, and thus epitomized the move away from established domains for culture. Many of Pearse's plays and pageants took place at St Enda's, itself a byword for alternative identity and culture. As explored more fully in Brian Crowley's essay in this volume, Pearse's pageants were remarkable for this innovative use of outdoor spaces like St Enda's school grounds and Jones' Road sports ground (now Croke Park). *Owen* was staged during a Fianna *céilí* at the Mansion House, home of the lord mayor and scene of many nationalist concerts, and later at the hall associated with the Colmcille branch of the Gaelic League, where three companies of the 1st Battalion of the Irish Volunteers also trained. *The master* was produced at the Irish Theatre (along with a revival of *Íosagán* and the short *Dúnlaing Óg agus an Leannán Sidhe*). While other productions of Pearse's work at the Abbey Theatre, such as *An rí* and *An Pháis*, provided the imprimatur of more mainstream cultural leaders like Yeats and Lady Gregory.

Recent work by scholars such as Mary Trotter has drawn attention to the ramifications of the wider performative nature of the revival era, citing, among other examples, the speaking of Irish and the buying of Irish goods. She concludes that the 'performance of an Irish identity in everyday life as an act of anti-colonial resistance would inform the practices of nationalist theatres – and their audiences'.[16] Theatre was a space for exploring radical ideas, a space in which to rethink and reperform concepts of Irish identity. The productions at St Enda's were not commercial enterprises but rather opportunities to influence the carefully invited audience of movers and shakers in the Dublin, and the wider Irish, cultural and political scene. If

15 Ibid., p. 16.   16 Trotter, *Modern Irish theatre*, p. 9.

Pearse used theatre as a way of bringing occluded Gaelic texts and contexts to a modern metropolitan audience, it is equally clear that he mobilized an audience for a marginalized culture. Philip O'Leary has drawn attention to Pearse's use of original sources from classical Gaelic literature in his dramatic writing.[17] The 1909 *Macghníomhartha Chúchulainn*, for example, was borne out of a deepening interest in the heroic Rúraíocht or Ulster cycle; later pageants would draw on the Fiannaíocht cycle. Like many of his fellow revivalists, Pearse turned to these texts as a way of tapping into (or reinventing) the essence of the Irish experience, which had been occluded by an education system that for a long time made no accommodation for Irish culture. Revivalist interest in Gaelic literature meant that scholarly editions of Fiannaíocht and Rúraíocht texts had been published; in some cases translations or popular versions were also available. A drive to bring these seminal Gaelic texts to further public prominence clearly informed the production of the massive outdoor pageants that consumed so much of Pearse's energies in 1913–14: *The defence of the ford*; *The Fianna of Fionn* and *Fionn: a dramatic spectacle*.

The fabric of subject-matters, settings and themes embraced by Pearse's work for the theatre provides a fascinating insight into the development of a mind finely tuned to the cultural contours of his time. If we look to *Íosagán* (1910), *An Pháis / The Passion play* (1911), *An rí / The king* (1912) and *The master* (1915), for example, we see how each in their different ways drew on a religious or quasi-religious narrative to explore the human condition as it is confronted by the problems, urgencies and consequences of the political. The message is by no means that of the conventional Catholicism sometimes identified as informing Pearse. Anne Markey's study of the development of Pearse's 'Íosagán' from short-story to play recalls the didactic story of an old man, Matthias, who can be identified as a Fenian. Matthias has been left isolated by the church (which often denounced radical oath-bound republicanism) but only he – and innocent children – can see Christ in their midst. During the old man's final hours it is the same young Christ-like child who appears to herald him; the priest, summoned by the same child, learns that there is discernment outside clerical pronouncements. Likewise, *An rí* revolves around the wisdom, bravery and purity of the young. While his monastery companions squabble over which of them should hold power in the future, the young Giolla na Naomh ('servant of the saints') thinks only of service. In the end it is he who will take on the mantle of the king and enter a battle

17 Philip O'Leary, *Prose literature of the Gaelic revival, 1881–1921* (University Park, PA, 1994).

that he knows will lead to his death. It is a death, as Elaine Sisson's essay demonstrates so finely, with much to tell us about Pearse's evolving sense of sacrifice in the political realm. As Sisson and others in this volume remind us, the intrusion of political violence into the calm of a secluded cloister is also the theme of *The master*, a play in which the new order of Christianity is pitted against the old pagan worldview, and in which another young pupil is prepared to put his life in danger to protect his teacher against the external forces of corrupt power. James Moran's careful reconsideration of *The master* in this volume also reveals the ways in which Pearse looked beyond Ireland in a manner that showed clear affinities with a broader, international set of ideas about the experimental in the realm of performance and politics.

Most famously, the Christological narrative of sacrifice and redemption provided Pearse with his powerful – and controversial – image of revolutionary violence in *The singer* (1916), the play he was writing in the months immediately before the Easter Rising. This is the play for which Pearse the playwright is best remembered – or at least its final lines are those most frequently recalled, when MacDara, the singer of the title, declares on going out to meet the English: 'One man can free a people as one Man redeemed the world. I will take no pike. I will go into the battle with bare hands. I will stand up before the Gall as Christ hung naked before men on the tree!'[18] Unsurprisingly – given the proximity of this play to the Rising, and, indeed, the piece's rather troubled cultural afterlife – *The singer* is treated extensively by several of the essays in this volume. Drawing on a remarkable range of philosophical and theological sources in his contribution to this volume, Maciej Ruczaj argues for a reading of the play that sees it as not simply concerned with national awakening but also with the radical emancipation of the self. Two further essays show how differing critical lenses can draw multiple meanings from a seemingly straightforward text. Michael Cronin's subtle response to *The singer* locates a matrix of politicized desires in the eroticized male body at the centre of the play, while Eugene McNulty situates the play within a discourse of legal exceptionality borne out of Irish nationalism's refusal of colonial jurisprudence. Fittingly for Pearse, whose day job was headmaster in the school he had founded, the figures of educator and pupil feature in works as otherwise diverse as *An rí/The king*, *The master* and *Owen* (1913). The last of these is in its own way as open to critique as the messianic imagery at the conclusion of *The singer*. Through the character of Owen,

---

18 Patrick Pearse, *The singer*, in Ní Ghairbhí and McNulty (eds), *Patrick Pearse: collected plays*, p. 228.

Pearse presented his audience with the special and unbreakable bond that can develop between a teacher and his pupil. But in this case the bond is so strong that it leads to the child sacrificing his life to protect the teacher, who has been revealed as a Fenian leader. While slight, and not often produced, *Owen* is certainly of note for its revelation of the real-life price of rebellion.

There is little doubt that in all of this Pearse was acutely conscious of the critical and historical context for his dramatic experiments. As a result, his theatrical productions were consistently framed by a careful process of contextualization. A master of what we would now term marketing and publicity, through the use of advance notices, newspaper articles, postcards and programme notes Pearse ensured that his work was highly visible in the thriving cultural scene of early twentieth-century Dublin. Performances were often heralded by speeches by Pearse and other prominent cultural leaders, and those attending would turn up in the knowledge that they would be rubbing shoulders with many of the city's leading cultural and political figures. Pearse used St Enda's school journal, *An Macaomh*, to announce his plays and to document his own musings on the significance of his works and their impact. He published the scripts for some of his plays during his own lifetime and arranged that his chosen literary executer, Desmond Ryan, would publish further texts after his death.[19] This careful curation of productions and publications means that the initial immediate context for Pearse's plays is relatively well signposted, even if some of the sources were for a long time relatively difficult to access, marginalized or even forgotten. As the essays in this volume remind us, the productions of Pearse's plays and pageants often took place alongside other events and performances and these provide for us an additional cultural and political context. Síle Denvir's contribution recalls for us Pearse's close connections and collaborations with musicians and the important role of music and song in his productions, and in the revival in general. While the help given to Pearse before and during productions reflected loyal support from the broad spectrum of nationalism there are also indications within the plays, and their production, of Pearse's growing alliance with advanced nationalism. Pearse's former teaching colleague Thomas Mac Donagh had a cameo in *An Pháis/The Passion play*, and various members of the Theatre of Ireland would help out at rehearsals at St Enda's. The list of those involved in the fête and pageants held at Jones' Road in June 1913, to help raise funds for St Enda's, reads like a who's who of Dublin

19 For more on this history of production and reception see Ní Ghairbhí and McNulty (eds), *Patrick Pearse: collected plays*.

radicalism: the radical artist Jack Morrow helped organize lighting and choreography; James Larkin printed extensive publicity material at his own expense;
and Sean O'Casey sent a letter promoting the fête to *The Irish Worker*. The fête
itself was publicized on the front page of *Irish Freedom*, the paper of advanced
nationalism. Some of the guest performers are also noteworthy: the
programme for the fête lists members of numerous bands, piping groups,
choirs, dancing groups, and, significantly, displays from Na Fianna Éireann.
Kerryman Thomas Ashe, who died while being force-fed on hunger strike in
1917, was a member of the Lusk Pipers who played at the fête; another group
of guest performers, the Emmet Choir, was as republican-leaning as its name
suggests. A surviving postcard from Willie Pearse also recalls the involvement
of Éamonn Ceannt, proclamation signatory, Gaelic Leaguer and piper. The
advanced nationalist – and theatre practitioner – Bulmer Hobson presided
over the fête's organizing committee. Marnie Hay's essay in this volume
provides a fascinating comparative study of the lives and careers of Pearse and
Hobson.

  While Pearse's growing radicalization can be charted through his plays, this
should not be our only lens for examining his work in theatre. The story of
the development of twentieth-century Irish theatre has undoubtedly become
more nuanced, particularly for drama in the English language. Irish-language
theatre history, however, is still in its early stages and much work remains to
be done. As Róisín Ní Ghairbhí notes in her essay in this volume, there was
much crossover between the English- and Irish-language strands of the
cultural revival. Pageantry and *tableaux vivants* played important parts in early
revivalist depictions of Gaelic literature and Irish history. In this regard it is
clear that Pearse saw his own production of *Macghníomhartha Chúchulainn* as part
of a vibrant and socially relevant cultural form. Similarly, the 1911 production
of *An Pháis/The Passion play* took place at a time of increased interest in (and
controversy regarding) passion plays and their potential to interrogate the
modern condition. The founding of the Irish Theatre in 1914 by Thomas
MacDonagh, Joseph Plunkett and Edward Martyn demonstrated the keen
interest shown by Pearse's peer group in European modernist theatre (for
more on these European connections see James Moran's essay). The Irish
Theatre would stage works by the likes of Chekhov and Ibsen and provide a
source of inspiration for the founding of the Gate Theatre in 1928.

  The essays published in this collection were generated following a
symposium, 'Pearse and the theatre/Pádraic Mac Piarais agus an
Amharclann', which was held in Coláiste Phádraig/St Patrick's College

(Dublin City University) in November 2013. Conscious of the plays' geneses in the vibrant and diverse world of the cultural revival, the approach of the organizers (the editors of this volume) was deliberately bilingual and inter-disciplinary. One of the aims of the symposium was to encourage fresh creative interpretations of Pearse's plays. Two performative strands allowed for creative interaction and reflection on the plays as theatre, and not simply as moribund historical texts. The workshop on *The singer* was attended by an enthusiastic mix of academics and theatre practitioners. Colm Hefferon, the workshop facilitator, aimed to avoid rigid ideological interpretations by 'exploring the human aspect of the plays'.[20] The workshop drew on the democratic and participatory approach of forum theatre in order to allow those participating to speculate on the multiple meanings that various production approaches might bring about. A public performance of *Caithréim*, a concert curated by Síle Denvir with graphics arranged by Ciarán Ó Súilleabháin, brought the music and song of Pearse's theatre to life.[21]

If the symposium drew part of its energy from the renewed interest in the events and consequences of the 'Revolutionary Decade', various commemo-rative events during the centenary year of 2016 have added further to our strategies for assessing Pearse's life inside and outside the theatre. The re-enactments of long-forgotten 1916 mobilizations by descendants of Volunteers from Gaeltacht areas in Kerry and Galway, for example, remind us that *The singer* (which featured a cultural leader exhorting Gaeltacht men to mobilize) was not merely propaganda but also witness. In this regard, Barry Houlihan's essay usefully reminds us that the process of commemoration, and particularly its performative dimensions, has done much to shape and reshape our sense of Pearse and the Rising at key moments over the last century. In a different sense it also helps to remind us that our understanding of Pearse (and of the Easter Rising) is deeply informed by how history has unfolded in the years that stand between us and 1916. One could argue, for example, that the manner in which Pearse's drama was produced in some ways antici-pated modern-day movements such as Ngugi Wa Thiongo's postcolonial theatre practice (e.g. *Ngaahika Ndeenda*) or Augusto Boal's idea of the 'spect-actor' and his 'theatre of the oppressed'. It is also possible (though admittedly anachronistic) to think about the Easter Rising in terms derived from Bertolt

20 Colm Hefferon, in conversation with the editors.   21 The original participants were musicians Síle Denvir, Thomas Johnston, Aoife Ní Argáin, Síomha Mulligan and Éadaoin Ní Mhaicín. *Caithréim* was performed again at Scoil Gheimhridh Merriman (the Merriman Winter School). A CD recording of the music that featured in *Caithréim* was issued by Cló Iar-Chonnacht in May 2016.

Brecht's formulation of 'epic theatre'. This is a form of theatre that 'turns the spectator into an observer', but in so doing 'arouses his capacity for action' and 'forces him to take decisions'. In such theatre, the audience is 'brought to the point of recognition'.[22] Recalling the end result that Brecht hoped for through such art, one cannot help but think of the dynamism that the Easter rebels intended to provoke with their actions:

> We need a type of theatre which not only releases the feelings, insights and impulses possible within the particular historical field of human relations in which the action takes place, but employs and encourages those thoughts and feelings which help transform the field itself.[23]

The symmetry is, of course, not merely coincidental. Brecht sought to bring the ideological contours of political revolution into the theatre; earlier in the century, Pearse had worked his way along a performative journey in the opposite direction. Read in this way the opening lines of the Proclamation certainly carry with them a Brechtian sense of the meta-performative, as the signatories declare themselves as mediating bodies channelling 'characters':

> IRISHMEN AND IRISHWOMEN: In the name of God and of the dead generations from which she receives her old tradition of nationhood, Ireland, through us, summons her children to her flag and strikes for her freedom.

It is a declaration that self-consciously positioned the signatories as performative cyphers birthing history by inhabiting its ghostly remains. Pearse's plays likewise act as ghostly presences that haunt the stage of history and provoke us into further consideration of the ideas they embody and of the place and time that first received them. The plays, like Pearse's politics, will always be contested. But that should not preclude critics and theatre practitioners from interpreting them – and Pearse – in new ways. For Yeats in 'The statues' the ultimate arena for interrogating Irish culture was not politics but creativity – the inspiration of 'our proper dark'.[24] Evolving contexts and evolving criticism allow Pearse's plays to function with all the dynamism that theatre enables. Writing about Gaelic literature in 1913 Pearse expressed his

---

22 Bertolt Brecht, 'The modern theatre is the epic theatre' (1930) in John Willet (ed.), *Brecht on theatre* (London, 1964), p. 37. 23 Bertolt Brecht, 'A short organum for the theatre' (1948) in Willet (ed.), *Brecht on theatre* (London, 1964), p. 190. 24 W.B. Yeats, 'The statues', *The collected poems of W.B. Yeats*.

wish that 'the old truths will find new mouths, the old sorrows and ecstasies new interpretation'.[25] The editors of this book embrace a similar aim and hope that further new voices will engage with Pearse's theatre and with the ideas expressed by the contributors here. Tá súil againn go spreagfaidh múnla dátheangach an leabhair seo comhrá idir scoláirí Béarla agus scoláirí Gaeilge: comhrá dá leithéid a ghin cuid mhaith de chruthaitheacht ré na hAthbheochana.

25 Patrick Pearse, 'By way of comment', *An Macaomh*, 2:2 (May 1913), 8.

1 / Performing Irish nationalism on and off the stage: Bulmer Hobson and Patrick Pearse

MARNIE HAY

The revolutionary generation in Ireland viewed theatre as a vital part of their efforts to raise nationalist consciousness.[1] Bulmer Hobson (1883–1969) and Patrick Pearse (1879–1916) were two notable members of this generation who engaged creatively with theatre as a 'nationalising force' in the early twentieth century.[2] Hobson and Pearse also recognized the importance of providing children with an overtly Irish nationalist education and demonstrated a commitment to preparing Irish boys for their future roles in the Irish nationalist movement. Hobson revealed this through his formation in 1902 and 1909 of two separate incarnations of a nationalist youth group called Na Fianna Éireann, while Pearse did so through the establishment of St Enda's School for boys in 1908.[3] In each case these endeavours engaged with theatre, and portrayed the young male as a metaphor for the nascent Irish nation state. This essay explores the parallels between these two nationalist activists, who were not only inspired by the Irish cultural revival, but also made an active contribution to that revival through their use of theatre as a nationalizing force.

Other parallels between Hobson and Pearse are also striking. Both men joined the Gaelic League in their late teens, though Hobson's efforts at attaining fluency in Irish were less successful than Pearse's. They were acclaimed public speakers who undertook American lecture tours: Hobson in 1907 to promote the new Sinn Féin ('ourselves') movement, and Pearse in 1914 to raise money for St Enda's. They were founding members of the Irish Volunteers, a paramilitary organization established in Dublin in November 1913 as a nationalist counterblast to the Ulster Volunteer Force, which had been formed earlier in the year to coordinate Ulster unionist paramilitary

1 See chapter 3 of R.F. Foster, *Vivid faces: the revolutionary generation in Ireland, 1890–1923* (London, 2014). 2 Ibid., p. 75. 3 For a more detailed look at these endeavours, see Marnie Hay, 'The foundation and development of Na Fianna Éireann, 1909–16', *Irish Historical Studies*, 36:141 (May 2008), 53–71; Marnie Hay, 'An Irish nationalist adolescence: Na Fianna Éireann, 1909–23' in Catherine Cox and Susannah Riordan (eds), *Adolescence in modern Irish history* (Basingstoke, 2015), pp 103–28; Elaine Sisson, *Pearse's patriots: St Enda's and the cult of boyhood* (Cork, 2004); Brendan Walsh, *The pedagogy of protest: the educational thought and work of Patrick H. Pearse* (Oxford, 2007).

activities in opposition to the 1912 home rule bill. Hobson and Pearse were also members of the Irish Republican Brotherhood (IRB), a secret society committed to the establishment of an Irish republic through the use of physical force if necessary. Hobson's membership predated Pearse's by more than a decade, demonstrating a lengthier commitment to republican nationalism. Hobson, who had joined the IRB in 1904, swore Pearse into the organization in late 1913 in anticipation of his lecture tour of the United States, which Hobson helped to organize.[4] Both men engineered opportunities to perform acts of Irish nationalism on and off the stage, most famously during the 1916 Easter Rising, the event that would ensure Pearse's posthumous fame and destroy Hobson's nationalist career.

Hobson and Pearse were both of mixed Irish and English parentage, but their family backgrounds and educational and career trajectories differed. Hobson grew up in Belfast in a comfortable, middle-class Quaker family. His father, Benjamin Hobson Jnr, who hailed from a Co. Armagh farming family, was a commercial traveller by trade and a Gladstonian home ruler in politics. His mother, Mary Ann Bulmer, was a women's rights activist, amateur archaeologist and theatre enthusiast from Darlington, in the north of England. The Hobson children attended the Friends' School, a Quaker boarding school in Lisburn. After leaving school, Hobson became an apprentice printer, and later a journalist.[5]

Pearse, who was four years older than Hobson, grew up in Dublin. His father, James Pearse, was a stonemason and monumental sculptor from a London working-class family, while his mother Margaret Brady, James' second wife, was a shop assistant from an Irish Catholic nationalist family. Patrick felt a strong bond with his maternal great-aunt Margaret, who regaled him with stories and songs of an Irish nationalist flavour. He was initially privately educated before attending the Christian Brothers School at Westland Row, where his love of the Irish language and its literature was further kindled. Academically inclined, he graduated with a BA in modern languages and a law degree. He acted as a barrister on two documented occasions,[6] but

---

4 Bulmer Hobson, *Ireland yesterday and tomorrow* (Tralee, 1968), pp 31, 75; Joost Augusteijn, *Patrick Pearse: the making of a revolutionary* (Basingstoke, 2010), p. 205; Bulmer Hobson, witness statement, 26 Jan. 1948 (Military Archives [MA], Bureau of Military History [BMH], WS 84), p. 1. 5 Marnie Hay, *Bulmer Hobson and the nationalist movement in twentieth-century Ireland* (Manchester, 2009), pp 6–10. The 1901 census records him as an 18-year-old apprentice printer, while the 1911 census lists him as 28-year-old journalist, census.nationalarchives.ie/pages/1901/Antrim/Clifton_Ward_Belfast/Hopefield_Avenue/1004537/; census.nationalarchives.ie/pages/911/Down/Holywood_Urban/Ballycultra/232384/ (accessed online 11 Jan. 2011). 6 For more on Pearse's limited activities as a barrister, see Eugene McNulty's essay in this

directed most of his energies to his work in the Gaelic League and the running of his father's business. He founded his school, St Enda's, in 1908.

Both Hobson and Pearse engaged with drama from a young age, though Pearse appears to have done so to a greater extent. On rainy days Hobson and his siblings, Florence and Harold, dressed up the family's Irish terrier, Beppo, and staged pantomimes.[7] Pearse's sister Mary Brigid recalled that her older brother was a prolific playwright from about the age of nine and regularly led his siblings in the production of his plays, which featured plots derived from history and melodramatic romance.[8] Hobson, however, was the first of the two to manifest his interest in theatre on the public stage, which he did while still a young adult in north Belfast.

Hobson's neighbours, the poets Alice Milligan and Anna Johnston ('Ethna Carbery'), sparked his interest in the Irish cultural revival. They provided him with inspirational reading material, such as Standish O'Grady's retellings of Irish heroic tales and their nationalist newspaper the *Shan Van Vocht*, and encouraged him to join the Gaelic League. Milligan was a noted producer of *tableaux vivants* ('living pictures') and her influence was evident in Hobson's first public theatrical venture. Inspired by *tableaux vivants* produced by the Belfast Gaelic League, Hobson organized a similar enterprise under the auspices of the Ulster Debating Club for boys, which he had founded at the age of seventeen.[9] Johnston revealed: 'It is evident that [Hobson] was anything but unobservant during our rehearsals, for he has drawn up half a dozen different series of episodes in Irish history, suitable for *tableaux*, in the cleverest way.'[10] The boys' club exhibited its *tableaux* on 27 December 1900 at the Avenue Minor Hall, with the Gaelic League's P.J. O'Shea providing a description of the scenes.[11] The *United Irishman* pronounced the venture a success, noting that the venue was crowded.[12]

Hobson soon embarked on other ventures that used theatre as a vehicle for promoting Irish nationalism. In June 1902 he established his first incarnation of the youth group Na Fianna Éireann in Belfast. It held inter-club hurling and Gaelic football competitions and classes in Irish language and history, but also dabbled in drama. In October 1902 at a meeting of the executive of the Belfast Fianna, Hobson announced that 'he intended to form a dramatic

collection.   7 Mary Hobson, *Memoirs of six generations* (Belfast, 1947), p. 52.   8 Róisín Ní Ghairbhí and Eugene McNulty (eds), *Patrick Pearse: collected plays/Drámaí an Phiarsaigh* (Dublin, 2013), p. 7.   9 *United Irishman*, 10 Nov. 1900.   10 Anna Johnston ('Ethna Carbery') to Seamus O'Kelly, 11 Nov. 1900 (National Library of Ireland (NLI), Bulmer Hobson Papers, MS 18,461).   11 *United Irishman*, 22 Dec. 1900; Hobson, *Ireland*, p. 14.   12 *United Irishman*, 5 Jan. 1901.

section from the various clubs', and a meeting of qualified boys was scheduled for 4 November 1902.[13] Séamus Robinson, who joined the Belfast Fianna circa 1903, recalled 'an attempt by Hobson to produce a play written by him on Wolfe Tone', but could not remember 'if the play was ever produced'.[14]

Around the same time that Hobson was trying to form a dramatic section of the Fianna, he was also engaged in setting up the Ulster Branch of the Irish Literary Theatre, the forerunner of the Ulster Literary Theatre (ULT).[15] Hobson and his friend David Parkhill had been impressed by the work of the Irish National Dramatic Company and journeyed to Dublin in autumn 1902 in order to meet the company's members.[16] With the production talents of the Fay brothers and the help of W.B. Yeats and George Russell (AE), the Dublin-based company produced Irish plays in small halls. Máire Quinn, one of the company's actors, took Hobson and Parkhill to the rehearsal hall at 34 Camden Street (coincidentally, the future hall of the first Dublin Fianna troop), where they 'met the whole crowd', which included Yeats, AE, James Cousins, the Fays and Fred Ryan.[17] Pearse would later come into contact with many of these individuals through his affiliation with the Theatre of Ireland, which was formed in 1906 as a breakaway group from the Irish National Theatre Society (in effect, the Abbey Theatre), the successor to the Irish National Dramatic Company.[18] Thus, both Hobson and Pearse were associated with theatrical companies that challenged and supplemented the Yeats-centric vision of the Irish national theatre movement.

The object of Hobson and Parkhill's visit was to gain permission to perform the company's plays and to solicit help from their actors. Hobson described everyone as 'most cordial and helpful except Yeats – haughty and aloof'.[19] Yeats refused their request for permission to perform *Cathleen Ni Houlihan*, a play in which the eponymous Cathleen, symbolizing Ireland, inspires a young bridegroom to join the United Irishmen's rebellion of 1798. In addition to his alleged 'antipathy towards all things Ulster',[20] Yeats probably resented the pair's goal of bringing Ulster more fully into the Irish literary revival because the project would be outside of his sphere of control.[21]

13 Fianna minute book, 1902 (NLI, Hobson Papers, MS 18,461).   14 Séamus Robinson, witness statement, 26 Oct. 1948 (MA, BMH, WS 156), pp 3–4.   15 For a detailed examination of the ULT, see Eugene McNulty, *The Ulster Literary Theatre and the Northern revival* (Cork, 2008). For a more detailed discussion of Hobson's involvement in the ULT, see ch. 2 of Hay, *Bulmer Hobson*.   16 Sam Hanna Bell, *The theatre in Ulster* (Dublin, 1972), p. 1.   17 Hobson to Bell, 2 July 1965, quoted in Bell, *Theatre in Ulster*, p. 2.   18 Ní Ghairbhí and McNulty (eds), *Patrick Pearse: collected plays*, pp 12–13.   19 Hobson to Bell, 2 July 1965, quoted in Bell, *Theatre in Ulster*, p. 2.   20 Bell, *Theatre in Ulster*, p. 2.   21 Mark Phelan, 'The rise and fall of the Ulster Literary Theatre' (MPhil, Trinity College Dublin, 1998), p. 49.

Maud Gonne overrode Yeats' refusal, and so *Cathleen Ni Houlihan* and James Cousins' *The racing lug* were staged by the newly formed Ulster Branch of the Irish Literary Theatre in November 1902 at St Mary's Minor Hall in Belfast. Despite its small size, the hall was far too big for the audiences that attended the plays' two-night run.[22]

Sam Hanna Bell reported that the Protestant National Society, an association co-founded by Hobson, was the force behind this first production;[23] however, this society was not formed until February 1903.[24] Thus, it is more likely that Hobson, Parkhill and William McDonald later formed the Protestant National Society to provide a formal structure for their various efforts to propagate the ideology of Theobald Wolfe Tone and the United Irishmen among young Ulster Protestants. Hobson's espousal of republicanism and non-sectarianism had been sparked by the centenary of the 1798 rebellion.[25] Having met with 'little noticeable success' in their quest to convert Ulster protestants to nationalism, the society decided to try using theatre for propaganda purposes.[26] This decision likely led to the next recorded production of the Ulster Branch of the Irish Literary Theatre.

In early 1904, the company revived *Cathleen Ni Houlihan* and added George Russell's *Deirdre* to the bill, playing to 'sparse audiences' and harvesting 'poor receipts', possibly because the overt 'Irishness' of the plays did not appeal to a Belfast audience.[27] As Harry Morrow ('Gerald MacNamara') put it, 'The Belfast public [...] were not taken by *Cathleen Ni Houlihan*. Ninety-nine per cent of the population had never heard of the lady – and cared less; in fact someone in the audience said that the show was going "rightly" til *she* came on.'[28] MacNamara's recollection reflects the challenges that Hobson and his colleagues faced in Ireland's northern bastion of 'British' culture.

They soon faced another challenge when George Roberts, the secretary of the Irish National Theatre Society, sent them 'an indignant letter' stating that they had no right to use the society's former name (Irish Literary Theatre) and demanding royalties for the production of its plays.[29] In response, the Belfast company changed its name to the Ulster Literary Theatre and began to write its own plays,[30] beginning with the staging of *Brian of Banba* by Hobson and *The reformers* by Parkhill ('Lewis Purcell') on four nights in November and December 1904 in the Ulster Minor Hall.[31]

22 Bell, *Theatre in Ulster*, pp 2–3. 23 Ibid. 24 *United Irishman*, 28 Feb. 1903. 25 Hobson, *Ireland*, p. 2. 26 Bell, *Theatre in Ulster*, p. 3. 27 Ibid. 28 Quoted in ibid., pp 3–4. 29 George Russell to Lady Gregory, *c.*Apr. 1904, quoted in R.F. Foster, *W.B. Yeats: a life*, i: *The apprentice mage, 1865–1914* (Oxford, 1998), p. 320. 30 Bell, *Theatre in Ulster*, p. 2. 31 ULT ticket and programme, 1904 (NLI, Hobson Papers, MS

Brian of Banba, which had been published in the *United Irishman* on 2 August 1902, is divided into two scenes and lasts about half an hour. It opens in the death chamber of Cennedigh Mac-Lorcan, where the ailing king of Thomond, heir to the Munster kingship, shares out the inheritances of his two sons, Mahon and Brian. While Mahon is content to be a tributary king under the Vikings, Brian prefers to fight the Northmen, against his father's advice. Disguised as a beggar, Brian later returns home to admonish his brother Mahon, the new king, for not providing him with aid when he first set out. Fired by Brian's tales of victory, Mahon agrees to support his next campaign against the Vikings. Eugene McNulty has read the play 'as a coded call for nationalists throughout Ireland to remember, and thus not leave isolated, their northern "counterparts", who were feeling ever more squeezed by the ideological pressures building around them'.[32] The character of Brian can also be seen as symbolizing Hobson's own project to propagate advanced Irish nationalism in the north of Ireland. In this reading, the Vikings are equated to the British, while Mahon and Cennedigh are interpreted as home rulers or even unionists in need of advanced nationalist conversion. As contemporary critics were quick to point out, *Brian of Banba* was derivative of Yeats' mythological plays. Christopher Morash has compared it to Alice Milligan's *The last feast of the Fianna* and James Cousins' *The sleep of the king*: all three plays featured 'heroes wearing horned helmets [spouting] interminable purple prose'.[33]

Contemporary reaction to the play was mixed, and in his monograph on the ULT, McNulty even concluded that *Brian of Banba* was 'something of a flop'.[34] Fred Morrow's direction and scenery and Jack Morrow's costumes attracted praise, whereas Hobson's performance in the title role provoked a comment that his 'written conception' of Brian 'was certainly better than his acted one'.[35] Writing in the ULT's own journal, *Uladh*, James Winder Good opined that Brian and Mahon were 'abiding types' whose possibilities Hobson had not realized to the full. He added that Hobson's work was 'hampered by the fact that it suggests, inevitably, a contrast with the plays of Mr Yeats; and there are few living poets who can bear the comparison unscathed'.[36] Hobson's playwriting needed a little more originality and a little

13,175). **32** McNulty, *Ulster Literary Theatre*, p. 101. **33** Christopher Morash, *A history of Irish theatre, 1601–2000* (Cambridge, 2002), pp 120–1. **34** McNulty, *Ulster Literary Theatre*, p. 101. **35** *Belfast Evening Telegraph*, 9 Dec. 1904. **36** *Uladh*, Feb. 1905, p. 6. For a discussion of *Uladh*, which Hobson co-founded, see ch. 4 of McNulty, *Ulster Literary Theatre*; Marnie Hay, 'Explaining *Uladh*: cultural nationalism in Ulster' in Betsey Taylor FitzSimon and James H. Murphy (eds), *The Irish revival reappraised* (Dublin, 2004), pp 119–31; Eugene McNulty, '"Draw it not too rigidly": *Ulad* and the cultural partition debate' in Alison O'Malley-

less emulation. The play garnered a more positive review from the *Irish News* critic, who described it as 'a picture-play and a very beautiful one at that' and praised 'a *caoine* sung by three female voices at the close of the first scene' for being 'full of a sad haunting sweetness'.[37] In contrast, the *United Irishman* considered the *caoine* to be the 'gravest' fault of construction in the play because 'it refused to blend with the drama, and remained a thing apart'.[38]

Brian of Banba was later presented, along with Purcell's *The enthusiast*, at a *feis* (festival) in Toomebridge, Co. Antrim, in early August 1905.[39] The performances stayed in the memory of one thirteen-year-old member of the audience, future journalist and labour activist Cathal O'Shannon:

> I was interested enough in *Brian of Banba*, because I knew the story [...] but what really did impress me was *The Enthusiast*, because for the first time I saw the kind of people that I knew and lived among in County Antrim and County Derry were there alive and talking as they talked at home.[40]

O'Shannon's opinion predicted the ULT's future, which lay in contemporary plays with a regional accent, like *The enthusiast*, rather than what Morash has called the cul-de-sac of the Irish mythological play.[41] As its commercial success grew, the ULT abandoned its derivative, propagandist roots, as exemplified by Hobson's play, in favour of works that promoted a blossoming regional identity.[42]

The primary focus of Hobson's nationalist activities gradually shifted from cultural to political concerns as he became increasingly involved in the Sinn Féin movement and the IRB, although he continued to recognize the importance of cultural performances for promoting Irish nationalism. When he and Countess Markievicz established a new incarnation of Na Fianna Éireann as a nationalist boy-scout group in Dublin in 1909, they created an organization that offered its members a combination of military training, outdoor activities and Irish cultural pursuits. Members with the requisite talent and inclination were afforded many opportunities to display their dramatic and musical abilities. For instance, a Dublin-based drama group called the Fianna Players performed a number of Irish plays; however, it was

Younger and Frank Beardow (eds), *Representing Ireland: past, present and future* (Sunderland, 2005).   37 *Irish News*, 8 Dec. 1904.   38 *United Irishman*, 24 Dec. 1904.   39 *Uladh*, Sept. 1905, p. 2.   40 Quoted in Bell, *Theatre in Ulster*, p. 25.   41 Morash, *Irish theatre*, p. 120.   42 David Kennedy, 'Ulster unionism and the new nationalism' in Kevin B. Nowlan (ed.), *The making of 1916* (Dublin, 1969), pp 74–5.

Markievicz, rather than Hobson, who spearheaded this endeavour. Among the plays performed by the group was Padraic Colum's *The Saxon shilling*.[43] Colum was a writer associated with the Irish literary revival, whose play had been rejected previously by the Irish National Theatre Society on the grounds that it was merely anti-military-recruitment propaganda.[44] The play's message, however, was in keeping with the promise made by Fianna members 'never to join England's armed forces'.[45] Elsewhere in Ireland, the Fianna troop in Tuam, Co. Galway, held a dramatic class and Belfast Fianna members performed in two plays at their annual concert in 1914.[46]

The Fianna also lent their talents to fundraising events, such as the Lang Benefit Concert held in Dublin in early 1915, at which members were among the performers of Irish songs, dances, recitations and sketches.[47] The Fianna hall on Camden Street in Dublin and the meeting rooms of other troops served as the venues for *céilís* and other social occasions 'at which nothing but Irish songs and dances were permitted'. According to Dublin Fianna member Seán Prendergast, hosting such fundraising events helped the youth group to gain 'friends' among older nationalists – and 'among the cailíní [girls]'.[48]

Hobson's public involvement in theatre may have started earlier than Pearse's, but the latter proved the more talented and prolific playwright. Of Pearse's plays written between 1909 and 1916, nine scripts survive (one of which, *Eoghan Gabha*, remained unfinished), while three scripts are lost.[49] Pearse's first formal affiliation with a theatrical company came in 1906 through his membership on the first committee of the Theatre of Ireland.[50] When Pearse launched St Enda's in 1908, theatrical productions became a regular part of school life and helped to raise public awareness of the school's approach to providing a progressive and thoroughly Irish education. Pearse produced St Enda's first dramatic productions in February 1909, staging Standish O'Grady's *The coming of Fionn* and Douglas Hyde's *An naomh ar iarraidh*

43 Seumas Mac Caisin (James Cashen), witness statement, 8 June 1947 (MA, BMH, WS 8), pp 5–6. The members of the Fianna Players were Seumas Mac Caisin, Percy Reynolds, Con Colbert, Theo Fitzgerald, Sean (Jack) Shallow, [?] MacGowan, Andy Dunne, Harry Walpole and Brian Callender as well as Countess Markievicz and Helena Molony.   44 Robert Welch (ed.), *The concise Oxford companion to Irish literature* (Oxford: 2000), pp 64–5.   45 'Na Fianna Éireann', *Irish Freedom*, Sept. 1912.   46 Liam Ó Maoil Íosa (Liam Mellows), 'Boy Scouts organising notes', *Irish Volunteer*, 7 Feb. 1914; 'Boy Scouts organising notes', *Irish Volunteer*, 28 Mar. 1914.   47 Photocopy of Lang Benefit Concert programme (MA, BMH, James FitzGerald Collection, CD 91/5).   48 Seán Prendergast, witness statement, no date (MA, BMH, WS 755), p. 25.   49 Extant scripts and treatments of the 'scriptless' plays are included in Ní Ghairbhí and McNulty (eds), *Patrick Pearse: collected plays*. A manuscript source for *The master* has recently come to light. See Barbara McCormack, 'Patrick Pearse: The master' in David Bracken (ed.), *The end of all things earthly* (Dublin, 2016).   50 Ní Ghairbhí and McNulty (eds), *Patrick Pearse: collected plays*, pp 12–13.

(*The lost saint*), but soon began writing his own plays. He wrote the pageant *Macghníomhartha Chúchulainn* (*The boyhood deeds of Cuchulainn*) in May 1909, staging it at St Enda's on the grounds of Cullenswood House on 22 June 1909.[51] As this example illustrates, the Ulster and Fionn cycles of heroic tales inspired some of Pearse's theatrical work, particularly the pageants. Christian imagery provided another source of inspiration. His miracle play *Íosagán*, which was first produced at St Enda's in February 1910, features a manifestation of the child Jesus in Connemara. An expanded version of the play was performed in the Abbey Theatre in April 1910.[52] Pearse's plays *Owen* (1913) and *The master* (1915) explore the bond between teacher and pupil, a rather chilling theme given future events: *Owen* features the motif of a sacrificial child, and almost the entire cast of the original production of *The master* went on to participate in the Easter Rising.[53] Róisín Ní Ghairbhí and Eugene McNulty have demonstrated that 'at the time of their first performance Pearse's plays were viewed by a who's who of the Dublin literati and were reported on and discussed widely and positively in the press'.[54] The same cannot be said for Hobson's *Brian of Banba*.

   The youth-oriented endeavours of Pearse and Hobson converged in June 1913 when the boys of St Enda's and the Fianna braved rainy weather conditions to participate in public presentations at the St Enda's fête held at Jones' Road (now Croke Park) to raise money for the school's building fund. Hobson served on the fête's organizing committee.[55] While St Enda's students performed in Pearse's pageants *The Fianna of Fionn* and *The defence of the ford*, Hobson's Fianna boys provided a different type of performance – a display of tent-pitching, camp work, skirmishing and military drill.[56] Elaine Sisson has asserted that 'St Enda's secured national identity to the body of the male youth and paraded youthful male bodies as a visual metaphor for the nation state', adding that this exercise 'was reflected in European-wide [*sic*] practices of annexing the "physical culture" of masculinity to moral strength'.[57] This uncomfortable link with an aspect of fascism holds true for the Fianna as well. Na Fianna Éireann exhibited young male bodies as 'a visual metaphor for the nation state' during stage performances, route marches, nationalist parades and public demonstrations of the practical skills that the boys had gained through camping and military training, such as their display at the St Enda's fête. The purpose of such training was to prepare the boys for their

51 Ibid., pp 16, 24.   52 Ibid., pp 16, 27–30.   53 Ibid., pp 36, 39.   54 Ibid., p. 2.   55 Ibid., pp 18, 22.
56 'Touching the St Enda's Fête', *An Macaomh* (May 1913), 46.   57 Sisson, *Pearse's patriots*, p. 113.

future role in the Irish revolution, the first act of which was the Easter Rising of April 1916.

The paths of Pearse and Hobson diverged due to the rebellion. As one of the leaders of the Rising, Pearse staged his most legendary theatrical performance when he proclaimed the Irish republic against the backdrop of the General Post Office on Easter Monday 1916. Hobson, in dramatic contrast, was incarcerated in the home of an IRB member at 76 Cabra Park in Phibsborough, north Dublin, where his republican brothers were holding him at gunpoint. Hobson had opposed the rebellion, instead favouring a policy of guerrilla warfare should the British government attempt to disarm the Irish Volunteers or impose conscription on Ireland. As general secretary of the Irish Volunteers and chairman of the Dublin Centres Board of the IRB, Hobson possessed the capacity to scupper the insurrection. To avert this possibility, the IRB kidnapped him on Good Friday.[58]

Pearse apparently told Irish Volunteers at St Enda's that although 'he did not share Hobson's policy or approve his attitude' in relation to the rebellion, 'Hobson was not lacking in physical courage', but in 'the imagination and decision of a revolutionary leader'.[59] Hobson's retrospective view of Pearse was far less gracious:

> He was a sentimental egotist, full of curious Old Testament theories about being the scapegoat for the people, and he became convinced of the necessity for a periodic blood sacrifice to keep the national spirit alive. There was a certain strain of abnormality in all this. He did not contribute greatly to the hard grinding work of building up the movement, but as soon as we had succeeded in getting a small organisation [the Irish Volunteers] and a handful of arms he seized the opportunity to bring about the blood sacrifice.[60]

In Pearse's opinion, Hobson did not have what it took to be a revolutionary leader. For Hobson, Pearse was – in relation to the republican movement – a johnny-come-lately with a death wish.

In contrast to Hobson, many former and current members of the Fianna participated in the Rising as commanders, fighters, dispatch carriers and scouts. Seven were killed during the rebellion. The estimated number of past

---

58 Marnie Hay, 'Kidnapped: Bulmer Hobson, the IRB and the 1916 Easter Rising', *Canadian Journal of Irish Studies*, 35:1 (Spring 2009), 55–6.   59 Louis N. Le Roux, *Patrick H. Pearse* (Dublin, 1932), p. 337.   60 Bulmer Hobson, witness statement, 26 Jan. 1948 (MA, BMH, WS 84), p. 2.

pupils of St Enda's who joined the Rising ranges between twelve and seventeen. Among the fifteen individuals executed for their roles in the rebellion were two young men connected with the Fianna: Seán Heuston and Con Colbert. The latter also taught physical drill at St Enda's and was among the five men associated with the school who were executed, the others being Patrick and Willie Pearse, Thomas MacDonagh and Joseph Plunkett. Hobson's co-founder of the Fianna, Countess Markievicz, who had been one of the commanders at St Stephen's Green and the College of Surgeons, was spared the same fate because of her gender.[61]

While Pearse's execution for his leadership of the Rising ensured an afterlife of fame, Hobson lived a life of relative obscurity after 1916. He went into hiding after the rebellion and successfully evaded arrest. His opposition to the Rising and subsequent disappearance fuelled scurrilous rumours that he was a coward and a traitor. When he emerged after the amnesty in June 1917, he found himself frozen out of the nationalist movement and withdrew from public life, playing no part in the subsequent events that led to the foundation of the Irish Free State in 1922. He initially worked in book publishing before becoming a civil servant in the Office of the Revenue Commissioners.[62]

In his free time Hobson reawakened his interest in theatre. In the late 1920s he and his wife Claire (née Gregan), whom he had married while on the run in June 1916, supported the establishment of the Gate Theatre in Dublin. An *Irish Times* columnist described Claire Hobson as 'strikingly handsome' and praised her 'sound judgment' in relation to literature and theatre. The Hobsons were known for hosting gatherings at their south Dublin home, the Mill House on Whitechurch Road in Rathfarnham, at which 'the most diffident artists' were encouraged 'to express themselves'.[63]

The actor Hilton Edwards pitched his plan for the foundation of a new theatre for the production of international and Irish plays to a group of Dublin residents one spring night in 1928. This meeting took place in the Little Theatre, one of the few nightclubs in Dublin at the time. Run by

61 Hay, 'Foundation and development of Na Fianna', 69; Brendan Walsh, 'Radicalising the classroom: Pearse, pedagogy of progressivism' in Roisín Higgins and Regina Uí Chollatáin (eds), *The life and after-life of P.H. Pearse* (Dublin, 2009), p. 230; Sisson, *Pearse's patriots*, p. 156. Among the Fianna members killed was dispatch carrier Gerald Keogh, whom Sisson has cited as the only St Enda's boy killed.   62 For a discussion of Hobson's post-1916 career, see Marnie Hay, 'From rogue revolutionary to rogue civil servant: the resurrection of Bulmer Hobson' in Diarmaid Ferriter and Susannah Riordan (eds), *Years of turbulence: the Irish revolution and its aftermath* (Dublin, 2015), pp 209–23.   63 Quidnunc, 'An Irishman's Diary', *Irish Times*, 26 Feb. 1958.

Madame Daisy Bannard Cogley – known as 'Toto' – and her partner Gearóid Ó Lochlainn, it could be found 'in an obscure thoroughfare at the back of Grafton Street'.[64] Cogley, a petite French woman who had married an Irish republican, held a cabaret there every Saturday night.[65] The writer Mervyn Wall recalled that Claire Hobson 'was one of a bohemian group who frequented' this nightclub during the Emergency years,[66] possibly after the break-up of her marriage to Hobson circa 1940–1.[67]

In late 1928 Cogley and Ó Lochlainn joined Edwards and Micheál Mac Liammóir as the founding directors of what was to become the Gate Theatre. To fund the theatre's first season of plays, Edwards asked interested people to pay a one guinea subscription.[68] The Hobsons joined a committee to organize the business side of the burgeoning theatre company,[69] and helped Mac Liammóir to research famous episodes in Dublin history for a pageant in honour of the city's annual civic week in September 1929. *The ford of the hurdles* was a historic epic covering the period from the Viking invasion to the Easter Rising.[70] In 1934 Hobson edited an attractively illustrated book, entitled *The Gate Theatre*, which summarized the theatrical company's first six years of existence and served as a fundraiser for future productions. Hobson's book included an account of a production of Pearse's *The singer* in the Gate.[71]

In conclusion, Hobson and Pearse were not only inspired by the Irish cultural revival, but also made an active contribution to that revival through their use of theatre as a nationalizing force. Hobson served a brief stint as an actor and playwright and helped to set up two theatrical companies. Pearse also helped to build up a theatrical company, but, more significantly, appears 'to have been involved in almost every element of the production of his plays', particularly at St Enda's.[72] Hobson and Pearse challenged Yeats' hegemonic grip on the Irish national theatre movement through their involvement with the ULT and the Theatre of Ireland, respectively. In time, ULT productions and Pearse's work were performed on the Abbey stage. As a dramatist, Pearse was the more talented and prolific of the two. A serious performance practitioner, his commitment to the creation of theatrical productions was deeper and more sustained. Hobson, at least during his Belfast years, seems to have

---

64 W.D.J., 'The making of the theatre' in Bulmer Hobson (ed.), *The Gate Theatre* (Dublin, 1934), pp 11–12. 65 Phyllis Ryan, *The company I kept* (Dublin, 1996), p. 134. 66 Mervyn Wall to Des Gunning, 16 Jan. 1995 (photocopy of letter in possession of author). 67 Roger Mitchell to Marnie Hay, 9 June 2012 (email in possession of author). 68 Micheál Mac Liammóir, *All for Hecuba* (Dublin, 1961), pp 60–1. 69 Mac Liammóir, *All for Hecuba*, pp 87–8. 70 Mac Liammóir, *All for Hecuba*, pp 82–3; W.D.J., 'The making of the theatre', p. 15. 71 See Hobson (ed.), *The Gate Theatre*. 72 Ní Ghairbhí and McNulty (eds), *Patrick Pearse: collected plays*, p. 19.

been more interested in using theatre as a vehicle for propagating Irish nation-alism. His later involvement in the foundation of the Gate Theatre reflected his commitment to building up the cultural institutions of the new state. Finally, both men recognized the importance of youth to the nationalist movement and engineered opportunities for boys to perform acts of Irish nationalism both on and off the stage, most famously during the Easter Rising, the event that would ensure Pearse's posthumous fame and destroy Hobson's nationalist career.

2 / Patrick Pearse: literary pioneer and propagandist

ANNE MARKEY

In 1896, Patrick Pearse joined the Gaelic League, which had been founded three years previously to promote the preservation and revival of Irish as both an oral and literary medium. The young Dubliner soon became one of the League's most enthusiastic and prominent members, being co-opted onto the executive committee in the autumn of 1898.[1] The next year, convinced that the restitution of the Irish language was an essential precursor not only to the creation of a corpus of modern Irish literature but also to the establishment of an authentically Irish nation, Pearse declared:

> Newspapers, politicians, literary societies are all but forms of one gigantic heresy, that like a poison has eaten its way into the vitals of Irish nationality, that has paralysed the nation's energy and intellect. That heresy is the idea that there can be an Ireland, that there can be an Irish literature, an Irish social life whilst the language of Ireland is English.[2]

As Joost Augusteijn persuasively argues, Pearse, at the beginning of his public life, believed that 'the restoration of the language was the essence of being Irish; political nationalism should and could only come second'.[3] By 1916, his early conviction that the regeneration of the language was an indispensable prerequisite of Irish independence had been superseded by what turned out to be a fatal dedication to armed insurrection. Tracing Pearse's development as a writer, this essay investigates the relationship between Pearse's fiction and drama by exploring the publication, translation, adaptation and performance history of a selection of his stories and plays. That investigation reveals that over the course of his literary career Pearse displayed an acute awareness of the importance of different readerships and audiences and an increasingly manipulative use of literature for varying propagandist purposes. When he set aside attempts to revitalize Irish through the creation of a modern prose literature in that language to write instead

1 Ruth Dudley Edwards, *Patrick Pearse: the triumph of failure* (Dublin, 2006), p. 26.   2 Séamas Ó Buachalla (ed.), *The letters of P.H. Pearse* (Dublin, 1980), pp 8–9.   3 Joost Augusteijn, 'The road to rebellion: the

dramas for his pupils in St Enda's and nationalist English-language juvenile fiction for a wider readership outside the school, he recycled plots and settings between his stories and plays. Moving between genres and languages in a constant process of remediation, his work displays an escalating willingness to subordinate cultural ideals for political ends.

Pearse's youthful enthusiasm for the creation of a body of prose literature in the Irish language was fuelled by his appointment in 1900 as honorary secretary of the League's recently established publications committee.[4] The committee's task, as Ríona Nic Congáil explains, was to create 'a new literature *ab initio*, including educational text-books for learners, new print editions of old tales previously in manuscript form, and a creative literature for competent native speakers and those who were gaining in proficiency through their attendance at Gaelic League classes across the country'.[5] Pearse threw himself wholeheartedly into commissioning and editing work, corresponding with contributors, and correcting proofs, with the result that the publishing wing of the Gaelic League quickly became a successful business.[6] In 1903, despite not being a native speaker of Irish, he was appointed editor of *An Claidheamh Soluis*, the League's weekly newspaper. He continued in that capacity until 1909.

As Secretary to the publications committee and as editor of *An Claidheamh Soluis*, Pearse had considerable influence over what was and was not published by the Gaelic League. He was not averse to publishing his own creative work, which often appeared pseudonymously and was adroitly tailored to appeal to and meet the needs of different readerships. Between 1903 and 1904, he published in the pages of the League's newspaper his own edition of 'Bodach an chóta lachna' ('The clown in the grey coat'). Pearse rendered this traditional tale from the *fiannaíocht* cycle of stories about the mythic hero Fionn Mac Cumhaill in modern, vernacular Irish. 'Bruidhean chaorthainn' ('Hostel of the rowan tree'), another tale from the Fianna cycle adapted from various manuscript sources by Pearse, was published in *An Claidheamh Soluis* in 1907.[7] Both stories were also published separately as full-length works that could be

development of Patrick Pearse's political thought, 1879–1914' in Roisín Higgins and Regina Uí Chollatáin (eds), *The life and after-life of P.H. Pearse* (Dublin, 2009), p. 11.   4 Edwards, *Patrick Pearse*, p. 41.   5 Ríona Nic Congáil, '"Some of you will curse her": women's writing during the Irish-language revival', *Proceedings of the Harvard Celtic Colloquium*, 29 (2009), 205.   6 Edwards, *Patrick Pearse*, pp 42–3.   7 For a discussion of the editorial choices and practices adopted by Pearse in his version of 'Bruidhean Chaorthainn', see Caoimhín Breatnach, 'Exploiting the past: Pearse as editor and interpreter of *fiannaíocht* literature' in Higgins and Uí Chollatáin (eds), *The life and after-life of P.H. Pearse*, pp 195–202.

used as textbooks by adult learners interested in the Irish language and its associated cultural and literary traditions.

Acutely aware that if the language was to flourish children had to be brought into the revivalist fold, he set about providing engaging reading material for them. Using the pseudonym Siúbhan Pháidín Sheaghainín, he composed a series of Irish-language adaptations of various international folktales, which were published in *An Claidheamh Soluis* between 1905 and 1907. Written in simple, vernacular Irish, the series included variants of such tales as 'Chicken licken' (Aarne-Thompson-Uther type 20C); 'The three little pigs' (Aarne-Thompson-Uther type 124); 'The mouse's tale' (Aarne-Thompson-Uther type 2032); 'The billy goats gruff' (Aarne-Thompson-Uther type 122F) and 'The clever little tailor' (Aarne-Thompson-Uther type 850).[8] On their publication as a two-volume collection – *Maingín scéal* – by the Talbot Press and the Educational Company in the 1930s, Siúbhan Pháidín Sheaghainín's Irish-language versions of these stories were incontrovertibly attributed to Pearse; not only was he named as author on the title pages of both volumes, but in a note included in the first volume his sister, Margaret, also acknowledged his authorship and thanked the Gaelic League for granting permission to republish his work.[9] Given his adoption of a woman's name as a pseudonym, it is perhaps unsurprising that none of these stories ever appeared under Pearse's own name during his lifetime. It is, however, more surprising that subsequent critics have had nothing to say about Pearse's pioneering role in producing entertaining, Irish-language versions of folktales for children.[10]

Recognizing the need for the more widespread use of the language among the young, Pearse also created original Irish-language fiction for children. Using the pseudonym of Colm Ó Conaire, he wrote *Poll an phíobaire* (*The piper's cave*), which was serialized in three parts in *An Claidheamh Soluis* in March 1905. Addressed to a young readership of both native speakers and learners of Irish, this contemporary cautionary tale is an adventure story about two schoolboy truants from Connemara. It is the first example of a work in which Pearse at least partly sets the action in a schoolroom and focuses on the relationship between students and teacher, a scenario to which he would return in later Irish- and English-language plays and stories. *Poll an phíobaire*, again attributed

8 The Aarne-Thompson-Uther classification system is set out in Hans-Jörg Uther, *The types of the international folktale: a classification and bibliography* (Helsinki, 2004). 9 Patrick Pearse, *Maingín scéal* (Dublin, 1936), n.p. 10 I am grateful to Ríona Nic Congáil for confirming that these stories by Siúbhan Pháidín Sheaghainín were the first Irish-language folktales published for children.

to Colm Ó Conaire, was published in book form by the Gaelic League in 1906, complete with a glossary to make it suitable for use as a school textbook, testifying to Pearse's awareness of the needs of different types of young readers.

During his editorship of *An Claidheamh Soluis*, Pearse was involved in often acrimonious debates about the form that contemporary Irish literature should take. In 1907, he declared: 'Literature which is in Irish is Irish literature; literature which is not in Irish is not Irish literature.'[11] However, even those who agreed with him that literature written in English could not be regarded as authentically Irish disagreed on the idiom and type of narrative form that should be adopted in the creation of contemporary Irish-language literature. As Philip O'Leary has demonstrated, Gaelic revivalists were split on the related issues of the desirability of writing in vernacular Irish and of using folk narratives as models for contemporary fiction. O'Leary has described how 'nativists' (such as Father Richard Henebry/Risteárd de hIndeberg) insisted that Irish-language authors should replicate the classical standards associated with the seventeenth-century historian Geoffrey Keating, and maintained that folklore should provide narrative templates for a revival of Gaelic literature; 'progressivists', meanwhile (and here we could note figures such as Pádraic Ó Conaire), believed that writers should use the language of everyday speech and draw on contemporary international literary forms and genres.[12] Pearse sided with the progressivists, declaring: 'we lay down the proposition that a living modern literature *cannot* (and if it could, should not) be built on the folktale.' Urging Irish writers to look abroad for inspiration 'in France, in Russia, in Norway, in Finland, in Bohemia, in Hungary, wherever, in short, vital literature is being produced', he explained:

> we would have our literature modern not only in the sense of freely borrowing every modern form which it does not possess and which it is capable of assimilating, but also in texture, tone and outlook. This is the twentieth century and no literature can take root in the twentieth century which is not of the twentieth century.[13]

11 Patrick Pearse, 'Irish Literature', *An Claidheamh Soluis*, 13 Apr. 1907, p. 9. 12 See O'Leary, *Prose literature of the Gaelic revival, 1881–1921*. For more on this debate see Philip O'Leary, 'The Irish Renaissance, 1880–1940: literature in Irish' in Margaret Kelleher and Philip O'Leary (eds), *The Cambridge history of Irish literature*, 2 vols (Cambridge, 2006), ii, pp 226–69, esp. pp 236–50. 13 Patrick Pearse, 'About literature', *An Claidheamh Soluis*, 26 May 1906.

He also declared that the short story was the form 'in which the renascent prose literature in Ireland is likely to achieve its chief successes'.[14]

Believing that if the Irish language was to flourish as a literary medium it had to engage with modern life, Pearse wrote more thematically complex and formally innovative fiction at the same time that he was producing modern versions of tales from ancient sagas and various types of children's stories. Between February 1905 and December 1906, four short stories by Pearse, once more using the pseudonym Colm Ó Conaire, appeared on the pages of *An Claidheamh Soluis*. These stories, which were all set in a contemporary if idealized Connemara, were published in book form as *Íosagán agus sgéalta eile* (*Íosagán and other stories*) and attributed to Pearse by the Gaelic League in 1907. Again, the volume contained a glossary to render it suitable for use as a textbook. Not all contemporary commentators were impressed with Pearse's original fiction; the progressivist lexicographer, Patrick Dinneen, for example, claimed that *Poll an phíobaire* 'smacks more like the margarine of the slums than pure mountain butter', while the nativist Richard Henebry objected to Pearse's use of vernacular Irish and detected in 'Íosagán' 'a false Keltic note born out of ignorance and the "English" poetry produced in Dublin'.[15] Pearse responded in combative mode, declaring: 'If Dr Henebry thinks he is going to impose dead linguistic and literary forms on a living language, then he is mistaken. Irish literature has taken its path – the path of the living speech'.[16] As both *Poll an phíobaire* and *Íosagán agus sgéalta eile* were put on the curriculum for the Intermediate Certificate, they played an important role in the preservation and spread of the Irish language for decades to come. Pearse's early forays into fiction, then, reflected his commitment to that language and his desire to see it prosper. In the context of Edwardian Ireland, this undoubtedly was a political aim, but at that stage Pearse's primary literary purpose was to promote the regeneration of the Irish language either through the provision of modern renditions of traditional stories or the creation of original fiction.

Following the foundation of St Enda's in 1908, as the pressures of running a school began to take precedence over his involvement with the Gaelic League, Pearse switched from writing Irish-language fiction to writing drama. In October 1908, just a month after the opening of the school, a group went from St Enda's to the Abbey Theatre to attend a performance of *When the dawn*

14 Patrick Pearse, 'Recent booklets', *An Claidheamh Soluis*, 7 Oct. 1905. 15 Patrick Dinneen, '*Poll an phíobaire*', *Irish People*, 5 May 1906, cited in Philip O'Leary, *The prose literature of the Gaelic revival, 1881–1921: ideology and innovation* (University Park, PA, 1994), p. 120; Fr Richard Henebry, 'Revival Irish', *The Leader*, 6 Feb. 1909, p. 587. 16 Cited in Edwards, *Patrick Pearse*, p. 91.

is come, written by the deputy headmaster, Thomas MacDonagh. Although MacDonagh's play, set in Ireland fifty years in the future, at a time of insurrection against British rule, was not very well received by critics, it appealed to the group from St Enda's. Pearse, struck by the capacity of drama to inspire nationalist, even revolutionary, fervour reported: 'Our younger boys came home yearning for guns'.[17] He quickly realized that drama could play a role in promoting St Enda's and theatrical productions soon became a significant element of school life. The first plays staged in St Enda's and performed by the pupils were Douglas Hyde's *An naomh ar iarraidh* (*The lost saint*) and Standish James O'Grady's *The coming of Fionn*, which ran 21–3 March 1909. Pearse was delighted by the favourable publicity garnered for the school by these productions, written by established and respected authors who were sympathetic to the school's nationalist ethos. However, finding more plays, particularly Irish-language plays, which reflected that ethos and were suitable for a cast composed mainly of schoolboys was no easy task, so Pearse rose to the challenge by writing some himself.

The young heroes of ancient Irish sagas were held up as role models to the boys of St Enda's, and Pearse drew on material from the Ulster cycle in the creation of his first dramatic work, entitled *Macghníomhartha Chúchulainn* (*The boyhood deeds of Cuchulainn*). This elaborate pageant, with a very large cast, played to an audience of over five hundred guests in June 1909, marking the end of St Enda's first year of operation. Róisín Ní Ghairbhí and Eugene McNulty remark on the formality of the play's diction, not only in the dialogue but also in the descriptive passages that function as stage directions, noting that Pearse himself had declared that he had 'kept close to the *Táin* [...] merely modernising (but altering as little as possible) the magnificent phrase of the epic'.[18] It is striking that Pearse, the former advocate of the living speech of the people as a literary medium who had insisted that Irish literature should engage with 'the mind of contemporary Europe' and be modern in 'texture, tone and outlook', deliberately adopted a stylized diction in his first dramatic work while sticking closely to the text of a medieval Irish saga.[19] His previous commitment to modernity was a casualty of his movement from fiction to drama, from page to stage, because Pearse was no longer simply pursuing the grand ideal of revitalizing the Irish language through the creation of a new literature but was instead promoting St Enda's.

---

17 Patrick Pearse, 'School annals', *An Macaomh* (Midsummer 1909), 82.   18 Róisín Ní Ghairbhí and Eugene McNulty (eds), *Patrick Pearse: collected plays / Drámaí an Phiarsaigh* (Dublin, 2013), p. 25. Patrick Pearse, 'By way of comment', *An Macaomh* (Midsummer 1909), 15.   19 Pearse, 'About literature', p. 7.

He explained that his motivation for writing *Macghníomhartha Chúchulainn* was the desire to 'crown our first year's work with something worthy and symbolic', so he used an ancient saga for his source and employed a dignified form of diction to underline the epic nature of his project in St Enda's.[20] Aware that not all attendees would understand the play, he pragmatically provided an English-language summary in the original programme and published the Irish-language script in the first edition of *An Macaomh*, the school journal, which appeared in the summer of 1909. The in-house publication of the play signals a significant shift in Pearse's intended audience, as he was no longer addressing a nationwide readership of native speakers and supporters of the Gaelic League as had been the case when he published fiction in *An Claidheamh Soluis*.

In the next issue of *An Macaomh*, Pearse announced his intention to stage a 'miracle play in Irish', which would 'probably be a dramatised version of "Íosagán"'. Here, he was referring to his original story, 'Íosagán', which had initially been published in the December 1906 issue of *An Claidheamh Soluis* before being reprinted as the title story of his first collection of fiction in 1907. In *An Macaomh*, Pearse went on to explain: '"Íosagán" is not a play for ordinary theatres or for ordinary players. [. . .] It has in fact been written for performance in a particular place and by particular players.'[21] Even a cursory reading of the text of *Íosagán* the play, which was included in *An Macaomh*, reveals that it was very obviously based on Pearse's earlier story of the same name. In adapting the story for the school stage, Pearse continued to use the vernacular Irish to which Fr Henebry had objected and kept the kernel of the story's focus on the miraculous appearance of the child Jesus who has come to redeem Matthias, a kindly, old Connemara man who has not attended Mass for years. However, to make the play suitable for performance by the boys of St Enda's, Pearse edited out elements of the original story, including the girls who chattered happily, the women who spoke to each other in low whispers, and the anxious mother who worried about the old man's influence on the village children. Because there are no female characters, the play deals only with relationships between men and, unlike the story, is concerned with the construction of a distinctively Gaelic form of muscular Catholicism. Instead of just playing on the green, as the children in the story did, the group of boys among whom Íosagán appears in the play have been swimming in the sea before competing at jumping, and planning a game of handball. Pearse

---

20 Pearse, 'By way of comment', *An Macaomh* (Midsummer 1909), 15.   21 Ibid., 18.

believed in promoting the physical as well as the moral and intellectual development of his pupils. The 1909–10 St Enda's prospectus states that the school
aimed to develop 'a manly self reliance' and 'the formation of a sense of civic
and social duty', while paying 'careful attention [...] to Physical Culture':
'The boys are taught to prize bodily vigour, grace and cleanliness, and the
advantages of an active outdoor life are constantly insisted on.'[22] The hardy,
manly Connemara boys in the dramatic version of *Íosagán* were models for the
pupils who played them, so Pearse altered the story to create a play in which
they take centre stage, reflecting and promoting the ethos of the school.

Not surprisingly, the dramatic version of *Íosagán* was enthusiastically
received by a group of invited guests on its first performance in St Enda's in
February 1910. A slightly expanded version, which was staged at a benefit
night in the Abbey in April of that year and attended by many prominent
revivalists, attracted similar praise. The play was staged again at a *feis* for
Dublin children learning Irish in June 1910, when 'the pupils of St Enda's were
presented as exemplifying Irish Ireland'.[23] This success spurred Pearse to write
an English-language translation of the play, presumably in the hope of
bringing the school and the talents of its pupils to the attention of a wider
audience. By 1910, then, Pearse's interest in encouraging the development of a
modern Irish-language prose literature had been replaced by a desire to
promote the financially troubled St Enda's to English-speaking parents.
Although the English-language version of *Íosagán* does not appear to have
been staged during his lifetime, it was included in the volume entitled *Plays,
stories, poems* of the *Collected works of Pádraic H. Pearse*, published by Maunsell and
Co. in 1917. That Pearse adapted a story written to foster the development of
Irish-language fiction into a play staged to support St Enda's and then later
translated that play into English suggests that he pragmatically set aside his
earlier commitment to the development of the Irish language in order to help
the cause of St Enda's.

Pearse was a founding member of the Irish Volunteers in November 1913
and the following month was sworn in as a member of the Irish Republican
Brotherhood. His increasing support for violent nationalism was reflected in
at least some of his later works, such as *Owen*, which was staged in its original
Irish version for young audiences in two Dublin venues during the winter of
1913. There is no known surviving copy of the original Irish-language version,
but an English translation by Pearse reveals that the action takes place just

22 *Scoil Éanna* [St Enda's prospectus], 1909–10, n.p.   23 Ní Ghairbhí and McNulty (eds), *Patrick Pearse:
collected plays*, p. 30.

before the outbreak of the Fenian rising of 1867.[24] It opens, as *Poll an phíobaire* did, in a country schoolroom, but the play quickly introduces an overt political charge that was not in the earlier, more conservative story. At the opening of the dramatic action, the schoolmaster is reading aloud a section on effective fire cover from a military manual when a ballad singer selling the sheets of nationalist songs such as 'The wearing o' the green' and 'Bold Robert Emmet' arrives at the door of the classroom. The singer and the master exchange the Fenian codeword of 'The hawk of the hill', which Pearse explains was 'the name given to the organiser of the Irish Republican Brotherhood'.[25] Next, the ballad singer delivers a message to the effect that the rebellion will begin that evening. The ballad singer goes on his way; school finishes for the day, and all the boys, with the exception of Owen, go home. Not realizing that Owen is watching him, the master takes a rifle, ammunition and a sword from under the floorboards. When he sees the boy, he shows him how to arm the rifle and how to fire it. After telling Owen that he is going to fight the English that night, he asks the boy to promise that he will not tell anyone, not even his mother or father or any of the lads, about the gun or the bullets or the sword. The boy makes the promise just before the police descend on the school. The master hides the weapons and manages to escape thanks to the assistance of Owen, who retrieves and fires the rifle only to be killed in a return of fire. The teacher is portrayed as a brave and daring Fenian captain, but the real hero of the play is the young boy who promises not to let even his parents know that the master is a Fenian, and who sacrifices his life to ensure that the rebellion can proceed.

In this short play, as Ní Ghairbhí and McNulty point out, 'Pearse explicitly links education with preparation for military action.'[26] Noting that the play 'gave ammunition to those who condemned Pearse after the Rising for training revolutionaries at St Enda's', Ruth Dudley Edwards acknowledges that the charge is 'not wholly fair, being based on an over-literal interpretation' of the text.[27] Pearse's influence on the pupils under his care is difficult to determine, not only because estimates of the number of former St Enda's students who took part in the Rising vary, but also because alumni differ in their assessment of the extent to which the headmaster's politics influenced his pupils. Denis Gwynn, who played Conchubar Mac Nessa, the king of Ulster, in *Macghníomhartha Chúchulainn* and later went on to fight in the British army during the First World War, claimed that Pearse used St Enda's to

24 The English-language version, *Owen*, is included in Ní Ghairbhí and McNulty (eds), *Patrick Pearse: collected plays*, pp 167–74. 25 Ibid., p. 167. 26 Ibid., p. 175. 27 Edwards, *Patrick Pearse*, p. 204.

'provide himself with the nucleus of a young band of politicians who would follow him to the scaffold'.[28] By contrast, Desmond Ryan, an ex-pupil who fought in the Rising, recalled that during the early years of the school, the headmaster 'only spoke once to us as a convinced revolutionary, and that to his senior students as an aside'.[29] Ryan acknowledged that in later years, 'he spoke oftener to his boys of past efforts to gain Irish independence', but insists that:

> there was no undue political propaganda except where Irish history retold is in itself a very powerful visualisation of the great men and the great glories and the great mistakes of the past and a very powerful incentive to youth.[30]

It would be impossible to prove that *Owen* sent out 'certain men/the English shot'.[31] Nevertheless, it was undoubtedly a highly political and nationalist play that drew on Irish history to offer revolutionary ideals to youth, not only in St Enda's but also in the other venues in which it was staged during the winter of 1913.

In February 1914, Pearse offered a similar message 'To the boys of Ireland' in an anonymously written address of that title published in the republican newspaper *Irish Freedom*. There, he drew on Irish mythology and history to encourage his young readers to join Fianna Éireann, a nationalist youth group established by Constance Markievicz and Bulmer Hobson in 1909. According to Marnie Hay, 'the official Fianna organisation, as well as individual members, published propaganda aimed mainly at boys in their pre-teen and teen years in advanced nationalist newspapers'.[32] In *Irish Freedom*, Pearse endorsed Fianna Éireann's aim 'to train the boys of Ireland to fight Ireland's battle when they are men'.[33] When Patsy O'Connor and Percy Reynolds launched *Fianna*, the organization's unofficial monthly paper, in 1915, Pearse was one of their first and most loyal contributors. His unfinished adventure story, *The Wandering Hawk*, was serialized in its pages between February 1915 and

28 Cited in Brendan J. Walsh, 'The progressive credentials of Patrick Henry Pearse: a response to David Limond', *History of Education Review*, 35:2 (2006) at http://www.freepatentsonline.com/article/History-Education-Review/164638619.html, accessed 4 Jan. 2016.   29 Desmond Ryan, *Remembering Sion: a chronicle of storm and quiet* (London, 1934), p. 96.   30 Ibid., p. 117.   31 The phrase comes from Yeats' poem, 'The man and the echo', in which the poet speculates that *Cathleen Ni Houlihan*, the 1902 play he co-wrote with Lady Gregory, inspired Irish men to become active revolutionaries.   32 Marnie Hay, 'The propaganda of Na Fianna Éireann, 1909–1926' in Mary Shine Thompson (ed.), *Young Irelands* (Dublin, 2011), pp 47–56, p. 19.   33 Patrick Pearse, *Collected works of Pádraic H. Pearse: political writings and speeches* (Dublin, 1916), p. 53.

January 1916, just a month before the journal ceased publication and only two months before the Easter Rising. In *Fianna*, it was claimed that each episode was originally written in Irish, but, as Séamas Ó Buachalla points out, Pearse himself said it was originally written in English.[34] Set in a fictitious boarding school named St Fintan's, *The Wandering Hawk* reworks and expands *Owen* to tell how a Fenian teacher inspires his pupils with tales of Irish history and nationalism. As in the earlier play, education is explicitly linked with the promotion of violent republicanism and with preparation for military action. *The Wandering Hawk* promotes the very qualities – bravery, loyalty, athleticism – fostered in public schools, promulgated through popular adventure stories, and associated with the *esprit de corps* and aggressive model of masculinity that underpinned British imperialism.[35] Here, though, Pearse suggests that Irish boys should develop those character traits and place them in the service of freeing Mother Ireland. By serializing the story in *Fianna*, Pearse was extending his influence beyond the confines of the school and issuing a general call to arms to the youth of Ireland.

In *The Wandering Hawk*, a charismatic teacher, Owen Kilgallon, inspires his senior pupils, one of whom narrates the story, with tales of Ireland's past wars and current conflicts. One day, a travelling tin whistler comes to the school and speaks covertly in Irish to Kilgallon, whom the young narrator dubs the 'Little Captain' because he reminds him of Napoleon. As the action progresses it becomes clear that Kilgallon is a Fenian, who goes by the name of 'The Wandering Hawk' in honour of James Stephens. When the authorities descend on the school, Kilgallon flees but the tin whistler is arrested. The teacher's loyal band of pupils do everything they can to help further the fight for Irish freedom. They pass messages between Kilgallon's comrades, take the Fenian oath, use smuggled guns to fight the British navy, and help to free a Fenian prisoner. The story breaks off at the point where the boys, at Kilgallon's command, have arranged to have telegraph wires cut so that the authorities cannot send for reinforcements after a successful Fenian ambush. Although named after an American pupil at St Enda's who went on to fight in the GPO, Kilgallon reflects aspects both of Pearse's ideal self and of his friend, Thomas MacDonagh, who, in common with Pearse and Kilgallon, admired Napoleon and was an inspirational teacher. To ensure that the story would excite the young readers of *Fianna*, Pearse read extracts from *The Wandering Hawk* to his senior pupils in St Enda's. Fearing that the episode in

34 Séamas Ó Buachalla (ed.), *The literary writings of Patrick Pearse* (Dublin, 1979), p. 10.   35 Jonathan Rutherford, *Forever England: reflections on masculinity and empire* (London, 1997), p. 15.

which Kilgallon and his acolytes destroy a British gunboat was too melodramatic, Pearse was relieved when one St Enda's boy replied: 'Only one gunboat! How moderate! Why not half the British fleet!'[36] Describing the attack on the gunboat, the young narrator of *The Wandering Hawk* recalls:

> We blazed. I shot as coolly as if I had been shooting at a row of magpies in a fair. I saw men go down with as much satisfaction as I would have seen a magpie topple. It was as interesting as, and not more exciting than, shooting magpies. I felt a sort of artistic pleasure in doing my work well.[37]

This cold-blooded, blasé account of a violent guerrilla attack reveals a disturbingly gung-ho acceptance of arming schoolboys in the nationalist cause. While the boys of St Enda's may well have responded positively to the story, one hundred years later global concerns about terrorism and the militarization of the young render problematic this type of propagandist children's fiction.

Owen appeared in the December 1915 edition of *Fianna*. By translating the play into English and publishing it in a newspaper produced for members of a nationalist youth movement, Pearse was again aiming to incite young nationalists to violent action on Ireland's behalf. In a prefatory note, he observed: 'Companies of the Fianna may find the English version suitable for performance at some of their Céilithe [events that usually included music and dance].'[38] This observation suggests that he wanted the call to arms encoded in the play to reach as wide an audience as possible. Having first used a school setting in *Poll an phíobaire*, a story that aimed to entertain young readers while helping them to gain fluency in Irish, Pearse went on to use a similar setting in works in both Irish and English that not only reflected his increasing commitment to violent nationalism, but also aimed to convert others, particularly boys, to that cause. It is telling that Pearse's play *The master*, though ostensibly written in Irish, was performed in English in 1915, while his final play, *The singer*, was written in English (though set in Connemara). Both plays evoked the theme of militant nationalism, as had the pageants produced by Pearse in Croke Park in 1913.

It is important to acknowledge that Pearse did not entirely abandon his attempts to contribute to the creation of modern Irish-language fiction.

36 Ryan, *Remembering Sion*, p. 117.   37 Ó Buachalla (ed.), *The literary writings of Patrick Pearse*, p. 232.   38 Ní Ghairbhí and McNulty (eds), *Patrick Pearse: collected plays*, p. 167.

Following a hiatus of six years in his short-story writing, he published 'An mháthair' ('The mother') in *An Claidheamh Soluis* in December 1913. This went on to become the title story of his second book of short fiction, *An mháthair agus sgéalta eile* (*The mother and other stories*), a thematically diverse collection published by Dundealgan Press in January 1916. Pearse contributed short excerpts from an unfinished dual-language story entitled 'An choill' in Irish and 'The wood' in English to the *Irish Review* in 1914. The posthumously published *Collected works of Pádraic H. Pearse: plays, stories, poems* (1917) did not include *The Wandering Hawk*, the English-language excerpts from 'The wood' or any of Pearse's Irish-language fiction, but it did contain translations by the poet Joseph Campbell of all the stories that had featured in *Íosagán agus sgéalta eile*, and *An mháthair agus sgéalta eile*. Those stories, explained a reviewer in the aftermath of the 1916 Rising, were written 'to fill a want in Irish literature'. The reviewer went on to claim that Pearse valued active patriotism over his own literary talents: 'As he saw his duty to Ireland, it called for the sacrifice of his career as a writer.'[39] It might have been more accurate to claim that what Pearse saw as his duty to Ireland influenced his career as a writer. While editor of *An Claidheamh Soluis*, he helped to develop children's literature in Irish by writing versions of popular folktales in Irish for young readers, a novella-length children's adventure story and short fiction for children. From 1909, he wrote and staged plays that were closely connected with the publicizing of his school, St Enda's. Although his interest in modernising Irish-language literature continued, most notably in his poetry collection, *Suantraidhe agus Goltraidhe* (1914), his attention increasingly turned to politics. In the years immediately preceding the Rising he effectively became a propagandist for revolutionary nationalism, with the intention of inciting young actors, audiences and readers to violent action on Ireland's behalf. Notwithstanding his ongoing commitment to the Irish language, in the final years of his life Pearse produced not only an unfinished propagandist school story but also a corpus of nationalist youth drama in English. Regardless of the literary or dramatic merits of these late plays, their ideological charge underlines the problematic nature of both Pearse's attitude to young people during his lifetime and of his legacy a century after his death.

---

39 C. O'B, 'Review: *"The works of P.H. Pearse: plays, stories, poems"'*, *Studies: An Irish Quarterly Review*, 6:23 (Sep. 1917), 510–12 at 510–11.

3 / Escaping the 'Suburban Groove': Pearse, theatre and the landscape of Scoil Éanna

BRIAN CROWLEY

When I sent out the last number of *An Macaomh* from Cullenswood House I had no more idea that within twelve months I should be sending out this number from a slope of the Dublin mountains than that I should be sending it out from the plains of Timbuctoo. Yet very soon afterwards I had convinced myself that the work I had planned to do for my pupils was impossible of accomplishment at Cullenswood. We were, so to speak, too much in the Suburban Groove. The city was too near; the hills were too far.[1]

Patrick Pearse's introductory essay in the 1910 Christmas edition of the Scoil Éanna magazine, *An Macaomh*, was largely devoted to explaining and celebrating his school's new home in The Hermitage in Rathfarnham, a large eighteenth-century villa set in fifty acres of parkland at the foot of the Dublin mountains. He had launched the school two years earlier in the relatively modest surroundings of Cullenswood House on Oakley Road, roughly midway between the prosperous Dublin middle-class suburbs of Rathmines and Ranelagh. It had been set up 'with the object of providing an elementary and secondary education distinctively Irish in complexion, bilingual in method, and of a high modern type generally'.[2] In the very first edition of *An Macaomh*, Pearse promises to use the pages of the magazine to 'record the fortunes of our adventure at Scoil Éanna'.[3] He makes particular reference to the historical events associated with the area in the medieval period and remarks on the school's good fortune in being located in one of the 'noble old Georgian mansions of Dublin', which had been the birthplace of the great Irish historian, W.H. Lecky. The Cullenswood years were arguably the richest and most exciting in the school's history. Its theatrical productions and other activities drew support and praise from many of the leading figures of the Irish cultural revival. Pearse had a particularly strong

1 'By way of comment', *An Macaomh*, 2:3 (Christmas 1910), 9. 2 Séamas Ó Buachalla, *A significant Irish educationalist: the educational writings of P.H. Pearse* (Cork, 1980), p. 317. 3 'By way of comment', *An Macaomh*, 1:1 (Midsummer 1909), 7–8.

bond with the boys from those earlier years and several of them would later fight alongside him in the 1916 Rising. However, despite the success he had experienced in Cullenswood House, its rich history and its beautiful gardens, in 1910 Pearse left it – and 'the Suburban Groove' – for the wild beauty of the Dublin foothills.

The phrase, 'the Suburban Groove', related not just to the geographical location of the school: it was also a theatrical reference which would have been recognized by contemporary readers. The phrase came from the title of a play by W.F. Clancy, which was first performed in the Abbey Theatre in October 1908, coinciding, more or less, with the opening of Scoil Éanna in Cullenswood House. *The Suburban Groove* was to be a popular play in the Abbey repertoire and had several revivals, including three separate runs in 1910. It was set on a Sunday evening in the dining room of the O'Connor family of Rathmines, where a friend of the son of the house, Dick Dalton, bristles at the confines and limitations of life in this most 'respectable' of Dublin suburbs. Rathmines at that time had become a shorthand term for a particular type of narrow, middle-class mediocrity. In her memoir, *The years flew by*, the republican and Rathmines native Sidney Gifford wrote that the area was the:

> butt of local humour for a couple of generations because its residents seemed to typify the flunky Irishman; with their strange synthetic English accent, their snobbery, and their half-hearted desire to be a ruling caste. Rathmines was a phenomenon. It was not a racial group nor a political stronghold, but a spiritual condition.[4]

In the play, Dalton has a secure clerkship with an insurance company at £200 a year, but longs to escape the 'drab little world of Sunday evenings' and pursue a career as a journalist in London. He shares a Pearsean belief that 'every man should find out – if he can – what his special line is, and then go for that for all he is worth'. He rejects the 'respectable' West Briton, middle-class values of Mrs O'Connor and his love rival, Claude Callan, a typical 'Rathmines Johnnie', who are in thrall to the doings of the vice-regal court. He is determined to escape but his love for Una O'Connor, the daughter of the house, causes him to give up his dream of pursuing journalism in London, and the play ends with their engagement and his decision to stay with his old life in Dublin. There is an ambiguity about this ostensibly conventional ending to the play. James O'Connor, his now future father-in-law, warns him that he has 'shut the door on all the big ideas ... you've chosen the small world, you're going to stick in the old groove'. He goes on to say that 'Life is all like that, it's all giving up, all compromises.'[5]

The reference to Clancy's play in the 1910 *An Macaomh* would have been an in-joke between Pearse and his readers, who were made up of supporters of the school, his pupils and their parents. Most of the boys who attended Scoil Éanna were drawn from nationalist families who were involved, or at least supportive, of the Irish cultural revival. Many of them were regular visitors to the Abbey Theatre and would have immediately understood Pearse's topical cultural reference. He was also indicating to his readership that the Scoil Éanna project should be seen as a challenge to the narrow culture of the small drawing rooms of Rathmines. Scoil Éanna was to be no domestic drama, but something altogether more epic in scale. He makes this point within a theatrical context because performance had been one of the most defining characteristics of the school in those early years. Pearse founded Scoil Éanna to fill the need for a school that could educate through the Irish language. However, from the beginning, Scoil Éanna was always much more than just an Irish-language school. Pearse wanted it to provide an education that was distinctly Irish and would 'recreate and perpetuate'[6] the values and traditions of ancient Ireland and, in particular, the mythical boy-corps of Eamhain Macha, the Ulster seat of King Conchubar Mac Nessa and the *Fianna* of Fionn. While Pearse promoted the school as a revival of ancient traditions, it also embodied what were then radically modern ideas of a child-centred education in which the pupils were encouraged to develop into their own best selves and pursue their individual talents.

Pearse needed the school to have a prominent public profile, and, in its early years in particular, theatre offered a way of not only promoting the school, but also demonstrating to Irish society what was distinctive and different about it. The quality and sophistication of the plays the boys performed became one of Scoil Éanna's defining characteristics. They were an opportunity to gain support from important figures in the revival movement and show them the work of the school. The school's sometime architect and an inveterate playgoer, Joseph Holloway, regularly attended, and in his descriptions of the performances he also made note of the distinguished

5 W.F. Clancy, *The Suburban Groove*, NLI, MS 29, 123. 6 'By way of comment', *An Macaomh*, 1:1 (Midsummer 1909), 9.

guests from the Irish cultural scene who attended. These included Standish O'Grady, W.B. Yeats, Padraic Colum, the Markieviczes, Agnes O'Farrelly, Mary Hayden, Eoin Mac Neill and Oliver Sheppard. At such performances, the audience would be led through the garden, which was lit by Chinese lanterns, to the school theatre, a temporary building of corrugated iron. In a sense, the whole evening was a performance, a public display of the school's values and Pearse's vision for it.

During the Cullenswood years the Scoil Éanna pupils performed five plays: *The coming of Fionn* by Standish O'Grady and *An naomh ar iarraidh* by Douglas Hyde in February 1909, Pearse's pageant, *Macghníomhartha Chúchulainn* (*The boyhood deeds of Cuchulainn*) in June 1909 and a double bill of Padraic Colum's *The destruction of the hostel* and Pearse's adaption of his short story, 'Íosagán', in February 1910. All but the Cúchulainn pageant were produced in the Abbey in April 1910. The choice of plays by Padraic Colum, Douglas Hyde and Standish O'Grady positioned the school very clearly within the Gaelic revival. The plays the boys performed had either a Christian theme (*The destruction of the hostel*, *Íosagán* and *An naomh ar iarraidh*) or were inspired by the mythology of ancient Ireland (*The coming of Fionn*, *Macghníomhartha Chúchulainn*). Indeed, in his programme notes, Pearse seemed intent on emphasizing the thematic connections between *The coming of Fionn*, which was inspired by Ireland's cycles of heroic literature, and the Christian story of Hyde's *An naomh ar iarraidh*.[7] This reflected his wider attempts to blend the values of Christianity with those of the ancient Gaelic heroic age of Fionn and Cúchulainn in the education he provided in Scoil Éanna.

The plays were a great success, critically and ideologically. Pearse intended them to embody the school's mission to revive the Gaelic heroic tradition and impress upon both the audience and wider Irish society that Scoil Éanna represented nothing short of a rebirth of these ancient traditions. W.P. Ryan's review of *The coming of Fionn*, which appeared in *The Nation*, and which Pearse reproduced at length in *An Macaomh*, sums up the blurring of performance and reality which Pearse intended these productions to achieve:

> In 'The coming of Fionn' one could easily lose sight of the fact that it was dramatic representation; the boys for the time were part of heroic antiquity; dressed in the way they were, and intense and interested as they were, one could picture them in Tara or Emania without much

7 Elaine Sisson, *Pearse's patriots: St Enda's and the cult of boyhood* (Cork, 2004), p. 57.

straining of the imagination. The heroic spirit had entered into their hearts and their minds, and one realised very early indeed that the evening's life and spirit were not something isolated, a phase and charm to be dropped when they re-appeared in ordinary garb. The evening's sense was a natural continuation of that of many evenings and days when the spirit of Fionn and his heroic comrades had been instilled into their minds by those for whom the noble old-time lore had a vivid and ever-active and effective meaning. Fionn and Cuchulainn and their high heroic kin had become part of the mental life of the teachers and the taught. With much modern culture they had imbibed things of dateless age, things that time had tested and found perennially human and alive.[8]

While performances of plays by O'Grady, Hyde and Colum positioned the school within the context of the wider Gaelic revival, it was Pearse's own compositions for his pupils that allowed him to use theatre as a way of articulating his vision for Scoil Éanna. The first of these was his outdoor pageant, *Macghníomhartha Chúchulainn / The boyhood deeds of Cuchulainn*, which was performed on the lawn of Cullenswood House at the end of the first school year in June 1909. Shortly before the first performance, Pearse wrote about his hope that the production would:

> crown our first year's work with something worthy and symbolic; anxious to send our boys home with the knightly image of Cuchulainn in their hearts and his knightly words ringing in their ears. They will leave St Enda's under the spell of the magic of their most beloved hero, the *Macaomh* who is, after all, the greatest figure in the epic of their country, indeed as I think the greatest epic of the world.[9]

There was no question of any other story other than that of Cuchulainn being the subject matter for this defining school production. In those early years in particular, Cuchulainn and his education under Conchubar Mac Nessa in Eamhain Macha was the principal historical antecedent on which Scoil Éanna sought to model itself. One of the pupils would later remark that Cuchulainn was mentioned so often in the school in the early years that it was as if he was 'an important, if invisible, member of staff'.[10]

Even before the first performance, Pearse seemed able to visualize the

8 'By way of comment', *An Macaomh*, 1:1 (Midsummer 1909), 14.   9 Ibid., 16.   10 Desmond Ryan, *The story of a success: being a record of St Enda's College, September 1908 to Easter 1916* (Dublin, 1919), p. 90.

performance and in particular how his pupils would act out the roles he had assigned to them. He imagined Denis Gwynn as Conchubar Mac Nessa, Eamonn Bulfin as Cathbhadh the Druid and Frank Dowling 'in face and figure and manner, my own high ideal of the child Cúchulainn'. Pearse saw in him a modern personification of the ancient descriptions of a 'small, dark, sad boy, comeliest of all the boys of Éire', who would embody Pearse's ideal of a boy: 'modest in a boy's winning way, with a boy's aloofness and a boy's mystery, with a boy's grave earnestness broken ever and anon by a boy's irresponsible gaiety'.[11] To reinforce this sense, the words spoken by the boys would be drawn from the original language of the *Táin*, extracted and slightly modernized by Pearse. An outdoor production would also release the performance from the confines of the proscenium arch and the theatre building; the entire school would be transformed into the ancient seat of Eamhain Macha. There is a sense that for Pearse this performance went far beyond play-acting. By re-enacting the heroic past the boys were able to make the values and ideals it represented manifest and real in the present. In the moment of performance, in other words, the boys became a living embodiment of Pearse's vision for the school.

The boyhood deeds of Cuchulainn was the most elaborate production so far in the school's history – with horses, a chariot and scenery provided by the Morrow brothers.[12] The artistic design of this production and the actual staging also owed much to Pearse's artist brother, William. The play featured several impressive set pieces in which the boys marched around the field – a feature that also had the welcome consequence of allowing a large number of the boys to be part of the event, always an important consideration for any school production. Joseph Holloway praised the earnestness and effectiveness with which the boys fulfilled their roles, feeling that in performing the pageant they had done 'something worthy of Ireland'. Following the play he joined the rest of the audience for tea, prize-giving and speeches. Holloway was as impressed by the audience as he was by the performance:

> It was a cheering sight to see those notable people present to do honour to the occasion – the first anniversary of the opening of the school. There is hope yet in Ireland when so many people feel enthusiasm over an event like this.[13]

11 'By way of comment', *An Macaomh*, 1:1 (Midsummer 1909), 16.   12 For more on the history of the Morrow brothers and their involvement in Irish theatre (in Belfast as well as Dublin) see Eugene McNulty, *The Ulster Literary Theatre and the Northern revival* (Cork, 2008).   13 Joseph Holloway, diary entry

While Pearse was undoubtedly pleased by the success of his pageant, its epic quality may also have highlighted the shortcomings of the school's location. Cullenswood was firmly located in staid suburbia, where Pearse had to deal with the challenge of running a boys' school in close proximity to solidly middle-class neighbours, who did not hesitate to take up their pens to complain about damage caused by balls kicked over walls, faces pulled at ladies through the windows of their drawing rooms and some choice language emanating from Pearse's pure-lipped *macaomh*s. A second performance the following year at the Castlebellingham *feis* may also have shown Pearse the effectiveness of an inspiring backdrop, one that was far from the narrowness of Rathmines. Castlebellingham was located on the edge of the Cooley peninsula, the birthplace of Cúchulainn, and the *feis* took place in the grounds of Castlebellingham castle. Reflecting on the Castlebellingham performance in 1910 Pearse wrote:

> I think that was the most spacious day in all our two years since we had come together to Scoil Éanna. I shall remember long the march of the boys round the field in their heroic gear, with their spears, their swords, their hounds, their horses; the sun shining on comely fair heads and straight sturdy bare limbs; the buoyant sense of youth and life and strength that was there. There was another march with our pipes and our banners to the station; and then home through the lamplit streets of Dublin.[14]

Seeing the pageant in such an appropriate and sympathetic location may well have reaffirmed Pearse's belief that the school needed a new home. In that same Christmas issue of *An Macaomh* Pearse would reveal that he was now writing from the school's new location in The Hermitage, Rathfarnham.

The move of Scoil Éanna to the elegant and impressive surroundings of The Hermitage in Rathfarnham was inspired by nothing as mundane or pedestrian as an estate agent. In the 1910 Christmas edition of *An Macaomh*, Pearse described how he had been reading Stephen Gwynn's book about the rebel Robert Emmet and 'came out to Rathfarnham in the wake of Emmet, tracing him from Marshalsea Lane to Harold's Cross, from Harold's Cross to Butterfield House, from Butterfield House to the Priory and the Hermitage'. Pearse goes on to say that a man called Edward Hudson made a home in The

23 June 1909, Joseph Holloway Papers, NLI.   **14** 'By way of comment', *An Macaomh*, 2:3 (Christmas 1910), 19.

Hermitage 'dotting his woods and fields with the picturesque bridges and arches and grottoes on which eighteenth-century proprietors spent the money that their descendants (if they had it) would spend on motor-cars'.[15] Legend had it that Emmet would have clandestine trysts in the grounds with his sweetheart, Sarah Curran. She lived in The Priory across the road, but her father disapproved of Emmet so they relied on the kindness of Edward Hudson who facilitated the two young people in their love affair. In the park Pearse found a path – known as 'Emmet's Walk' – where the lovers presumably took romantic strolls. There was also a lodge built in imitation of a military fort called 'Emmet's Fort' and an obelisk that Pearse believed to be a memorial to the horse owned by Curran. (In fact, the horse it commemorated belonged to one of the later nineteenth-century owners of the house.) Pearse even ate grapes from what was called 'Emmet's Vine'. Pearse's description of his 'discovery' of this property very clearly suggests to the reader that his move to Rathfarnham owes more to destiny than to happy accident. Although never explicitly stated, the subtext is clear: it is the spirit of Emmet who has led Pearse to the school's new and more worthy home.

Pearse noted that whereas he had spoken most often of Cúchulainn and his contemporaries while based in Cullenswood House, in The Hermitage it was Emmet and his band of rebels who most occupied his thoughts and those of his pupils. Pearse was unsure whether this was as a result of a change in him or the effect of 'the associations that cling to these old stones and trees'. While Emmet may have replaced Cúchulainn as the school's chief inspiration, he fulfilled this role in a very different fashion. In Cullenswood, Pearse sought to evoke the spirit of Cúchulainn by re-enacting the ancient sagas and using theatre to transform suburban Dublin into the mythic realm of Eamhain Macha. In contrast, in The Hermitage, the memory of Emmet infused the landscape:

> We know that Emmet walked under these trees (some of them were already old when with bent head he passed underneath their branches up the walk, tapping the ground with his cane as was his wont); he must often have sat in this room where I now sit, and, lifting his eyes, have seen the mountain as I see it now (it is Kilmashogue, amid whose bracken he was to couch the night the soldiers were in Butterfield House), bathed in a purple haze as a yellow wintry sun sets, while

---

15 Ibid., 11–12.

Tibraddon has grown dark behind it. I do not think that a house could have a richer memory to treasure, or a school a finer inspiration, than that of that quiet figure with its eyes on Kilmashogue.[16]

No further evocation of the school's new inspiration, no pageant or performance, was needed. Pearse did not employ the Morrow brothers to paint murals depicting the deeds of Emmet, as he had done in Cullenswood with Cúchulainn. Instead, there was a clear theatricality in how Pearse writes about the spirit of Emmet and how he used the dramatic backdrop of the grounds of The Hermitage to vivify his tale of Emmet's heroic deeds. Visitors to the school were told the story of Emmet and were shown the areas associated with him so that the school and the story of Emmet became completely interwoven.

Pearse's susceptibility to the historic associations of The Hermitage was no doubt aided by its dramatic combination of natural beauty and man-made features. The house itself was a modest-sized, severe neo-classical mansion. Its principal feature was a Doric portico, which gave the school the kind of gravitas and dignity it needed to compete with the elite Irish Catholic schools like Clongowes Wood College in Kildare, or Blackrock College in Co. Dublin. Pearse wrote that as the school had the 'highest aim in education of any school in Ireland: it must have the worthiest home'.[17] Dominated by the impressive backdrop of the Dublin mountains, the school grounds also contained a rugged river valley, woods and rocky outcrops. These features had been enhanced at the turn of the nineteenth century by the original owner, Edward Hudson, who had laid out the grounds in the Romantic or pictur-esque style, with carefully designed vistas and views that aimed to create a landscape both wild and mysterious. Like many similar gardens and parklands at the time, it was dotted with sham ruins or follies. However, what made it particularly distinctive was that these 'ruins' were not inspired by classical or Gothic models, but were built in imitation of ancient Irish field monuments. Both Edward Hudson and his son, William Elliot Hudson, were keen antiquarians. Within the grounds were a faux cromlech, a dolmen, an ogham stone and a walled enclosure containing a structure built in imitation of an ancient portal. The name of the house and grounds, The Hermitage, was reflected in the construction of a hermit's cave and various ecclesiastically inspired arches. The figure of the isolated, melancholic hermit who retreated

16 Ibid., 12.   17 Ibid., 9.

from the world to pursue a life of contemplation was popular during the Romantic period and there are numerous examples of hermitages being constructed to evoke their presence. Pearse responded to both the inherent theatricality of the landscape and its playful possibilities. In 1913, for example, he wrote a series of articles entitled 'From a hermitage', in which he rather impishly adopted the persona of 'the real (or imaginary) hermit who once lived (or did not live) in this place'.[18]

Despite his enthusiasm for the school's new home, in practical terms the move to Rathfarnham had major implications for the nature of the school's theatrical performances. The school was now a considerable distance from the city centre with no direct public transport, so evening performances in an indoor theatre within the school itself were no longer an option. With the exception of outdoor pageants, all future performances would now take place in city-centre theatres. This coincided with Pearse's development and increasing confidence as a playwright. While his motivation in writing plays still originated from his need to provide appropriate theatrical vehicles for his pupils, in terms of stagecraft and writing, his plays from this point became more sophisticated and accomplished. They were also increasingly more reflective of his personal political, philosophical and artistic preoccupations.

The school had already performed in the Abbey Theatre in April 1910, prior to their move to Rathfarnham. These were revivals of several plays previously performed in the school's theatre. Pearse's first play written specifically for the Abbey stage was an Irish-language Passion play. Pearse adapted the dialogue directly from the biblical text. In addition to presenting the story in Irish, he also incorporated distinctly Irish elements into it, including a traditional 'keen' or lament. The production was highly praised and included modern stage techniques while remaining true to Passion play traditions. From Joseph Holloway's description, it is clear that Pearse took advantage of the technical resources that came with performing in a professional theatre:

> The lighting of this whole scene from beginning to end could not be more effectively managed and the whole scheme was of unsurpassable beauty. As the people pray on the hillside the ominous sound of hammering is heard and soon after our Lord's voice and those of the thieves who hang on either side of him are heard away in the distance

18 Patrick Pearse, *Collected works of Pádraic H. Pearse: political writings and speeches* (Dublin, 1924), p. 143.

until at last all is still and the stage darkens and the thunder rolls and
the lightning flash and in awe we feel all is over and the greatest tragedy
of the world consummated and all who had followed the incidents were
deeply and wonderfully moved. The students of St Enda's and St Ita's
had in a simple and unaffected way re-created the tragedy of the king of
the world for us again and we felt all the better for the sight. Never had
I seen a more profoundly impressive and beautiful picture than that I
had beheld during the Crucifixion. William Pearse was excellent as
Pilate, I was greatly struck by what, with simple means, great effects can
be produced and illusion interpreted on the stage. The crucifixion for
instance, was far more intensely sorrowful 'off' than had the picture been
really presented to the eye.[19]

While these performances in the city raised the profile of Pearse's school
and garnered praise for his educational experiment, to truly showcase the
school and its new home Pearse would have to attract visitors out to
Rathfarnham. The school's next production took place the following year and
was a play called *An rí* (*The king*), which was initially written as an outdoor
performance piece. It was set in a monastery school in early medieval Ireland
and opened with a group of boys discussing the travails of their king, who
they can hear riding by in the distance as he heads to battle. The king is
defeated, and, bloodied and humbled, he wanders into the monastery and
announces that God has abandoned him because of his evil ways. He begs the
abbot to replace him as king with whoever among the pupils is purest of
heart. This new king alone can defeat their enemies and save the kingdom. All
in the monastery agree that the chosen leader must be a young boy called
Giolla na Naomh ('servant of the saints'). Arrayed in the robes of a king, this
young boy leads the army to victory but is slain in battle. The play ends with
his dead body being borne back to the monastery for burial. Unlike the other
plays Pearse had written for his pupils to perform, this was not an adaptation
but a completely original piece. Its themes of childlike innocence and purity,
heroism, and self-sacrifice for the greater good were reflective of Pearse's own
personal preoccupations. However it was also shaped by many practical
considerations, which reflect its origins as a school play, not least of which
was that its cast was largely made up of young boys, with plenty of non-
speaking roles for members of the student body. The lead role of Giolla na

19 Joseph Holloway, diary entry, 8 Apr. 1911, Joseph Holloway Papers, NLI.

Naomh was played by Desmond Carney, one of the school's brightest intellectual stars at the time. He was photographed in costume and this image featured in the school magazine. As always, the costuming was of a high standard and featured a winged headdress that must have given the production a distinctly Wagnerian air.

The performance formed part of the school's annual open day, or *aeridheacht*, which rounded the school year off in June 1912. It was also a way of showcasing the school's impressive new home by taking advantage of the opportunities it offered for more ambitious staging and heightened dramatic effects. Pearse wrote the following year that it had been staged with 'much pageantry of horses and marchings, at a place in our grounds where an old castellated bridge, not unlike the entrance to a monastery, is thrown over a stream'.[20] The faux ruins that had been built in the eighteenth century to evoke the spirit of a hermitage now allowed Pearse to draw parallels between his school and the ancient centres of Irish monastic scholarship. As he wrote in 1910:

> Edward Hudson in the eighteenth century, had his eyes on the sixth century, but he was building for us in the twentieth. His quarrying had ends he did not foresee, and his piled stones have found at last their destined use.[21]

Pearse may well have had the area by the castellated bridge in mind when writing the piece, and the setting proved to be a crucial part of the play's success. The reviewer in the *Irish Times* could imagine 'No more fitting locale' for the performance. The grounds of St Enda's were 'specially favoured by nature', the 'secluded spot sheltered by tall elms' where the play was enacted formed the 'perfect background' and a 'natural stage'. Moreover, the reviewer continued, the 'youthful players in their Gaelic dress, fitted into the scene as perfectly as if they were part of it'.[22] It was as if the landscape within the walls of The Hermitage had enabled them to blur the distinction between the play and the school itself. Once again this outdoor performance had gone beyond mere play-acting: the performance and the school had become one organic whole.

While Pearse may have found a home for the school that was an ideal location in which to realize his educational vision, that home would soon

20 'By way of comment', *An Macaomh*, 2:3 (May 1913), 9.   21 'By way of comment', *An Macaomh*, 2:3 (Christmas 1910), 13.   22 *Irish Times*, 17 June 1912.

threaten the school's very existence. Pearse had outstanding bills even before the move to Rathfarnham, and the move precipitated a financial crisis from which he and the school were never able to escape. According to his former pupil Denis Gwynn, Pearse was disappointed with the rate of Irish language learning in the school, particularly among the day pupils, who were returning to anglophone homes every evening. His hope in moving out to Rathfarnham was that these day pupils would become boarders. His vision of a 'child-republic' would only be fully realized if the students learned and lived together. However, many of the parents of Pearse's day-pupils did not send their boys as boarders to Rathfarnham; instead, the distance from the city combined with a lack of public transport meant that the school lost pupils year on year. The resultant loss of revenue was compounded by debts run up as a result of alterations to the building to adapt it for use as a school. In addition, in 1910 Pearse had also opened a girls' school, Scoil Íde in Cullenswood House, which closed just two years later, leaving more unpaid bills. Fundraising became an increasingly urgent priority, and Pearse attempted to harness the school's theatrical reputation to shore up its precarious finances. At the invitation of W.B. Yeats, a fundraising double-bill of *An rí* (with additional dialogue) and Rabindranath Tagore's *The post office* took place in the Abbey Theatre in May 1913.

While the productions in the Abbey were highly praised, the next event in aid of the building fund of St Enda's was less successful. Between 9–14 June 1913 the St Enda's fête took place in the athletic grounds on Jones' Road (now Croke Park stadium). There was a mixed programme of music, dancing and performance but the highlight of each day was to be a pageant performed by the boys of Scoil Éanna. There were three in all which were performed on different nights: a revival of *An rí*; a new work, *The defence of the ford*, which Pearse based on the story of Cúchulainn and the cattle raid of Cooley; and *The Fianna of Fionn*. According to the programme, *The Fianna of Fionn* did not 'tell any story, but is in the nature of a rhythmical march symbolizing the activities of the ancient fianna'. Sean O'Casey was an enthusiastic volunteer at the event and recorded in his autobiography his often humorous observations of how things unfolded. While he was never slow to prick the pomposity of the Gaelic revivalists, he seems to have been genuinely moved by the boys' performance. Despite these theatrical triumphs, the event itself proved overly ambitions and ill-fated. There was torrential rain throughout the week, and both Pearse and his audience appeared dispirited.[23] He also had

23 See Sean O'Casey, *Drums under the window* (London, 1945), pp 278–84.

to contend with an obstinate organ grinder, who refused to silence his music so that the words of Cúchulainn could be heard, and on the last night a fire destroyed two dressing rooms. Even the normally supportive Joseph Holloway was unimpressed, though admittedly his disapproval was directed against the lack of support for the event as much as the event itself:

> There was a want of organisation about this Fête that depressed me – it lacked the dignity that should halo such an occasion – an Irish Fête set up for the maintenance of an Irish College! It was more on a level with a fair green on market day! It did not inspire! Irish Ireland entertainments, sad to relate, seldom do! How is it? What is wrong with them? Now Gaels don't all answer at once![24]

The lack-lustre nature of the Jones' Road fête may well have given Pearse pause for thought. Five years since the start of his educational adventure he had achieved much, and yet the project was increasingly troubled financially and his pupil numbers continued to decline (there were only thirty boys enrolled by 1915–16). While their school performances could move and inspire those who came to see them in the theatre or the rarefied surroundings of The Hermitage, the failure to translate that success to the more worldly location of Jones' Road was in many ways emblematic of the failure of Scoil Éanna to affect wider change beyond its walls. Pearse's attempts to expand the school and thus its influence had largely met with failure and even the medium-term future of Scoil Éanna was far from secure. Significantly, this period of decline for the school coincided with a period of heightened political activity in Irish society, which increasingly preoccupied Pearse's energies in much the way that Scoil Éanna once had. Reflecting on this time, Pearse regarded it as a period that would one day 'be regarded as the most important in recent Irish history'.[25] By the end of 1913, Pearse was one of the founding members of the new Irish Volunteers force and had also been secretly sworn into the revolutionary Irish Republican Brotherhood.

This new direction was reflected in the school's next theatrical offering that year. *Owen* was performed at the winter *ceilí* in the Mansion House, with Desmond Carney in the lead role once again. Significantly, the setting for this play was not an ancient monastery, but rather Ireland at the time of the 1867 Fenian rebellion. Like Giolla na Naomh, Owen must also sacrifice his life,

24 Joseph Holloway Papers, NLI.   25 Pearse, *Collected works*, p. 141.

this time to save his rebel teacher, who is going on the run to evade capture by the authorities. Owen is killed when he shoots a rifle at the police as they break down the door of the school. The Fenian rebellion was also the subject of Pearse's journalism at the time, and he looked to it as the last meaningful occasion when an attempt at revolution had been made. The play also reflects one of Pearse's other preoccupations in his newspaper articles at the time: the need for weapons. *Owen* contains a very pointed sequence in which the young boy expresses a fascination with the rifles he sees his teacher remove from a hiding place under the floorboards in preparation for the uprising. A photograph of Desmond Carney in the role of Owen showed him in the final scene of the play, on one knee, aiming a rifle. While this play was set in a school and its cast featured several boys, its inspiration would seem to owe more to Pearse's political interests than to Scoil Éanna.

The last of the Scoil Éanna outdoor performances took place at the annual *aeridheacht* on 13 June 1914. Entitled *Fionn: a dramatic spectacle*, it seems to have owed much to the *tableau vivant* form, which was very popular at the time. No script survives, but a detailed description of the action, including key lines of dialogue, was reproduced in the playbill. It told the story of how Fionn came to be the leader of the *Fianna* when he saved Tara and the high king, Conn of a Hundred Battles, from an onslaught by the son of Miodhna. William Pearse was responsible for much of the production and also played the role of Conn. The extent of Patrick's involvement is less clear. He had just returned from a fundraising lecture trip to the United States the previous month, and had been busy with a 'rush of work' preparing for the open day, exams and his work with the Irish Volunteers. The title of the piece suggests that the main emphasis was on its staging rather than its dialogue. This may well have been for practical reasons, as it limited the amount of time Patrick needed to contribute to the project. Also, by their very nature, open-air performances were not best suited to a large amount of complex dialogue. This production seems much more reminiscent of the pageants from the Jones' Road fête —*The defence of the ford* and *The Fianna of Fionn* — in terms of the emphasis on pure spectacle. It was to be one of the last of this type of outdoor pageant, a change that reflected the shift in Pearse's priorities at that time.

The performance of Pearse's next play for the school, *The master*, formed part of a double bill with another revival of *Íosagán* in the Irish Theatre on Hardwicke Street in May 1915. Although it was not performed in the school itself, it is possible to sense the influence of The Hermitage in the choice of setting. Like *An rí*, it takes place in a monastery school in ancient Ireland.

Ciarán, a monk and teacher, is visited by his former playmate, a pagan king called Daire. When they meet, they clash over the different choices they have made in life. Daire wants Ciarán to abandon his faith and the monastery and join him as his 'right hand', to assist him in ruling the people. He accuses Ciarán of wasting his life in pursuit of 'shadows' and 'ghosts', while Ciarán criticizes Daire for seeking out empty worldly pursuits. Elaine Sisson has suggested that these exchanges play out 'personal conflicts in Pearse's psyche: the tension between public service and private belief and the integrity of intellectual thought versus the "manliness" of action'.[26] This conflict is made explicit in the very specific stage direction in relation to the set. The play is to be set within a little cloister in the middle of a woodland:

> The subdued sunlight of a forest place comes through the arches. On the left one arch gives a longer vista where the forest opens and the sun shines upon a fair hill. In the centre of the cloister two or three steps lead to an inner place, as it were a little chapel or cell.[27]

Sisson writes that, like *An rí*, the play portrays 'two psychological landscapes: the interior, private and domestic space of the cloister and the public world of outside'.[28] In representing these two worlds in terms of a cloister and an unknown horizon, full of possibilities, it is also possible to see it as a reflection of the choice Pearse was then making to pursue the path of revolution rather than remain, surrounded by his pupils, in the peace and contemplation of his own hermitage in Rathfarnham.

Pearse's final work for the theatre, *The singer*, featured an entirely adult cast and was not written with his pupils in mind. It told the story of a revolution against British rule that began among an Irish-speaking community in Connemara. The central character, MacDara, is a Christ-like figure who in many ways acts as a Pearse surrogate in the play. He is the inspirational singer of the title, whose words can inspire men to acts of heroism. After many years wandering the roads of Ireland, he returns home to assist his brother Colm in the uprising. The play climaxes with MacDara heading out to face the British forces, stripped naked 'as Christ hung naked before men on the tree'.[29] Just as he had used theatre to transport his school back to the ancient playing fields of Eamhain Macha, Pearse now transported the coming revolution to

26 Sisson, *Pearse's patriots*, p. 76 27 Róisín Ní Ghairbhí and Eugene McNulty (eds), *Patrick Pearse: collected plays/Drámaí an Phiarsaigh* (Dublin, 2013), p. 177. 28 Sisson, *Pearse's patriots*, p. 75. 29 Ní Ghairbhí and McNulty (eds), *Patrick Pearse: collected plays*, p. 228.

an idealized and thoroughly gaelicized west of Ireland. It was not performed during Pearse's lifetime for fear its subject matter might alert the authorities to the very real rebellion that was being planned at the time. The first performance took place in 1917 and the cast was largely made up of former Scoil Éanna pupils, many of whom had fought in the Easter Rising. This play is often viewed as a rehearsal for the coming insurrection, but it could be argued that the audience Pearse had in mind were those who would see the play after the Rising.

Amid the hectic activity leading up to Easter 1916, Pearse produced a surprisingly large body of writing. In addition to this play, he wrote a series of political pamphlets, poems and a large part of the Proclamation. All of these works sought to explain the necessity of an armed revolution and contextualized the Rising within the wider Irish revolutionary tradition. Pearse himself was steeped in this tradition and understood its inspirational and imaginative power. His choice in creating a theatrical representation of his vision for the coming revolution is testimony to the importance that theatre had assumed for him in the years since his first Cúchulainn play was performed on the lawns on Cullenswood House. Just as that production had allowed Pearse and his school to escape 'the Suburban Groove' for an afternoon and to imagine and be elevated into the realm of the heroic past, this final play enabled Pearse to gain an insight into the imaginative and symbolic significance of the approaching Easter Rising. Perhaps, indeed, it was this imaginative ability that allowed Pearse to shape an event the success of which lay not in military victory, but in the hold it managed to take on the imagination of Irish society.

4 / Angel delight: Patrick Pearse and modernist experiment

JAMES MORAN

The final play that Patrick Pearse brought to stage production before his death was his script *The master* (1915), set in Ireland during the country's evangelization by Christian missionaries. Here, in a monastery, a teacher named Ciarán instructs a group of boys about the new religious faith, until an evil king tries to test this belief and puts a sword to the throat of one of the master's favourite boys, Iollann. However, as the boy kneels, Pearse scripted the following denouement:

> CIARÁN (*aside.*): I dare not speak. My God, my God, why hast Thou forsaken me?
> IOLLANN: Fear not, little Master, I remember the word you taught me...Young Michael, stand near me!

> *The figure of a mighty warrior, winged, and clothed in light, seems to stand beside the boy. Ciarán bends on one knee [...] He falls forward, dead.*[1]

Upon first reading that section of text, the reader may be left with the impression that Pearse's dramaturgy is entirely backward looking, a retreat into Celtic myth and Irish Christianity (and by implication, Catholicism). After all, the young boy making such a brave stand, Iollann, has the same name as 'fair-haired Iollann', a warrior who fights and dies to protect others in the Ulster cycle.[2] The angel who appears is the Archangel Michael, who in the Book of Revelation leads the good angels against Satan during the war in heaven, with the result that Satan 'was cast out into the earth, and his angels were cast out with him' (Rev. 12:9). Meanwhile, the boy's tutor, Ciarán, not only spouts the words of Christ on the cross (Matt. 27:46), but also bears the name of the sixth-century Irish saint who founded the monastery at

1 Patrick Pearse, *The master* in Róisín Ní Ghairbhí and Eugene McNulty (eds), *Patrick Pearse: collected plays/Drámaí an Phiarsaigh* (Dublin, 2013), pp 177–99, pp 196–7.   2 As Ní Ghairbhí and McNulty point out, the name may also point to Iollann Iolchruthaith, 'Iollann the rejuvenator', who appears in a fourteenth-century poem by Gofraidh Fionn Ó Dálaigh. See *Patrick Pearse: collected plays*, p. 197.

Clonmacnoise in Co. Offaly. Pearse's minor characters are also named after various figures from Irish traditional story, history and religion.[3]

Patrick Pearse steered his readers towards seeing his dramatic writing as being formed from a set of oral tales that the author knew through the influence of his mother, a native Irish speaker from Meath. He explained that:

> One of my oldest recollections is of a kindly grey-haired *seanchaidhe* [storyteller], a woman of my mother's people, telling tales by a kitchen fireplace. She spoke more wisely and nobly of ancient heroic things than anyone else I have ever known. Her only object was to amuse me, yet she was the truest of all my teachers. One of her tales was of a king, the most famous king of his time in Ireland, who had gathered about him a number of boys, the children of his friends and kinsmen, whom he had organised into a little society, giving them a constitution and allowing them to make their own laws and elect their own leader.[4]

That particular story formed the basis for the text of both *The master* (1915) and Pearse's earlier play *The king* (1912), two scripts that revolve around young boys and their priestly teachers in monastic schools. But Pearse had clearly supplemented those stories with some of his own reading about Irish history: for example, when Pearse read the autobiography of Theobald Wolfe Tone (the Irish revolutionary who died after the rebellion of 1798), he would have encountered the section by Wolfe Tone's son that explains how, for Wolfe Tone, 'the consciousness of dying for his country, and in the cause of justice and liberty, illumined, like a bright halo, his last moments, and kept up his fortitude to the end [...] he expired without further effort'.[5] When Pearse came to write *The master*, he ensured that his main character surrendered to a similarly redeeming death, in an ecstasy of religious feeling. After all, ever since Pearse's students at St Enda's had presented a double bill of plays about Christianity and ancient warriors as their first dramatic production in 1909, he had wanted to remind his contemporaries of 'the day when Ireland was both a more religious and a more heroic land than she or any other land has ever at any other time been'.[6]

3 See James Moran (ed.), *Four Irish rebel plays* (Dublin, 2007), p. 101. 4 Patrick Pearse, 'By way of comment', *An Macaomh*, 1:2 (Christmas 1909), 11–18 at 13. 5 Xavier Carty, *In bloody protest: the tragedy of Patrick Pearse* (Dublin, 1978), p. 68. See William Theobald Wolfe Tone, 'A last effort; Tone's death', *The autobiography of Theobald Wolfe Tone, 1763–1798*, ed. R. Barry O'Brien, 2 vols (London, 1893), ii, pp 338–70 at p. 368. 6 Quoted by Raymond J. Porter, *P.H. Pearse* (New York, 1973), p. 94. The boys performed

Such an apparently backwards-looking and introspective artistic vision would confirm the worst assessments of those who later denigrated the Easter Rising. Ezra Pound, for example, had grown to know Yeats well by the time of the insurrection, and responded to events in Dublin by scripting the essay 'Provincialism the enemy', which was then serialized in the journal *The New Age* during the summer of 1917. Here Pound excoriated 'ignorance of the manners, customs and nature of people living outside one's own village, parish, or nation'.[7] He also believed that the rebels of 1916 had little connection to the Irish dramatic tradition that had been developed at the Abbey Theatre, commenting, 'I think the theatre, Yeats, Synge and co. had developed a wide sympathy for Ireland, which the revolutionaries have wiped utterly away.'[8]

However, what I would like to emphasize in this chapter is that Pearse's theatrical range was not simply informed by the kind of ideas that Pound denigrated as 'provincial'. By focusing mainly on the concluding moment of *The master*, the point at which the Archangel Michael appears, we can see that Pearse also looked beyond Ireland and showed affinities with a broader, international set of ideas about experiment in the realm of performance and politics. Indeed, some of those international ideas had developed not in opposition to what 'Yeats, Synge and co. had developed', but precisely because of what Pearse knew from the Abbey Theatre.

EXPRESSIONIST ANGELS

In the influential study, *Theory of the modern drama*, Peter Szondi identifies a 'crisis' that happened in drama in around 1880. At this point, he argues, the alienated subjects of modernity and their social ideas could not be adequately contained by the Aristotelian form, and so writers including Ibsen, Strindberg and Hauptmann unknowingly introduced epic elements into their works.[9] Gerhart Hauptmann's work certainly manifests such a development: he journeyed away from a relatively straightened version of theatrical realism and towards a more expansive imagining of the possibilities of the stage. His early

Douglas Hyde's *An naomh ar iarraidh* (*The lost saint*) and Standish O'Grady's *The coming of Fionn* in March 1909.   7 Ezra Pound, 'Provincialism the enemy', *The New Age*, 12 July 1917.   8 Interestingly, one month after the Rising, Yeats intended to install Pound as manager of the Abbey, in the place of St John Ervine, but Pound opted against the move, following advice from John Quinn. See Pound, *The selected letters of Ezra Pound to John Quinn, 1915–1924*, ed. Timothy Materer (Durham, NC, 1991), p. 169, p. 120.   9 Peter Szondi, *Theory of the modern drama*, ed. and trans. Michael Hays (Cambridge, 1987 [1956]).

work *Einsame Menschen* (*Solitary people*, 1891) has been characterized by Leroy R. Shaw as focusing upon 'a familiar world delineated by the things of everyday life, populated with the types of people known from one's work and society'.[10] Hauptmann even dedicated that work to 'those who have lived it'.[11] But when Hauptmann wrote his 1893 play *Hannele*, he did something quite different: here and in his 1905 play *Elga*, he presented dream plays, but not quite in the same way as Strindberg. The dream plays of Hauptmann involve a character the audience sees first in a waking state before that character falls asleep and into the dream of the play. Hauptmann's work thus sought to expand the range of the theatrical form, by providing a kind of framing device within which a dream play could take place. Thus, as David Nicholson points out, Hauptmann's *Hannele* is effectively a 'naturalistic fairy tale', which begins with what Nicholson calls 'a typically naturalistic scene' as the squabbling inhabitants of a poorhouse are confronted with the arrival of the horribly bruised Hannele, a girl of about 14, who fell into a freezing pond while trying to evade her brutal stepfather.[12] But the drama is transformed when Hannele falls asleep and a dream section of the play begins, in which Hannele sees the apparition of her dead mother, and '*A green-gold light suddenly floods the room. Three radiant Angels, crowned with roses, and having the forms of beautiful winged youths, appear and take up the song.*'[13]

Patrick Pearse's dramatic oeuvre, of course, includes both angels and ancient warriors, as well as the kind of 'peasant quality' realism that Seán Ó Faoláin so derided. (Pearse's subsequent 1916 play, *The singer*, is set in '*the wide kitchen of a country house*' amid '*a wild country with a background of lonely hills*'.)[14] It may be that Pearse was simply creating a stylistically confused mishmash, but his theatrical writing looks less idiosyncratic when set against the 'naturalistic fairy tale' of Hauptmann, a dramatist whose oeuvre incorporated the arrival of angels and warriors (such as the dreaming knight of *Elga*), but also the realism of *The weavers* (1892). Shortly before Pearse wrote *The master*, the Abbey Theatre had staged Hauptmann's *Hannele* (in February, April and October 1913). By this time, Pearse knew this playhouse well, of course, having staged his work *Íosagán* there in 1910 and *The king* in May 1913. If he saw or heard about

10 Leroy R. Shaw, *The playwright and historical change: dramatic strategies in Brecht, Hauptmann, Kaiser and Wedekind* (Madison, WI, 1970), pp 27–8.   11 Gerhart Hauptmann, *The dramatic works of Gerhart Hauptmann*, iii: *Domestic dramas*, ed. Ludwig Lewisohn (New York, 1914), p. 128.   12 David Nicholson, 'Hauptmann's Hannele: naturalistic fairy tale and dream play', *Modern Drama*, 24:3 (Fall 1981), 282–91 at 283. 13 Gerhart Hauptmann, *Hannele*, trans. Charles Henry Meltzer (New York, 1908), pp 58–9.   14 Patrick Pearse, *The singer* in Ní Ghairbhí and McNulty (eds), *Patrick Pearse: collected plays*, pp 201–33, p. 201.

Hauptmann's play, he may have been impressed by the way the German made a child into the focus of the dramatic action, and by the way Hauptmann had moved into representing a moment at which expressionistic elements, in angelic form, intrude into the stage world.

If *The master* echoes the dramaturgy of Hauptmann, the script is also influenced by Rabindranath Tagore's play *The post office*. Yeats had met Tagore in 1912, and rated his work highly: he arranged to have Tagore's dramatic text performed in English at the Abbey in May and October 1913, and his high opinion of the piece is shown in a preface that he contributed to a published version of it in 1914, in which he commented that: 'On the stage the little play shows that it is very perfectly constructed, and conveys to the right audience an emotion of gentleness and peace.'[15] After Yeats had read *The post office*, he passed the script to Pearse, who spied similarities between his own earlier work *The king* and Tagore's play, noting 'both of us had in our minds the same image of a humble boy and of the pomp of death'. The Abbey Theatre staged the plays as a double bill in 1913.[16] When Pearse sat down to write his next play, *The master*, he, like Tagore, included the anticipated arrival of the king, as well as glorified death, and portrayed one of the main characters as a carefree young boy who takes delight in the natural world. Intriguingly, almost two years in advance of the rebellion, Pearse also knew of the central image described in Tagore's play: the 'Post Office here right in front of your open window, with the golden flag flying'.[17]

STONE ANGELS

That concluding section of *The master*, in which the Archangel Michael appears '*winged, and clothed in light*', would have looked familiar to anyone who had seen the church architecture that had been designed by Patrick Pearse's father, an English nonconformist who had been born in London and who raised a family (of four children, although only two survived infancy) in Birmingham before moving to Dublin in about 1864, after the death of his first wife. James Pearse spent his working life as a sculptor, and after he passed away in 1900, Patrick took to describing himself, for a while, as 'Patrick H.

15 W.B. Yeats, 'Preface' in Rabindranath Tagore, *The post office*, trans. Devabrata Mukerjea (London, 1914), p. vi. 16 Quoted by Louis Le Roux, *Patrick H. Pearse*, trans. Desmond Ryan (Dublin, 1932), p. 133. 17 Rabindranath Tagore, *The post office*, trans. Devabrata Mukerjea (Dundrum, 1914), p. 15.

Pearse, sculptor', and ran the family stone-carving company for a further decade. The angel who appears in *The master*, then, was a familiar image for a man whose father had spent his time carving angels and icons such as Erin Go Breagh and the marriage of the Virgin and St Joseph for gravestones, churches and public buildings in Dublin.[18] Certainly, the earlier parts of *The master* obsess over the kind of vivid vignettes that fill nineteenth-century devotional art, with the characters talking about, for example, 'Peter that carries a sword', 'Lazarus, for whom He [Christ] wept' and 'Martha, who busied herself to make Him comfortable'.[19] Indeed, perhaps the entire setting of the play reveals the stonemason's eye, taking place as it does in '*A little cloister in a woodland. The subdued sunlight of a forest place comes through the arches [...] In the centre of the cloister two or three steps lead to an inner place, as it were a little chapel or cell*'.[20] Patrick Pearse's father had, after all, worked for the company that upholstered and maintained one of Pugin's masterworks – St Chad's Cathedral in Birmingham – and so would have seen the ideas that Pugin had originally learnt as a stage designer at Covent Garden. As Rosemary Hill puts it, one of Pugin's recurring architectural themes was 'The space within a space, the picturesque ideal of revelation by partial concealment'.[21] When Patrick Pearse chose to fight at the Dublin GPO in 1916, the classical architecture was hardly reminiscent of this Gothic style with which his father had been most familiar, but by directing the rebels to occupy the main building that dominated Dublin's central thoroughfare, Patrick Pearse showed that he still maintained his father's aesthetic sense of where onlookers might focus their attention, and to this day, the GPO portico remains the most iconic image of the 1916 battleground.

Patrick Pearse's father had become involved with a set of politically radical ideas when in England.[22] In Birmingham, a church-furnishing company at which James Pearse gained employment was based on Newhall Hill, proudly remembered by city residents as the site where hundreds of thousands had gathered to persuade the government to pass the great reform act of 1832. James Pearse then witnessed a revival in radical sentiment in Birmingham, and his own thinking was particularly influenced by the Quaker politician and local MP John Bright. James Pearse travelled to watch Bright, remembering in

18 Brian Crowley, '"His father's son": James and Pádraic Pearse', *Folk Life: Journal of Ethnological Studies*, 43 (2004–5), 71–88 at 79–80.   19 Ní Ghairbhí and McNulty (eds), *Patrick Pearse: collected plays*, pp 182–3.   20 Ibid., p. 177.   21 Rosemary Hill, *God's architect: Pugin and the building of Romantic Britain* (London, 2007), p. 83.   22 For more about the influence that James Pearse exerted on his son's political views, see James Moran, '"He calls his dada still": nineteenth-century English radicalism and the drama of Pádraic Pearse', *Kritika Kultura*, 14 (2010), 53–74.

the mid-1880s having heard him giving a speech consisting of a 'large and most touching appeal for justice to this country [Ireland]'.[23]

Under Bright's influence, James Pearse found himself drawn towards still more unconventional political views. Bright strongly supported the atheist MP Charles Bradlaugh, a figure who championed a number of advanced causes such as birth control, female suffrage and home rule for Ireland. James Pearse thus came to admire Bradlaugh, acquired the MP's biography and maintained a degree of personal contact with the controversial figure. In fact, James sent a letter to Bradlaugh's daughter to enquire about her father's health on the day of Bradlaugh's death.[24] If the angel that appears in *The master* was partly inspired by James Pearse's sculpture work, then this apparition was no straightforward depiction of conventional Catholic piety. Through the work of James Pearse, that angel may have been freighted with politically radical ideas, including the advancement of women and the death of God.

Furthermore, in *The master*, Pearse emphasizes some of the more socially unorthodox personal relationships that might be found in Irish myth. The boy Iollann is, for example, described by his classmates as having a distinctly feminine appearance:

> MAINE: He is more like a little maid, with his fair cheek that reddens when the master speaks to him.

> ART: Faith, you wouldn't call him a little maid when you'd see him strip to swim a river.

> RONAN: Or when you'd see him spring up to meet the ball in a hurley match [...]

> MAINE: He has a beautiful white body, and, therefore, you all love him; ay, the master and all. We have no women here and so we make love to our little Iollann.[25]

Irish revisionist historians have tended to regard such moments in Pearse's writing as straightforward expressions of Pearse's own desires. Such a reading is not implausible. But we should also note that this depiction of Iollann is also self-consciously literary. The words spoken by Iollann's classmates hark

23 James Pearse, 'England's duty to Ireland', NLI, MS 21,079, f.16.   24 Crowley, 'His father's son', 74.
25 Ní Ghairbhí and McNulty (eds), *Patrick Pearse: collected plays*, p. 178.

back to the Ulster cycle, where Cuchulainn is both famed for his skill with the hurley and suspected of being insufficiently masculine. Cuchulainn is 'a beardless boy', who at one point has to paint a false beard on his face in order to wage war.[26] Furthermore, although Pearse is not usually considered to be a friend to feminists, there is at least some acknowledgment of the injustices suffered by women in this play, when the master describes one of the biblical Marys as representing 'all lowly, hidden women, all the nameless women of the world'.[27] Pearse's drama may generally endorse a conservative view of family and social hierarchy, but he at least allows for the existence of a set of more subversive subcurrents.

THE PLEASURE OF BEING BOOED

As we look at these elements in Pearse's work, and at the denouement of *The master*, it therefore becomes clear that one of the most suitable optics through which to view his dramatic work is that of internationally aware, modernist performance. Pearse's most (in)famous statements include those that were dramatized in satirical form by Sean O'Casey, including the conclusion of Pearse's 1913 article 'The coming revolution':

> I should like to see any and every body of Irish citizens armed. We must accustom ourselves to the thought of arms, to the sight of arms, to the use of arms. We may make mistakes in the beginning and shoot the wrong people; but bloodshed is a cleansing and a sanctifying thing, and the nation which regards it as the final horror has lost its manhood. There are many things more horrible than bloodshed; and slavery is one of them.[28]

Yet, in the modernist age of manifestos and making it new, such a statement aligns with similar expressions in the realm of experimental writing and performance. After all, four years earlier, Filippo Tommaso Marinetti had made a near-identical statement to Pearse by printing the 1909 Futurist manifesto in *Le Figaro*, stating:

---

26 Winifred L. Faraday (trans.), *The cattle raid of Cualnge* (London, 1904), p. 57.   27 Ní Ghairbhí and McNulty (eds), *Patrick Pearse: collected plays*, p. 183.   28 Patrick Pearse, 'The coming revolution', *Collected works of Pádraic H. Pearse: political writings and speeches* (Dublin, 1924), pp 91–9 at pp 98–9.

We will glorify war – the world's only hygiene – militarism, patriotism, the destructive gesture of freedom-bringers, beautiful ideas worth dying for, and scorn for woman.[29]

In *The master*, Pearse's ideas come close to those of Marinetti's subsequent manifesto, 'The pleasure of being booed' (1911), which declared that truly significant art might not be appreciated immediately by an audience. Indeed, the genuinely meaningful artwork might be greeted with derision by audiences who were not schooled to expect novelty. Thus, as Marinetti explained, he aimed to:

teach *a horror of the immediate success* that normally crowns dull and mediocre works. The theater pieces that immediately take hold of each member of the audience, with no intermediaries or explanations, are more or less well-made works that lack any novelty or creative intelligence. [...] While waiting for this abolition, we teach authors and actors *the pleasure of being booed.*[30]

After all, a potentially avant-garde outlook can be detected in the closing sections of Pearse's *The master*, where the Archangel Michael comments that, 'I am he that waiteth at the portal. I am he that hasteneth. I am he that rideth before the squadron.'[31]

The master was the first play Pearse wrote after he enrolled in the IRB, at a time when he was aware that he was riding 'before the squadron', and that his brand of revolutionary nationalism was far in advance of broader public opinion. *The master* teaches its audience members that if they know what the truth is, they need not wait for endorsements from the opinions of others, but could triumph in isolation – and death, if necessary. After all, at the end of *The master*, Ciarán's victory comes from a prophetic ability to see the truth rather than from rational thought about how isolated he is, which leads only to doubt and hesitation. Shortly before the angel appears, all of Ciarán's pupils except for Iollann abandon the teacher, who is mocked by the king:

Daire: [...] Have you been a good teacher?
Ciarán: My pupils must answer.

29 F.T. Marinetti, 'The founding and manifesto of Futurism', *Marinetti: selected writings*, ed. R.W. Flint, trans. R.W. Flint and Arthur A. Coppotelli (London, 1972), pp 39–44, p. 42.   30 Marinetti, 'The pleasure of being booed', *Marinetti: selected writings*, pp 113–15.   31 Ní Ghairbhí and McNulty (eds), *Patrick Pearse: collected plays*, p. 197.

Daire: Where are your pupils?
Ciarán: True; they are not here.
Daire: They are at an ale-feast in my tent [...][32]

Ciarán nonetheless asks, 'May one not serve the people by bearing testimony in their midst to a true thing even as by feeding them with bread?'[33] Of course, the Christological resonances are undeniable here: Ciarán recalls both the Christ who is abandoned by his sleeping disciples at Gethsemane, and the Christ of Matthew 4:4, who reminds his tempter Satan that 'Man shall not live by bread alone.' But Ciarán also embodies the attitude of the Futurist, happy to assert the idea that one need not be frightened of the opinions of the populace whose *Weltanschauung* is not sufficiently developed to appreciate new forms of thinking. As Marinetti put it, 'Not everything booed is beautiful or new. But everything applauded immediately is certainly no better than the average intelligence and is therefore *something mediocre, dull, regurgitated, or too well digested.*'[34] Needless to say, for critics of modernism and for critics of the Easter Rising, this is very dangerous thinking, potentially showing a contempt for democracy that might lead from Marinetti to Mussolini and from Pearse to the Provisional IRA.

Pearse, of course, did gain a retrospective popular mandate for his actions, as he always anticipated he would do. This distinguishes him from that line of modernist thought that maintained a consistent distaste for Yeats' 'mob'. But Pearse's ideas about theatrical display do come close to those of Marinetti, who had a similar relationship with the audience, wanting to perform to it, yet also wanting to provoke it and avoid pandering to its current taste. Pearse came particularly close to the Marinettian idea of 'the pleasure of being booed' when in May 1913 he wrote:

I dreamt that I saw a pupil of mine, one of our boys at St Enda's, standing alone upon a platform above a mighty sea of people; and I understood that he was about to die there for some august cause, Ireland's or another [...] the great silent crowd regarded the boy with pity and wonder rather than with approval – as a fool who was throwing his life away rather than as a martyr that was doing his duty. It would have been so easy to die before an applauding crowd or before a hostile crowd: but to die before that silent, unsympathetic crowd![35]

32 Ibid., p. 192.   33 Ibid., p. 194.   34 Marinetti, 'The pleasure of being booed', p. 115.   35 Quoted in Vincent Quinn, 'Fostering the nation: Patrick Pearse and pedagogy', *New Formations*, 42 (2001), 71–84 at

Pearse saw that it would be good to gain either the approval or the hostility of the crowd: at least then the performer would know that his actions had made some kind of impact. The more terrible fate, as he saw it, was simply to be silently ignored and dismissed as a meaningless 'fool'.

In addition, immediately after staging *The master*, Pearse had a more visceral experience of what Marinetti called 'the pleasure of being booed'. Pearse produced *The master* at the Irish Theatre in Hardwicke Street on 20 May 1915, the same week he organized a large military parade of Dublin Volunteers in Limerick. The parade, like the production at the Irish Theatre, included musical accompaniment, carefully coordinated movements and an address from Pearse.[36] Indeed, Pearse published information about this 'great excursion' alongside an advertisement for *The master* in Dublin's revolutionary journal the *Irish Volunteer*.[37] For him, the parade and playhouse were part of a common endeavour, and St Enda's pupils such as Joseph Sweeney, who acted in *The master*, were led by their headmaster to march in Limerick. On the final night of performances at the Irish Theatre, Pearse warned these schoolboys that Dublin Castle had prepared an attack on them at Limerick the following day, and instructed everyone to carry 50 rounds of ammunition. Once in Limerick, the Volunteers found themselves jeered by a hostile crowd, bombarded with flotsam and jetsam and forced to defend themselves with rifle butts.[38] This reaction was exactly what, in the Irish Theatre, Pearse had anticipated and described. He felt the revolutionary vanguard ought to lead a nationalist rebellion in the face of such antagonism or indifference, and that, as Marinetti put it, 'Courage, audacity and revolt will be essential elements of our poetry.'[39]

Walter L. Adamson, in his wonderful description of Marinetti's staging of *serate* in the early twentieth century, draws attention to the way that, for Marinetti, the single performance event spilled out well beyond the confines of the playhouse walls. Adamson describes how the Futurists prepared for a *serata* by making prominent displays of themselves in public, placing themselves 'like the goods in a department store window' before 'enticement would be supplemented by printed advertisement: leaflets handed out on street corners, posters tacked up on walls'. The Futurists emphasized their

71. 36 'Remember Limerick: Whit Sunday', *The Volunteer*, 22 May 1915, p. 5. I am grateful to Brian Crowley for helping me locate Pearse's 'general orders' for the Limerick parade. 37 *The Volunteer*, 22 May 1915. 38 Joseph A. Sweeney, 'In the G.P.O.: the fighting men' in F.X. Martin (ed.), *The Easter Rising, 1916 and University College, Dublin* (Dublin, 1966), pp 96–105 at p. 98. 39 Marinetti, 'The founding and manifesto of Futurism', p. 41.

own difference from the masses by wearing special costumes, and would – when their moment finally came to emerge onto the stage – 'declaim their verse or manifesto', often to signs of intense audience disapproval, before trooping away in a post-performance procession.[40]

Historians of the Easter Rising will note the obvious affinities between such performance events and the way in which Pearse and his colleagues organized the Rising of 1916. During Easter Week the rebels became a distinctively costumed group whose members paraded in public before their rebellion, printed their own declaration, which was read by Pearse, and were marched towards a post-performance realm of imprisonment and execution. The staging of *The master* was, indeed, one of the ways in which Pearse could make a prominent display, prior to the rebellion, of the participants (a large proportion of the cast later took part in the Easter Rising), and reveals his complex and contradictory attitude towards the masses. Like Marinetti, Pearse realized that the wider public could be frustratingly docile and uncomprehending – *The master* makes much of this idea – yet both men also felt the compulsion to provoke and engage that audience. Ultimately, only a fundamental disturbance of the spectatorship, and the development of a new kind of relationship between onlookers and performers, would be the measure of success for both men. The Easter Rising was no Fabian exercise in preparing the ground: this was the shock of the new. As Róisín Ní Ghairbhí and Eugene McNulty put it in their discussion of *The master*, 'the costumes might be archaic but the message is extraordinarily modern'.[41]

40 Walter L. Adamson, *Embattled avant-gardes: modernism's resistance to commodity culture in Europe* (Berkeley, 2007), p. 89.   41 Ní Ghairbhí and McNulty, 'Introduction', *Patrick Pearse: collected plays*, pp 1–63 at p. 40.

5 / Waiting for the exceptional: Pearse's drama and the space between Law and law.

EUGENE McNULTY

> Only our conception of time makes it possible for us to call the day of the Last Judgment by that name; in reality it is a summary court in perpetual session.
>
> —Franz Kafka[1]

The question of time and its judgments haunts Patrick Pearse's work for the theatre. Time and again (a haunting phrase in itself) his plays concern themselves with the origin, agency and temporality of judgment. Indeed there is clearly something (but not all) of the Janus-faced modernist project in these works that look longingly towards a newly imagined future while processing a sublimated nostalgia for meanings lost in some now vanished originating moment.[2] In many of Pearse's plays we can detect a mind meditating not just on the nature and possibility of action but on the relationship between present action and its function in the posterity of the future. It is to be found, most obviously, in the sacrificial actions of key bodies in his three most complete works for the theatre: the young boy in *An rí/The king* (1912); the eponymous teacher-priest in *The master* (1915); and MacDara, the covert revolutionary balladeer in *The singer* (1916). In different ways, sometimes oblique, sometimes more directly, his drama resolves itself around the processes and agents through which radical action can be instigated. This onstage action is further shaped by the assumed relationship with the observing audience – those who have been implicated by their participation in the drama. In the space between the stage-action and the participating gaze, Pearse's work invites reflection upon the notion of judgment – its personality, mechanisms, modalities, agency and time frame. More specifically, this essay argues, at the heart of Pearse's drama is a

---

1 Franz Kafka, 'Reflections on sin, pain, hope and the true way' in *The Great Wall of China: stories and reflections* (New York, 1970), p. 287. 2 For a more developed discussion of Pearse as a modernist see Máire Ní Fhlathúin, 'The anti-colonial modernism of Patrick Pearse' in Howard J. Booth and Nigel Rigby (eds), *Modernism and empire* (Manchester, 2000), pp 156–74; Declan Kiberd, 'Patrick Pearse: Irish modernist' in Roisín Higgins and Regina Uí Chollatáin (eds), *The life and after-life of P.H. Pearse* (Dublin, 2009).

particular politico-cultural concern for the mechanisms of judgment as revealed by the regulatory powers of both the 'law', the diachronic marker of real-world legal process, and the 'Law', the synchronic marker of trans-historical justice. We can see something of this philosophic dichotomy at work in his 1916 pamphlet 'The sovereign people' in which Pearse draws a telling distinction between the originating 'natures' of a nation and an empire:

> The nation is a natural division, as natural as the family, and as inevitable. That is one reason why a nation is holy and why an empire is not holy [...]. The nation is the family in large; an empire is a commercial corporation in large. The nation is of God; the empire is of man — if it be not of the devil.[3]

It is the space created by this sacred/profane dialectic that allows Pearse to further assert that 'the right to the material ownership of a nation's soil coexists with the right to make laws for the nation and that both are inherent in the same authority, the sovereign people'.[4] Republicanism, in other words, functions through a law borne of the Law. Empire, or colonialism, functions through a rendering of the two:

> laws made or acts done by anybody purporting to represent the people but not really authorized by the people, either expressly or impliedly, to represent them and to act for them do not bind the people; are a usurpation, an impertinence, a nullity.[5]

The implications are clear — a properly constituted anti-colonialism would not only resist colonial law but seek to reveal a fundamental absence of authority at its core. Colonial law is here not so much wrong, as simply empty.

A central proposition in what follows is that it is in the dialectical space between the two — Law and law — that Pearse most fully inhabits the imaginative intersection between his cultural and political selfhoods. His most famous play, *The singer*, for example, ends with the eponymous singer, MacDara, declaring: 'I will take no pike. I will go into the battle with bare hands. I will stand up before the Gall as Christ hung naked before men on the tree!'[6] It is a declaration — not without its problematics — that connects

3 Patrick Pearse, 'The sovereign people', *Tracts for the Times*, 13 (Dublin, 1916), p. 7.   4 Ibid., p. 10.
5 Ibid., pp 5–6.   6 Patrick Pearse, *The singer* in Róisín Ní Ghairbhí and Eugene McNulty (eds), *Patrick*

the actions of military rebellion with divine judgment. At its heart stands an image of time: MacDara's actions, like Christ's, will find their full revelation only in retrospect; his present actions are fully readable only when placed in the context of a covenant with the future. It is an ending that functions as an ideological engine through which the present becomes an imagined utopian past.

In this regard Pearse's drama is very much of its revivalist moment – a moment whose key cultural turn was signalled by a concern for the re-articulation of Irish selfhood in its temporal, as well as spatial, psychical components. This is a period that has many of the contours of what Paul Ricoeur (following on from Karl Jaspers) would term a 'boundary situation'.[7] For Ricoeur, these are moments of crises 'such as war, suffering, guilt, death etc. in which the individual or community experiences a fundamental existential crisis'. Ricoeur goes on to argue that at 'such moments the whole community is put into question'; and if in extreme cases it feels itself to be 'threatened with destruction from without or from within' such a community 'is compelled to return to the very roots of its identity' – what he posits as the 'mytho-poetic' core of its existence.[8] While Ricoeur was clearly more concerned with the apocalyptic implications of extreme events (holocaust, genocide, world war), there is also a sense in which this thinking is translatable to those moments of cultural-nationalist self-interrogation or reinvention. Such moments are marked by a discourse in search not only of modes of resistance to imposed external structures but narratives of communal self-(re)definition.

At the heart of the nationalist 'boundary situation' driving the revivalist project, this essay contends, was a sustained and deep-set cultural interrogation of the pathways through which power was manifested through the translation of 'Law' into 'law'. Writing from Trieste in 1907, James Joyce, for example, in a newspaper piece entitled 'Ireland at the bar', sought to allegorize Ireland's troubled status – as a non-speaking actor on the stage of nations – by recourse to a narrative of legal inequity, centring on the infamous Maamtrasna murder trials of 1882:

Pearse: collected plays/Drámaí an Phiarsaigh (Dublin, 2013), p. 228. **7** Karl Jaspers uses the term *'grenzsituation'*, which can be translated variously as 'boundary situation', 'borderline situation' and 'ultimate situation'. For more on this idea in its original context see Karl Jaspers, *Philosophy*, ii: *Existential elucidation* (Chicago, 1969); Oswald O. Schrag, *Existence, existenz, and transcendence: an introduction to the philosophy of Karl Jaspers* (Pittsburgh, 1971). **8** Paul Ricoeur, 'Myth as the bearer of possible worlds' in Mark Patrick Hederman and Richard Kearney (eds), *Crane Bag book of Irish studies* (Dublin, 1982), pp 261–2.

Several years ago a sensational trial was held in Ireland. In a lonely place
[...] a murder was committed. Four or five townsmen [...] were
arrested. The oldest of them, the seventy year old Myles Joyce, was the
prime suspect. Public opinion at the time thought him innocent and
today considers him a martyr. Neither the old man nor the others
accused knew English. [...] The questioning, conducted through the
interpreter, was at times comic and at times tragic. On one side was the
excessively ceremonious interpreter, on the other the patriarch of a
miserable tribe unused to civilised customs, who seemed stupefied by all
the judicial ceremony.[9]

Much like Joseph K in Kafka's *The trial*, the old man is faced by a process of
law that he cannot comprehend, one he cannot access in any meaningful way.
Myles Joyce cannot 'read' or make visible the law that has him in its grip, he
cannot speak to it. Likewise, Joyce presents the law as having no proper access
to, or interest in, him as a subject in the world. It is a narrative that resonates
with Gayatri Spivak's assertion that colonial law was one of those processes
whose effect was to eradicate spaces of power within which the colonial
subject could articulate his or her proper subjectivity. As she puts it, along
with the production of scientific systems of knowledge, the 'institution of
the law' was one more discursive space wherein 'great care was taken to oblit-
erate the textual ingredients' through which the colonial subject could fully
occupy his/her agency in the matrix of power.[10] For his namesake James,
Myles Joyce becomes symbolic of Ireland as it stands subject to a law that
misreads it, as it stands exposed to a system that speaks 'differently'.

In terms generated by Giorgio Agamben's recent influential work, we might
also begin to read Myles Joyce as a kind of exceptional body, one that was
left exposed by a law that simultaneously abandoned and judged it. The old
man, Joyce, is in the end condemned by a law that strips him of all the
linguistic markers of proper subjectivity. We might here draw on Agamben's
thinking around the nature and function of sovereign power – with its
specific attention to sovereignty as executed through the 'Law'. This is work
that has centred on the recovered archaic and paradoxical figure of *Homo sacer*

9 James Joyce, 'Ireland at the Bar' in Ellmann and Mason (eds), *The critical writings of James Joyce* (London,
1959), p. 197. For more on Joyce's engagement with this historical event see James Fairhall, *James Joyce and
the question of history* (Cambridge, 1995).   10 Gayatri Chakravorty Spivak, 'Can the subaltern speak?' in
Patrick Williams and Laura Chrisman (eds), *Colonial discourse and post-colonial theory: a reader* (Harlow, 1994),
p. 75.

(sacred man), a figure Agamben re-presents as 'bare life'.[11] For Agamben this archaic figure (he traces its existence back through classical Greek and Roman juridical systems) was one from whom the usual protection of both the Law and religion had been removed. Thus: *Homo sacer* could be killed and yet not murdered – as defined in Law; *Homo sacer* could be killed and yet not sacrificed – as defined by religious codification.[12] Placed outside all modes of protection, sacred man is transformed into 'bare life', a body stripped down to the point where all that remains is its corporeal signification. It is in this passage from inclusion to exclusion that Agamben detects the proper significance of *Homo sacer* for the performance of the Law and, thus, sovereign power. In this version of the juridico-political order the Law includes us all in its purview exactly through its (ever-constant) potential to exclude us from its protection. This paradox of inclusion/exclusion is the juridical motor, Agamben argues, at the heart of the development of modern bio-politics. This is a development that we can in turn read as central to the very nature of modernity – as Agamben reminds us: 'It can even be said that the production of a bio-political body is the original activity of sovereign power.'[13] Sovereign power is thus the source of an ideological locus that has the 'right' to decide when the Law can be suspended – that is, withdrawn in a manner that leaves certain bodies in the position of 'bare life'.[14] At the heart of sovereignty, that most complex of abstractions, then, we find the power to define and create bare life, a power revealed as all too material in its execution on real bodies.[15]

The shift from Joyce to Pearse (with a nod to Kafka) is perhaps not the most obvious of moves to make. As Seamus Deane puts it, Pearse is this period's 'most famous minor writer and its major revolutionary figure';[16] one could argue, indeed, that it is the tensions between these designations that

11 For an extended discussion of this figure, in addition to Agamben, *Homo sacer: sovereign power and bare life* (Stanford, CA, 1998), see Agamben, *State of exception* (Chicago, 2005), and Sergei Prozorov, *Agamben and politics: a critical introduction* (Edinburgh, 2014). 12 As Agamben puts it, the proper significance of the *Homo sacer* figure is that it is 'situated at the intersection of a capacity to be killed and yet not sacrificed, outside both human and divine Law' (*Homo Sacer*, p. 73). 13 Agamben, *Homo sacer*, p. 6. 14 There is a particular paradox at work here, one that Agamben notes as 'the Law is outside itself', or alternatively as 'I, the sovereign, who am outside the Law, declare that there is nothing outside the Law' (*Homo sacer*, p. 15). For a powerful explication of the ramifications of this power in the context of post-Sept. 11 geopolitics see Judith Butler's *Precarious life: the powers of mourning and violence* (London, 2006) – particularly the essay 'Indefinite detention'. 15 In this respect Agamben's work sheds new light on Carl Schmitt's definition of sovereignty: 'Sovereign is he who decides on the state of exception.' For more on this relationship see *Homo sacer*, pp 8–19, and Carl Schmitt's *Political theology: four chapters on the concept of sovereignty* (Chicago, 2006). 16 Seamus Deane, *Celtic revivals: essays in modern Irish literature* (Winston-Salem, NC, 1987), p. 63.

leads Declan Kiberd to note that it can seem 'almost heretical to link Pearse to James Joyce'.[17] Yet both men were certainly interested in the transformatory possibilities offered by the imaginative re-ordering of the world. Moreover, many years before the turn to direct-action rebellion, Pearse too had been much concerned with the problems of the Law/law and the bodies that stand before it. In addition to his persona of schoolmaster turned revolutionary, Patrick Pearse also held a Law degree and around the same period when Joyce was writing in Trieste, Pearse took on what appears to have been one of his very few cases as a barrister in court. While much less serious in import and consequence, it is a case that echoes Myles Joyce's experience of communicative alienation. The case of R.V. MacBride (or MacGhiolla Bhrighde) concerned the use of Gaelic names on carts, and Pearse took the case on behalf of the Gaelic League. As Arthur Cleary, who was present in court, observed:

> It was in some ways a strong case. The events happened in a thoroughly Irish part of Tirconaill where Irish was the national language of everyone, and it might, therefore, seem reasonable that a native Irish speaker was justified in describing himself in that language on his cart. But this would not have accorded with the persecution of the Irish language, which was then, and is still largely, pursued. Consequently an R.I.C. constable had prosecuted him and there had been a conviction. Against this the proceedings in the King's Bench were, in effect, an appeal.[18]

Joyce's metaphorical concern for a law incapable of reading its subjects, and for bodies excluded from its *logos*, is transformed into the literal material of this case. The law here refuses the signification of identity inscribed in Irish letters on the man's cart, insisting instead on a transformation of the terms through which identity is expressed and thus made knowable to it. The presiding judge, indeed, after arguing 'in favour of Irish for a bit – a way of his when he was going to decide against you', eventually proposed 'some complications which involved the conception of an Irish-speaking police constable who knew no English' – a rather obfuscatory sidestepping of the relationship that was actually at stake in the case.[19] In its summing up the

17 Kiberd, 'Patrick Pearse: Irish modernist' (Dublin, 2009), p. 65.   18 Arthur Cleary, 'Patrick Pearse's only case' in Louis Walsh, *Old friends: being memories of men and places* (Dundalk, 1934), pp 113–14.   19 Ibid., p. 115.

court confirmed that 'letters meant English letters'.[20] Both the case of Myles Joyce and Pearse's experience of 'English' law in Ireland may be read as demonstrating the problem of what Jean-François Lyotard has termed 'the *différend*', namely (as Spivak parses it), 'the inaccessibility of, or untranslatability from, one mode of discourse in a dispute to another'.[21] Both cases, that is, reveal a discursive friction or disconnect between the hegemonic ambitions of British jurisprudence in Ireland and the actual bodies that it attempts to regulate and make knowable to itself. In their different ways, each of the narratives also reveals the ways in which what we might term the 'colonial *différend*' can result in the production of bodies placed beyond the law's protection.

It is an idea that returns us to Agamben, and indeed to Kafka. In the course of tracing the development of sovereign power and the law into the twentieth century, Agamben points us to a Franz Kafka short story that he reads as revelatory of the invasive reach of disciplining power in late modernity (as with much else in Kafka, this nightmare of legal totality can only seem evermore prescient to his twenty-first century readers). 'Before the law' (also sometimes titled 'At the door of the law'), a story perhaps better described as a parable, tells of a 'man from the country' who comes in search of admittance to the Law. He comes to an open door – an entrance to the Law we are told – but the attendant doorkeeper refuses to let him pass to what is beyond: 'The man thinks about it and then asks whether in that case he will be allowed in later. "Possibly", says the doorkeeper, "but not at the moment."'[22] This perpetual deferral – 'not yet' – is key to the story's power; its effect is to require the man to sit at the door awaiting his admittance. This pattern of request and refusal is continued for many years, with the man from the country now permanently camped at the threshold to the open door. In fact the man spends the rest of his life in just this position, summoning up points of clarification to be addressed to the intransigent doorkeeper (discussion is possible but the final answer is always a refusal to admit the desperate man), until he reaches the very final moments of his life:

> He has not long to live. Before he dies, everything he has learnt in the entire time becomes concentrated in his head into a question that he has not asked the doorkeeper hitherto. He beckons him to approach, for his body is growing stiff and he can no longer get up. The doorkeeper has

20 Ibid.   21 Spivak, 'Can the subaltern speak?', p. 96.   22 Franz Kafka, 'At the door of the law' in *Franz Kafka: stories, 1904–1924* (London, 1995), p. 194.

to bend right down to him, the difference in height between them having altered very much to the man's disadvantage. 'What do you want to know now?' the doorkeeper asks. 'You're insatiable.' 'Everybody seeks the Law', says the man, 'so how is it that in all these years no one but me has demanded admittance?' The doorkeeper sees that it is all over for the man, and to penetrate his growing deafness he shouts at him, 'No one else could gain admittance here because this entrance was meant for you alone. Now I am going to close it.'[23]

The seemingly counterintuitive denouement on further inspection reveals the real power of the Law. There is no place into which the man can enter, for as Derrida puts it in his reading of the story, the Law here is 'the guarding itself, only the guarding'.[24] According to Derrida, Kafka reveals the real heart and origin of the Law: 'The secret is nothing – and this is the secret that has to be kept well, nothing either present or presentable, but this nothing must be well kept. To this task of keeping, the nobility is delegated.'[25] The Law for Derrida, in other words, is present only in, and by way of, its happening – and this 'secret' is kept by the keepers of hegemonic power. For Derrida, then, while the diachronic 'law' may be recordable and traceable as a function of history, the synchronic 'Law' withholds itself and refuses its own historicity:

> The Law yields by withholding itself, without imparting its provenance and its site. This silence and discontinuity constitute the phenomenon of the Law. To enter into relations with the Law which says 'you must' and 'you must not' is to act as if it had no history or at any rate as if it no longer depended on its historical presentation. At the same time, it is to let oneself be enticed, provoked and hailed by the history of this non-history.[26]

While not suggesting Pearse was engaged with the kind of linguistic turn produced by post-structuralism, I do want to pick up on some resonances between his work and the reading of the Law proposed by Derrida. Pearse's work, I want to suggest, is populated with images of the colonial law as an empty signifier – an empty vessel that lacks historical roots and thus validity. Crucially, however, and here we need to relocate his work as essentially utopic, as opposed to the radical scepticism of Kafka (and indeed Derrida in this

23 Ibid., p. 195.   24 Jacques Derrida, 'Before the law' in Derek Attridge (ed.), *Jacques Derrida: acts of literature* (London, 1992), p. 206.   25 Derrida, 'Before the law', p. 205.   26 Ibid., p. 192.

instance), Pearse is occupied with the conceptualization of a Law that is capable of properly reading the Irish bodies within its purview. In his reading, these are bodies that are the very source of (authentic) sovereign power, and thus of 'the Law'. This is an idea that goes to the philosophic heart of republicanism in its broader European context of course; in such a political locus the Law is in effect reading itself. In this regard we might look to one of Pearse's most interesting and subversive short stories, 'The keening woman'/'An bhean chaointe' (1907/1916). Indeed Pearse's story now reads like an anti-colonial version of Kafka's 'Before the law' (1914).

Like Kafka's work, 'The keening woman' tells the story of waiting. We meet an old woman who has spent the last decades of her life waiting for the return of her son Coilin from prison. In the course of the story we discover that her son died many years ago in prison and that she has since gone mad; it is also suggested that Coilin was innocent of the murder for which he was imprisoned – the murder of a local landowner was actually carried out by a government agent. At the centre of the narrative stands a journey undertaken by the mother, who moves through a series of authority figures in search of justice for her son. As she tells us: 'I went to Galway. I saw the governor of the gaol. He told me that he wouldn't be able to do a taste, that it's the Dublin people who would be able to let him out of gaol, if his letting-out was to be got.'[27] While Kafka's man from the country gets to meet only one doorkeeper, Pearse's 'every-mother' moves through a series of doors but each is revealed as unable to deliver the law/Law. On finally reaching Dublin she tells us:

> The morning of the next day I enquired for the Castle. I was put on the way. I went there. They wouldn't let me in at first, but I was at them till I got leave of talk with some man. He put me on to another man, a man that was higher than himself. He sent me to another man. I said to them all I wanted was to see the lord lieutenant of the queen. I saw him at last. I told him my story. He said to me that he couldn't do anything. I gave my curse to the Castle of Dublin, and out the door with me.[28]

Once again the Law appears here as that which guards itself, as that which continually delays those who seek it; Pearse's story works to reveal colonial law as an absence that protects itself by a process of constant deferral. The story reaches its conclusion with the rather unlikely notion of the woman

27 Patrick Pearse, 'The keening woman' in Joseph Campbell (ed.), *Plays, stories, poems* (Dublin, 1980), p. 219. 28 Ibid., p. 220.

travelling to London to see the queen, a narrative device perhaps borrowed from the story of Grace O'Malley's (Gráinne Ní Mháille's) reputed journey of 1593 to petition Elizabeth I for the freedom of her brother and son. It is a move that allows Pearse to place 'Ireland' in direct confrontation with the putative sovereign origin of colonial law in Ireland:[29]

> When I came to London I asked knowledge of the queen's castle. I was told. I went there. They wouldn't let me in. I went there every day, hoping that I'd see the queen coming out. [...] I went over to the queen before she went in to her coach. There was a paper, a man in Dublin wrote for me, in my hand. [...] I spoke to the queen. She didn't understand me. I stretched the paper to her. She gave the paper to the officer, and he read it. He wrote certain words on the paper, and gave it back to me. The queen spoke to another woman that was along with her. The woman drew out a crown piece and gave it to me. I gave her back the crown piece, and I said that it's not silver I wanted, but my son. They laughed. It's my opinion they didn't understand me. I showed them the paper again. The officer laid his finger on the words he was after writing. I curtseyed to the queen and went off with me. A man read for me the words the officer wrote. It's what was in it, that they would write to me about Coilin without delay. I struck the road home then, hoping that, maybe, there would be a letter before me.[30]

The letter, of course, never arrives and the woman is left to wait before the law in a narrative that can offer her no resolution; the impossibility of communication condemns her to the state of trauma-induced psychosis in which we meet her at the story's outset. Importantly, however, Pearse's narrative does index a resolution for the reader; or at least the story's purpose seems to be to suggest for the reader possible starting points for resolution. The woman, of course, is 'Mother Ireland' and her textual journey from coast to coast in Ireland, and from Ireland to England and back again, has primarily established the need to look to herself for a Law (the letter of the law) that can properly read her, and which she can in turn read.

That image of an allegorized Ireland awaiting the arrival of a (in Pearse's terms) valid Law is one that we may now see as shadowing much of his work

---

29 For a really fruitful and suggestive reading of the role of gender in this story see Máire Ní Fhlathúin, 'The anti-colonial modernism of Patrick Pearse'.   30 Patrick Pearse, 'The keening woman', p. 221.

for the theatre. Indeed there is something almost Beckettian about Patrick Pearse's fascination with the act of waiting. His drama is saturated with characters whose very being seems regulated by the act of anticipation, by a gaze directed towards some future event or revelation. Almost all his plays and pageants occupy some form of temporal inter-zone, presenting his audience with in-between places burdened by the problematic consequences of the past and awaiting a future-defining event. It is into these inter-zones that Pearse places a series of 'exceptional' bodies. These are bodies whose exceptionality functions to signal, on the one hand, the problem of colonial law (it is revealed as 'empty'), and, on the other, the possibility of a re-articulated covenant with a self-authored Law. Pearse's key performative bodies, in other words, may be read as articulating sites of counter-sovereignty that symbolically emanate the utopic possibility of a new Law. More particularly, the image of the young male body as the site of a possible, or hoped for, newly articulated covenant with the concept of the Law is one that Pearse will return to time and again in his drama.

Indeed the male body as a site of a 'political theology' becomes the explicit framing device for the action of his early work, *Íosagán* (1910). Here the action inhabits a space that hovers somewhere between life and death, between this world and the next, between the profane and the sacred. It opens with a stage-image of an old man, Matthias, sitting, observing, waiting – it will soon become clear that it is death's arrival upon which he waits. As the action unfolds we learn that Matthias has fallen away from the Catholic church due to its disavowal of Fenianism and a priest's condemnation of his part in it. Matthias' days are now spent mostly in the company of the village's young boys, whose memories are too short to affect their sense of Matthias and his actions. It is one of these boys who sums up Matthias' situation:

> CUIMÍN: I heard Father Sean Eamonn saying it's the way he did some terrible sin at the start of his life, and when the priest wouldn't give him absolution in confession there came a raging anger on him, and he swore an oath he wouldn't touch priest or chapel for ever again.[31]

The notion that we are in a zone outside of the normative regulatory powers of church and (colonial) state is further reinforced by the introduction of Íosagán – the young Christ figure who will in the end be the

---

31 Patrick Pearse, *Íosagán* in Ní Ghairbhí and McNulty (eds), *Patrick Pearse: collected plays*, pp 120–1.

catalyst for Matthias' reconciliation with faith and divine power. Tellingly, Íosagán often joins the young boys in their play but slips away when the adults appear:

> CÓILÍN: … he goes from us when grown people come near us. He will go from us now as soon as the people begin coming from mass.[32]

Matthias' wait for acceptance by, and reconciliation with, the church – something in the end that is facilitated by Íosagán – locates the action in a limbo space, a space in which his republicanism has in effect been misread and judged too soon. In Pearse's vision the righteousness of republicanism will be confirmed retroactively by the judgment of the future; as another of the young boys puts it:

> PÁDRAIC: He's not a wicked person, *muise*. Don't you mind the day Íosagán said that his father told him Matthias would be among the saints on the Day of the Mountain?[33]

The reference to the Day of Last Judgment is illuminatory here; indeed it provides the key to the parable's action and intent.[34] Pearse presents his audience with a body speaking from a space unrestricted by the confines of profane history (as Íosagán tells Matthias, 'I was always here') and thus able to authorize Fenianism's rejection of colonial law.[35] By bleeding the sacred into the profane, in other words, Íosagán's body performs a teleological validation of the history of Irish republicanism.

The action of *An rí/ The king* (1912) is similarly poised in an inter-zone between a disappointed past and a newly rearticulated covenant with the future. It opens with another scene dominated by the act of waiting. This time it is a group of young boys who stand in the grounds of a monastery observing the action of a battle below. Their king is engaged in another campaign but there is little hope that he will be victorious – his rule has been tainted by un-kingly actions – and in their discussion of the situation the boys link 'the thousands [the king] has slain' and the 'churches he has plundered' with the 'battles he has lost'.[36] When the scene is joined by a group

32 Ibid., p.123.   33 Ibid., p.121.   34 Revelation 20:11–12: 'Then I saw a great white throne and the one who sat on it; the earth and the heaven fled from his presence, and no place was found for them. And I saw the dead, great and small, standing before the throne, and books were opened. And the dead were judged according to their works, as recorded in the books.'   35 Pearse, *Íosagán*, p. 123.   36 Patrick Pearse,

of monks and their abbot the allegorical signification of the battle below the ramparts becomes ever more apparent. The king's rule is conjured as a form of imperial folly, an internal process of colonization that has had tragic effects on the people. As the abbot puts it: 'This king has shed the blood of the innocent. He has made spoils and forays. He has oppressed the poor. He has forsaken the friendship of God and made friends with evil-doers.'[37] Pearse here sublimates his vision of British wrongdoing into this tyrannical kingly figure and his abuse of sovereign power. The abbot, moreover, suggests that such a rotten core at the centre of the Law/law should not be in a position to decide on the issues of life and death at stake in moments of crisis:

> THE ABBOT: It is an angel that should be sent to pour out the wine and to break the bread of this sacrifice. Not by an unholy king should the noble wine that is in the veins of good heroes be spilt; not at the behest of a guilty king should fair bodies be mangled. I say to you that the offering will not be accepted.[38]

The king thereafter becomes about the search for one who could more ably interpret the proper responsibilities of sovereignty as the origin of the Law, and thus as the keeper of a power over the bodies in its care/control. It is here too that the play takes it most obvious republican turn, with the suggestion that the real problem is the site of power in royal prerogative – a site that increasingly stands in Pearse's work as a symbol for British misrule in Ireland:

> THE ABBOT: The nation is guilty of the sins of its princes. I say to you that this nation shall not be freed until it chooses for itself a righteous king.
> SECOND MONK: Where shall a righteous king be found?
> THE ABBOT: I do not know, unless he be found among these little boys.[39]

In politico-theological terms what is needed is a new covenant between the people and he that leads them. But this is really a thinly veiled conceit for what Pearse is actually concerned with – the political revelation of (proto-) republican action. Once again – and this is clearly not unproblematic – the

The king in Ní Ghairbhí and McNulty (eds), *Patrick Pearse: collected plays*, p.151.   37 Ibid., p. 153.   38 Ibid. 39 Ibid.

carrier of a newly imagined future is the body of a young boy, who must die
to birth a new world of rebalanced power and authority. The search for (what
we might term) the 'postcolonial moment' thus finds its most precise
modality in Pearse's work in the broken body of young manhood.[40] While the
monks have been busy with their analysis of politics and power, the young
boys of the monastery have likewise been discussing their own position in the
hierarchy of the imagined nation. Most of them are boastful of the fact that
they come from the royal line and are thus worthy candidates to take over as
king. But one, named Giolla na Naomh ('servant of the saints'), refuses to
propose himself as a successor to the king, declaring instead: 'I would rather
be a monk that I might pray for the king.'[41] It is this righteous boy who takes
the king's place in battle. The resultant symbolic alteration in sovereignty, and
thus origin of the Law, changes the course of the conflict and the people are
victorious – winning their fight for freedom after seeing the young boy fall
and die in battle for them. Importantly, the old king gives way willingly and
kneels before the dead boy's fallen body, thus acknowledging this symbolic
representative of a previously abused people as the rightful site of power.
Once again Pearse invites his audience to witness a moment of transference
and transformation; the question of sovereignty is presented as mutable and
translatable, a crucially enabling conclusion in Pearse's project to rearticulate
colonial law and its enactment in Ireland.

The possible translation of the source of the Law in Ireland is an idea that
also speaks to the structure and action of *The master* (1915), a piece that
presents a confrontation between a noble teacher – named Ciarán but in many
ways a sublimated version of Pearse's self-image – and a king figure named
Daire. The play returns its audience to one of the key turning points in Irish
(proto-) history, the arrival of Christianity and the subsequent displacement
of older Druidic religious practices. Its message is once again the possibility
of transformation and the importance of those who are willing to face down
entrenched positions of power. Early in the piece three of Ciarán's pupils
discuss the king's opposition to his teachings:

ART: But why does the king come against Ciarán?
CEALLACH: It is the Druids that have incited him. They say that Ciarán
            is over-turning the ancient law of the people.
MAINE: The king has ordered him to leave the country.[42]

---

40 It is an image, as Michael Cronin demonstrates so brilliantly in his essay for this collection, that
would soon find its echoes on the battlefields of a Europe torn asunder by the First World War.
41 Pearse, *The king* in Ní Ghairbhí and McNulty (eds), *Patrick Pearse: collected plays*, p. 152.   42 Patrick

Thereafter the play proceeds by way of a biblical analogue: the Old Testament of royal power is challenged by the New Testament of an enlightened law represented by the teacher and his community of pupils. As with *Íosagán*, the audience is confronted with the codification of a politico-theological argument: colonial law is here seen as defunct and in need of the new covenant of a proto-republicanism. Tellingly, the play ends with a stage-image that leaves no doubt as to which of these forces is in the ascendancy. The Archangel Michael appears on stage – to protect Ciarán from the king's sword – proclaiming his arrival in terms that reinforce the alignment of republican action with a tactical rendering of the sacred as an alternative authorizing power:

> MICHAEL: I am he that waiteth at the portal. I am he that hasteneth. I am he that rideth before the squadron. I am he that holdeth a shield over the retreat of man's host when Satan cometh in war. I am he that turneth and smiteth. I am he that is Captain of the Host of God.[43]

As with the old man Matthias, Ciarán's politicized exceptional body is here protected, or validated, by the ultimate exceptionality of divine intervention. Faced with this divine confirmation that the old order must give way to the new, the king bends to his knee in supplication. Finally then, *The master's* return to a moment when the 'law of the people' was reimagined and radically translated away from the pagan towards the Christian provides an analogue for counter-hegemonic resistance.

CODA: *THE SINGER* (1916)

Long before the grand performative gesture of Easter 1916, then, Pearse had understood and explored the deep structural and symbolic possibilities of the dramatic space. It is this concern for the symbolic, and theatre's potential for delivering subversive ideas through codified language (somatic as well as spoken dialogue), that most fully informs Pearse's openly revolutionary play, *The singer*. Of course this is a very particular play in Pearse's career and life – at this stage he was not simply writing a play about revolution but helping to plan one in the real world. As a result it is the play for which Pearse (the

Pearse, *The master* in Ní Ghairbhí and McNulty (eds), *Patrick Pearse: collected plays*, p.179.   43 Ibid., p. 197.

playwright) is best remembered – it is also the piece that has provided the most ammunition for critics (cultural and political) who draw on it for evidence of a megalomaniacal (or indeed messianic) side to Pearse's clearly complex personality. It is not difficult to see why. *The singer* appears, after all, almost consumed with the seductions of redemptive violence and the purifying possibilities of blood spilt by young men marching towards their destiny (an image that would be forever changed in a Europe soon to witness the final logic of total warfare on the Somme). However, while there is clearly much that is problematic about the piece, proving or disproving the psychopathologies of the writer – who would soon turn his attention to a moment of revolutionary action saturated with symbolic intention and consequence – is in truth too much for any play to bear. All that said, positioning *The singer* in the longer view of Pearse's career in the theatre may help reveal its structural consistency within his dramatic vision and remove it from the more reductive readings sometimes assigned to it. More specifically, what we find here is a continuation of Pearse's symbolic interrogation of sovereignty and the origin of the Law/law.

As *The singer* opens once again we find ourselves in a dramatic space consumed by the act of waiting. The opening scene is occupied by two women (an old woman, Máire, and her foster-daughter, Sighle) burning the midnight oil as they await the return of the men of the house. The most immediate concern is the young man of the house (Colm) and his ragtag band of fellow rebels, all of whom are out on the mountainside for covert military training in preparation for the anticipated rebellion. But behind the scene's anticipatory tension there also lies the more mysterious fate of the house's elder son (MacDara) who has been forced away from the area because of his openly rebellious songs and poems. Indeed we'll soon learn that the women's passive waiting (as one of the men will later put it: "'Tis women that keep all the great vigils'[44]) stands in for a more generalized sense of passing time before some hoped-for radical action. Most obviously Colm and the local men are obsessed with their condition of being on hold as they await the messenger who will bring the word to trigger open rebellion. By the play's end it will become clear that MacDara is the near-mythical figure who has been travelling the country inspiring rebellion with his impassioned and eloquent words. Tellingly, the play's ending will bring with it the realization that everyone has 'waited too long'.[45]

---

44 Patrick Pearse, *The singer* in Ní Ghairbhí and McNulty (eds), *Patrick Pearse: collected plays*, p. 209.
45 Ibid., p. 222.

It is pretty clear that the character of MacDara is a projection of Pearse's idealized self on stage; but the play may be also be read as the culmination of Pearse's interest in the links between language and action, and the judgment of this action by an imagined future. When asked by his old teacher (Maoilsheachlainn) 'Is a poet not a maker?' MacDara responds by saying that cultural creativity is merely the first step on the road to full revolution:

> No, he is only a voice that cries out, a sigh that trembles into rest. The true teacher must suffer and do. He must break bread to the people: he must go into Gethsemane and toil up the steep of Golgotha.[46]

As with the earlier plays discussed above, this central image is not quite the straightforward Christian piety it may first appear. Rather, it allows Pearse to reference Christ as a prototype of the radical revolutionary, a model of transformatory possibility. Once again the idea of active resistance leads Pearse to the image of an exceptional body – or, rather, the image of 'the people' as a communal exceptional body (the body politic):

> The people, Maoilsheachlainn, the dumb, suffering people: reviled and outcast, yet pure and splendid and faithful. In them I saw, or seemed to see again, the Face of God. Ah, it is a tear-stained face, blood-stained, defiled with ordure, but it is the Holy Face.[47]

Not surprisingly, given the context within which Pearse was writing in early 1916, the sacred/profane conceit is more obviously politically loaded now. The theocentric imagery is thus a vehicle for a message of communal radicalization, and it is this that provides the meta-context for MacDara's claim that 'One man can free a people as one Man redeemed the world.'[48] The image of divinity – the ultimate exceptional body of Christ is the powerful absent presence on stage at this moment – is really an image of counter-sovereignty, an alternative site of Law (one that frees and redeems). In many ways, of course, such a reading merely adds grist to the mill of those arguments around Pearse's messianic tendencies. But when viewed through the longer lens of Pearse's career in the theatre, we may begin to see a more subversive philosophical scaffolding lying behind the seemingly reactionary religiosity. It is a philosophical scaffolding, moreover, that will ultimately help shape Pearse's involvement in radical events beyond the fourth wall.

46 Ibid., pp 219–20.   47 Ibid., p. 222.   48 Ibid., p. 228.

6 / The *Übermensch* of the Western world: self and nation in *The singer*[1]

MACIEJ RUCZAJ

Pearse's plays and pageants have often been disparaged as mere exercises in political propaganda. Most particularly, and understandably, it seems scarcely possible to deal with a play such as *The singer*, completed only weeks before the Easter Rising, without reference to the insurrection that the piece seems to herald. Any discussion of *The singer* thus requires one to balance on the uneasy border between literary text and history. As a dramatic text written in the run-up to the political performance of Easter Week, *The singer* reads, according to many critics, as a blueprint for the coming revolution, blurring the boundaries between performance and life, gesture and action, metaphor and reality.[2] The play has been described, with the benefit of hindsight, as a 'literary rehearsal of the act of liberation', an earlier draft of the final 'performance' played out in the streets of Dublin by the Volunteers.[3] While acknowledging Seamus Deane's argument that Pearse's texts must always be read functionally, in relation to the aims he pursued outside the realm of writing,[4] I would never-theless argue that *The singer*, and Pearse's writings in general, should not be presented as more or less accidental assemblages of propagandist tricks, but rather as documents tracing the formation of one of the most influential conceptualizations of Irish nationalism. Rather than functioning as 'mere adjuncts to an ideological journey' and 'propagandistic preparation for the "real action" ahead', they provided a space within which 'the very idea of what it is to be Irish was being explored and reinvented'.[5]

Shortly after the Rising, Padraic Colum wrote about Pearse as a 'great

---

1 *Übermensch* is the term deployed by Nietzsche in *Thus spoke Zarathustra* (1883) to signify 'over-man' or 'beyond-human' – it has regularly been translated as 'superman' but this translation is considered problematic by many Nietzschean scholars.   2 See, for example, Ben Levitas, *The theatre of nation: Irish drama and cultural nationalism, 1890–1916* (Oxford, 2002), pp 224–5; David Cairns and Shaun Richards, *Writing Ireland: colonialism, nationalism and culture* (Manchester, 1988), p. 110.   3 Cairns and Richards, *Writing Ireland*, p. 110. It is probable that the decision not to perform the play in the early spring of 1916 was motivated by fear of exposing the conspiracy. See, for example, Desmond Ryan, *The man called Pearse* (Dublin, 1919), p. 94; Róisín Ní Ghairbhí and Eugene McNulty, 'Introduction: Patrick Pearse and theatre', *Patrick Pearse: collected plays/Drámaí an Phiarsaigh* (Dublin, 2013), pp 40–1.   4 Seamus Deane, *Celtic revivals: essays in modern Irish literature, 1880–1980* (Winston-Salem, NC, 1987) p. 74.   5 Ní Ghairbhí and McNulty, 'Introduction', p. 5.

Catholic writer'; at the same time he described some of Pearse's texts as decisively 'Nietzschean' in spirit[6] – a paradoxical claim considering Nietzsche's reputation in Catholic Ireland at that time.[7] While Colum's comment about Pearse's Nietzschean 'gay and deliberate commitment to the dangerous courses'[8] may have been made in passing, it nevertheless sheds light on some of the central paradoxes of Pearse's thought, paradoxes that were inscribed very prominently into the text of his final play. Pearse's viewpoint, one might argue, combines adherence to a form of Catholic theology with an inherent tendency towards the emancipatory discourses of modernism. Pearse's writings, I argue here, are haunted by two major interconnected dilemmas. The first is the relationship between revolutionary nationalism and the religious sentiments of the majority of the members of the Irish nation. Without questioning the rootedness of contemporary Irish identity in the Catholic universe, Pearse attempts consistently to mould a system of 'national faith' based on what we might term an analogy to the religious creed. In his texts he transfers not only the theological vocabulary but also the basic structure of the Catholic narrative of salvation into the national context.

Secondly, there is a crucial tension between the ideas of emancipation and subjugation of the self in Pearse's writings. If we consider Pearse's literary and pedagogical practice separately from his political engagements, we encounter a very strong emphasis on the individual and the subjective.[9] On the other hand, the notion of total subjugation of the individual to the goals of the collective recurs in his writings almost as frequently as the defence of the subjective in education or literature, despite the fact that the two positions seem to point in exactly opposite directions. In the very same article in which he praises an educational system that instead of 'the code of rules' introduces 'the person' as its 'centre and inspiration', he proposes Cúchulainn and Columcille as role models for his students at St Enda's due to the fact that they represent life dedicated to 'a service so excessive as to annihilate all thought of the self'.[10] Acknowledging this paradox, Gal Gerson, quoting from Pearse's essay 'The coming revolution', claims that:

6 Padraic Colum, 'Padraic Pearse' in Maurice Joy (ed.), *The Irish rebellion of 1916 and its martyrs: Erin's tragic Easter* (New York, 1916), pp 291–4.   7 For Nietzsche's reception in the Ireland of Pearse's time see, for example, Austin Clarke's 'A centenary celebration', *Massachusetts Review*, 5:2 (1964), 307–10.   8 Padraic Colum, 'Padraic Pearse', pp 291–4.   9 See, for example, Philip O'Leary, *The prose literature of the Gaelic revival, 1881–1921* (University Park, PA, 1994), p. 108; and Declan Kiberd, 'Patrick Pearse: Irish modernist' in Roisín Higgins and Regina Uí Chollatáin (eds), *The life and after-life of P.H. Pearse* (Dublin, 2009), pp 65–80.   10 Patrick Pearse, 'An ideal in education', *Irish Review*, 4:41 (June 1914), 170–3.

Collective action, according to Pearse, did not depend on the commands
of an established hierarchy, but on an inner imperative, which would lead
different people in different paths to 'a common meeting place [...]
[where] on a certain day we shall stand together, with many more beside
us, ready [...] for a trial and a triumph to be endured and achieved in
common.'[11]

Gerson's phrase 'inner imperative', one that has obvious Kantian echoes,
brings us once more to the notion of the autonomous subject fostered in
Pearse's literary and pedagogical writings, this time in the context of political
nationalism. As Gerson sums up, Pearse repeatedly recognized 'the subjective
individual as the foundation of the nation'.[12] The answer to this paradoxical
pairing of individual autonomy and collective struggle can be traced in the
character of MacDara, the protagonist of *The singer*. MacDara is much more
than a Gaelic arch-propagandist of the nationalist cause; indeed his story
can/should be read as a *Bildungsdrama* of the Irish national hero. Following a
theoretical model proposed by the Polish historian of nationalism Nikodem
Bończa Tomaszewski, I wish to position *The singer* as a narrative simultaneously concerned with national awakening and with the emancipation of the
self. Seemingly contradictory 'Catholic' and 'Nietzschean' impulses may be
ultimately resolved, I argue, by inscribing Pearse's text into the tradition of
national messianism represented by the Polish Romantic poet Adam
Mickiewicz.

SELF AND NATION

In his biography of Nietzsche, Heidegger delineates the central process of
modern philosophy: the emancipation of *subiectum*, announced most prominently by the Cartesian *cogito*, and finding its climax (as well as its breaking
point) in Nietzschean philosophy.[13] According to Nikodem Bończa
Tomaszewski, the nineteenth century was, however, the age of the self in a
more popular sense: it was the time when the idea of *subiectum* – as the
autonomous, self-proclaimed and self-governing entity – left the university
departments of philosophy, entered the popular imagination and was articu-

11 Gal Gerson, 'Cultural subversion and the background of the Irish "Easter poets", *Journal of
Contemporary History*, 30:2 (1995), 333–47. 12 Ibid., 343. 13 See also Nikodem Bończa Tomaszewski,
Źródła narodowości [*Sources of nationalities*] (Wrocław, 2006), pp 53–4.

lated in novels, poetry and historiography. By the end of the nineteenth century, images of revolt against the tyranny of class distinctions and the official morality or political system had become commonplace, although one hundred years earlier such ideas would have been considered largely esoteric. In its extreme form, symbolized by Stendhal's Julian Sorel or Nietzsche's Zarathustra, the self is established as the sole lawmaker and sense-giver, perfectly autonomous and desiring total control of its universe.[14]

According to Tomaszewski, a distinct pattern can be detected in a vast number of nineteenth-century narratives of the self, from great works of art such Stendhal's *The red and the black* or Flaubert's *Sentimental education* to the private diaries and literary attempts of average members of the public. A cycle of psychological development starts with the discovery of subjectivity and its gradual establishment, concomitant with the rejection of limitations imposed by society and external reality, that is, of the forces that threaten the sovereignty of the subject. The process generates unbearable suffering, resulting from a feeling of 'cosmic loneliness'. For many of the literary and historical figures, such as Stendhal's Sorel or Flaubert's Moreau, this creation of a personal 'world-apart' provided the ultimate solution, the embracing of a full individuality. Nevertheless, as Tomaszewski claims, for the majority 'this was only the beginning of the journey'. 'Cosmic loneliness' leads to a desire for a new type of communal experience, and in the nineteenth century the most common harbour for the tormented self was the idea of nation.[15]

Tomaszewski argues that national consciousness – as an intrinsically modern construct – depends on the prior awakening of the separate, individual self and its emancipation from traditional social structures and loyalties. Only the interdependence of these two processes can resolve the paradox of the nineteenth century as both the age of the self and of the nation. Drawing on numerous literary works and autobiographies of the period, Tomaszewski constructs a typical 'national hero': a young male deeply attached to his *Heimat*,[16] yet alienated from it by the convulsions of modernity and passing through the process of self-discovery in total opposition to and rejection of the external world. The final affirmation of the 'I' results in the 'cosmic loneliness', often described by the metaphor of death, and leads to the desire for a reconstruction of the relation to the 'not I', but on different grounds that would reflect the newly gained subjectivity. One of the effects of this process is a powerful drive to 'change the world' – to remake the

14 Tomaszewski, pp 53–61.   15 Ibid., pp 58–61.   16 That is, his sense of being and its relationship to a specific place.

external reality after the image of the self, expressed in the Romantic 'philosophy of the deed'. Another was the appearance of the modern nation as a both an 'imagined' and a 'material' fellowship of equal, liberated individuals.[17]

The problem, however, with grasping the relationship between self and nation springs from an a priori definition (derived mainly from Hobbes) of nation as a *subiectum* in itself.[18] Nation, just as 'state-leviathan' in Hobbes' political philosophy, becomes 'man writ large': it acquires the quality of an abstract person, a collective self that automatically deprives the individual of subjectivity at the moment he becomes part of the superior entity. It is due to the application of this Hobbesian concept that nationalism came to be associated most commonly with 'the abandonment of the self' and of 'being gathered up' in the collective body of a nation.[19] Such a concept of nation naturally collides with the philosophy of personalism central to the Christian tradition,[20] and indeed with modern individualism.

A possible answer to this apparent contradiction between the emphasis on the subjective and the call for unity within the nation may be provided by recourse to the theological roots of Catholic social thought, which Tomaszewski has identified in the development of Polish national consciousness in the nineteenth century. According to Tomaszewski, the concept of the nation has its roots in the ancient understanding of communal bonds derived from Pauline theology and its idea of the community as a body (*soma/corpus*). This concept, however, has very little in common with the organicism of modern biological metaphors denoting socio-political entities. In the Greek context, *soma* is a part of man separated from the 'soul' (*psyche*), through which the 'I' participates in the external reality. In James Dunn's words, *soma* is a 'relational concept' the meaning of which 'transcends mere physical body' (*sarx*, i.e. 'flesh', in St Paul's vocabulary). It actually denotes the 'means by which "I" and the world can act upon each other'.[21] It thus enabled St Paul to visualize the establishment of a tightly bound community without denying the individual identity of each member. Crucially, in Paul's letters the idea of *soma/corpus* acquired a transcendental dimension: the unity of the church is guaranteed by the participation of each particular body in the *corpus*

---

17 Tomaszewski, pp 52–103.   18 Tomaszewski, pp 109–10; Thomas Hobbes, *Leviathan*, XVII.13.
19 Michael Mays, *Nation states: the cultures of Irish nationalism* (Lanham, MD, 2007), p. 42.   20 Personalism is a branch of philosophy concerned with fully describing the uniqueness of humanity against the backdrop of the natural world.   21 James D. G. Dunn, *The theology of Paul the Apostle* (Grand Rapids, MI, 2006), p. 56.   22 Ernst H. Kantorowicz, *The king's two bodies: a study in medieval political theology* (Princeton, 1957).

mysticum of Christ. In his seminal work on medieval political theology, Ernst Kantorowicz demonstrates how medieval jurists applied the theological concept to the political reality, creating by analogy the image of the 'king's two bodies' – one temporal, the other mystical. This second body, timeless and detached from the actual person, enabled each particular member to participate in the community.[22] By its differentiation between a particular ruler and the idea of kingship, it also led in the late Middle Ages (when the political and cultural boundaries between the main European proto-nations became stabilized) to the notion of the body of the *patria* – the unity of people and territory made possible and guaranteed by the person of the ruler.[23]

Both the Pauline theological concept of *corpus mysticum* and its medieval political re-writing were essentially vertical. The community was constituted and its perseverance guaranteed through the person of the ruler (Christ/king), even if this effect was achieved through their mystical, not earthly, bodies: 'To use modern apparatus – only a king has full subjectivity.'[24] According to Tomaszewski, the concept persists in modern nationalism, yet it underwent the process of secularization and horizontalization. Through the process of emancipation of the self, everyone 'becomes a king' and participates in the mystical body of the nation to the same degree, without the need for mediation via a central, unifying figure. On the other hand, the process reaches its fulfilment with the 'appropriation' of *patria* by the individual, that is, with identification and acceptance of its every aspect (from language and customs to landscape and climate) as 'one's own'.[25] Tomaszewski concludes his argument by re-emphasizing that 'although the idea of subjectivity lies at the basis of the national consciousness, it is not an attribute of the community as a whole, but of an individual participating in nation.'[26] Instead of Hobbesian 'total participation' in the body of state, where the individual is absorbed into the collective entity, the philosophy of *corpus* allows 'participation without a loss of autonomy' by constructing *patria* as an 'external manifestation of the subject'.[27]

---

23 Tomaszewski, pp 106–10.   24 Ibid., p. 125.   25 Ibid., pp 125–6.   26 Ibid., p. 138.   27 Ibid., pp 110, 126.

THE BODY OF THE NATION

Implicit intimations of the concept of the nation as a 'fellowship participating in the body of *patria*' constitute one of the central themes of Pearse's
The singer. In what follows, I attempt to reconstruct a spiritual biography of
its protagonist, reading Pearse's final dramatic utterance as an exemplification
of the mutual interdependence of the processes of individual emancipation
and the awakening of national consciousness, of the parallel matrices of
subjectivization and nationalization discussed above.

In MacDara's story, the process of emancipation of the self is structured
as a gradual transcending or transgressing of all external limitations imposed
on the awakening subject, in accordance with the Romantic scheme outlined
above. MacDara's nonconformist attitude forces him into a series of conflicts
with various types of authority: religious, political and communal. The
process of MacDara's emancipation starts with banishment from his *Heimat*
– in his case an 'every-village' in Connemara. He leaves behind the basic traditional structures of family and local community, with their limited horizons
and set rules that provide the existential and intellectual framework for
individual lives. During the ensuing journey, all other ties binding him to 'not
I' are loosened: as a man, he rejects the earthly love of a woman; as a teacher,
he is deprived of the love of his pupil; as a poet, he finally abandons and
rejects his vocation as a 'maker of songs'. He experiences a total alienation
from society, encapsulated in his resignation from its most basic rituals: 'I
could neither pray when I came to a holy well nor drink in the public house
when I had got a little money. One seemed to me as foolish as the other.'[28]

The process culminates with the final transgression, which consists in
rejecting the basis of the individual and communal existence:

> Once, as I knelt by the cross of Kilgobbin, it became clear to me, with
> an awful clearness, that there was no God. Why pray after that? I burst
> into a fit of laughter at the folly of men in thinking that there is a
> God.[29]

This newly acquired knowledge is, however, by no means a Nietzschean 'gay
science'.[30] Emancipation reveals itself as a process consisting of suffering,

---

28 Patrick Pearse, *The singer* in Ní Ghairbhí and McNulty (eds), *Patrick Pearse: collected plays*, p. 221.
29 Ibid.   30 At the last moment, MacDara, in fact, shrinks from becoming an Irish-peasant
Zarathustra, saying to himself: 'why take away their illusion [...] their hearts will be as lonely as mine'

imaginatively described as the 'death of the old self' or, in terms borrowed from mysticism, as a passage through the 'dark night' of the deepest depravation and deprivation. MacDara, stripped of 'all illusions' and his creative powers, appears to the people he meets on his way as 'a wandering, wicked spirit'.[31]

In a paradigmatic Romantic text, Adam Mickiewicz's *Dziady* (*Forefathers' Eve,* 1832), the protagonist erects a tombstone to symbolize the death of his former self and to mark a new beginning, highlighted by his change of name (from Gustaw to Konrad). He undergoes a similar process of loosening all ties with external reality, culminating in the act of defiance of God's authority (both in his symbolic suicide and in claiming his poetry as an act of creation equal to that of God). Nevertheless, both Mickiewicz's Gustaw-Konrad and Pearse's MacDara do not fully follow the path leading towards an equivalent of Nietzsche's *Übermensch.* The processes of the death of the old, 'enslaved' self and the birth of the emancipated subject are in their cases paralleled by, and inalienably bound to, a movement towards national illumination. Indeed we may find something of this at work in Nietzsche's suggestion that: 'The desire for individuation is merely one phase in life [...] there comes a point when we wish to go beyond the individual and idiosyncratic.'[32] Characteristically, when Roger Griffin, in his seminal work on political modernism, discusses the 'August madness' of 1914, he describes how the underlying notion of the individual revolt of 'Nietzsche's passive last men' against 'the old world' ended not in the spirit of Zarathustra but in the embracing of the nation as 'the womb, the home, and the horizon-framing myth'.[33]

According to Joep Leerssen, in the nineteenth century, in the dominant Ascendancy discourse (represented in this case by William Allingham), Ireland was perceived as a congregation of small communities, as a *Gemeinschaft* rather than *Gesellschaft.*[34] In this perspective, an Irishman has no country, but only a region, a homeland, a place of origin.[35] The question of a higher level of political and social organization remains somehow transcendent to the Irish context. *Gemeinschaft*, Leerssen adds, also implies stable power relations,

(ibid., p. 221).   **31** Ibid.   **32** Quoted in Otto Buhlmann, *Yeats and Nietzsche: an exploration of major Nietzschean echoes in the writings of W.B. Yeats* (Totowa, NJ, 1982), pp 123–5.   **33** Roger Griffin, *Modernism and fascism: the sense of a beginning under Mussolini and Hitler* (London, 2007), p. 154.   **34** *Gemeinschaft* denotes social relations built on close personal ties (such as family), while *Gesellschaft* indexes social relations built on more impersonal connections (such as duty to an organization).   **35** Joep Leerssen, *Remembrance and imagination: patterns in the historical and literary representation of Ireland in the nineteenth century* (Cork, 1996), p. 167.

based on unquestioned tradition and perpetuating the existent order.[36] When MacDara abandons the microcosm of his native village, the source of his creativity seems to wither as a result of his being an exile: 'When I first went away my heart was as if dead and dumb and I could not make any songs.'[37] Nevertheless, a gradual transfer from the level of *Heimat* to that of the wider fellowship of the nation is triggered. Whereas, for his fellow 'mountain men', the horizon reaches no further than Oughterard and Galway, MacDara's progress towards Dublin is concomitant with the widening of his 'imagined community'.[38] Crucially, he gradually learns to perceive it as 'his own': mapped, absorbed and articulated in a series of poems:

> The first song I made was about the children I saw playing in the street of *Kilconnell.* The next song that I made was about an old dark man that I met on the causeway of *Aughrim.* I made a glad, proud song when I saw the broad *Shannon* flow under the bridge of *Athlone.* I made many a song after that before I reached *Dublin.*[39] [Emphasis added.]

The people and the landscape, the human and the topographical elements all merge together into the first intimation of the *corpus* of the *patria.*[40] What used to be a mere emotion in his youthful poems ('love for the people' and 'great anger against the Gall'[41]) now becomes a material reality and gains a corporeal existence, a status which was earlier reserved only for the limited reality of his 'place of origin'.

The final step towards the birth of the subject in MacDara's story is linked to the symbolic deicide. As I have already mentioned, MacDara's fate in this respect copies both the path of a romantic rebel, defying the highest authority, and a typical *via mystica*, in which the moment of re-entering into a communion with God is preceded by the deepest fall. The moment of

36 Ibid., p. 170. 37 Pearse, *The singer* in Ní Ghairbhí and McNulty (eds), *Patrick Pearse: collected plays*, p. 218. 38 For more on the critical deployment of this term, see Benedict Anderson, *Imagined communities: reflections on the origins and spread of nationalism* (London, 1991). 39 Pearse, *The singer* in Ní Ghairbhí and McNulty (eds), *Patrick Pearse: collected plays*, p. 218. 40 We may compare this passage with Michelet's description of the 'individual/national genesis': 'And however large this patria may be, he [a member of the nation] enlarges his heart so as to embrace it all. He beholds it with the eyes of the mind and clasps it with the longings of desire. Ye mountains of the native land, which bound our sight but not our thoughts, be witness that if we do not clasp in one brotherly embrace the great family of France, it is already contained in our hearts. [...] ye sacred rivers, ye holy islands, where our altar was erected ...' (Jules Michelet, 'On the unity of fatherland' in Hans Kohn (ed.), *Nationalism: its meaning and history* (Princeton, 1955), pp 101–2. 41 Pearse, *The singer* in Ní Ghairbhí and McNulty (eds), *Patrick Pearse: collected plays*, p. 214.

MacDara's illumination and reawakening is again clothed in the imagery and language of mysticism: 'He has revealed His Face to me. His Face is terrible and sweet, Maoilsheachlainn. I know it well now.' The newly regained God reflects the transformative and generative power of suffering: 'His Name is suffering. His Name is loneliness. His Name is abjection.'[42] Crucially, MacDara's return to the community and his re-embracing of the divine are concomitant; they are in fact articulated in the same monologue and through one set of images:

> I have lived with the homeless and with the breadless. Oh, Maoilsheachlainn, the poor, the poor! I have seen such sad childings, such bare marriage feasts, such candleless wakes! In the pleasant country places I have seen them, but oftener in the dark, unquiet streets of the city. [...] The people, Maoilsheachlainn, the dumb, suffering people: reviled and outcast, yet pure and splendid and faithful. In them I saw, or seemed to see again, the Face of God. Ah, it is a tear-stained face, blood-stained, defiled with ordure, but it is the Holy Face![43]

In MacDara's story the religious illumination merges almost invisibly (and also indivisibly) with the national illumination. Communion with the people and communion with God becomes a single experience. MacDara's God is undoubtedly the tribal God of the Gaels, but at the same time retains essentially Christian features. As has been stated above, the unity of the church in theological terms results from individual participation in the body of Christ. At the same time, the image of Christ's body – due to its theological complexity and due to its function in popular religious practice – contains an inherent tension between the suffering human body of the crucified and the glorified mystical body of the resurrected.[44] The same tension is transferred in MacDara's monologue onto the national level, as he speaks of 'a tear-stained face, blood-stained, defiled with ordure' that nevertheless remains a splendid 'Holy face'.

In Tomaszewski's theory, nationalism – even if relying heavily on religious symbolism – is essentially a secular and secularizing movement. In contrast, Pearse's national 'communion' acquires a vertical dimension parallel to the mode of existence of *ecclesia* in St Paul's concept of *corpus mysticum*. In MacDara's monologue, quoted above, the community is established through

42 Ibid., p. 221.   43 Ibid., p. 222.   44 See Miri Rubin, *Corpus Christi: the Eucharist in late medieval church* (Cambridge, 1991), p. 302.

participation in the body of Christ – at the same time splendid and defiled – even if it stands here not for the universal brotherhood of the church, but for a particular community of the Gaels. The movement towards affirming the individual and the communal identity fails to eradicate the vertical, transcendent dimension. This theological turn in the narrative is, however, modified by the interplay with the discourse of Romantic messianism. The preservation of the vertical dimension of the construction of the community is followed by a full revelation of the status of MacDara within this community. He returns to the collectivity of the nation not merely as one of its members, but as the elected One.

MESSIAH OF THE GAELS

The singer is the third of Pearse's plays to perform the theme of communal deliverance by means of the radical act of the upturning of the existing order. It is also linked with *An rí* and *The master* due to its rootedness in the medieval dramatic modes of liturgical and mystery plays. Nevertheless, MacDara provides a very different model of the national hero than Giolla na Naomh, the youthful king from *An rí*, or Ciarán, the protagonist of *The master*, who is introducing Christianity to the Irish. Giolla na Naomh is a typical Girardian scapegoat, a 'spotless lamb' sacrificed in order to save the community.[45] Although he agrees to play this role in the play, he remains rather a passive object of the sacrificial story. Ciarán, on the other hand, fails due to personal doubts to confront the political powers that be in the name of his cause. The dramatic change of the socio-political order must be induced from outside – by the miraculous appearance of the Archangel Michael. In contrast, MacDara manages to imitate Christ's narrative to its utmost consequences, becoming both an offering and the offerer.[46]

An inherent characteristic of the emancipated *subiectum* is a will to act, to actively change the external reality. According to Romantic philosophy from Schelling to Carlyle, the subject fulfils itself through a deed.[47] In Tomaszewski's words, 'the deed for the Romantics is not simply *any* human activity but rather the act of transformation, which by itself creates the new world'.[48] The nineteenth-century obsession with the deed can be easily

---

45 For more on the scapegoat mechanism see René Girard, *The scapegoat* (Baltimore, MD, 1986).   46 Cf. *The short catechism extracted from the catechism* (Dublin, 1891), pp 20, 51.   47 Cf. Isaiah Berlin, *The roots of Romanticism* (Princeton, 2001), pp 13, 78, 88–90.   48 Tomaszewski, p. 84.

detected as one of the central features of Pearse's political writings, with constant attacks on the 'current generation' because of their reluctance to act and their preference for the politics of a 'debating society', which meant choosing passivity instead of an exercise of will.[49] Reading Pearse's diatribes against the majority, who had succumbed to the temptations of a comfortable and respectable life, as opposed to the 'rare phenomenon' of Man (with a capital 'M'[50]), one cannot but think of the Nietzschean dualism of the Last Man and the *Übermensch*.

The tension between deliberative rationalism and 'will to power' is directly reproduced in *The singer* through the debates of MacDara and his brother Colm with the 'elders' of the village about the legitimacy of the insurrection. The philosophy of the deed is articulated most explicitly in MacDara's statement:

Aye, they say that to be busy with the things of the spirit is better than to be busy with the things of the body. But I am not sure, master. Can the vision beautiful alone content a man? I think true man is divine in this, like God, he must needs create, he must needs do [...] The true teacher must suffer and do. He must break bread to the people, he must go into Gethsemane and toil up the steep of Golgotha.[51]

Again the language and imagery of religion and eternity are invoked, only to be translated into the political and temporary context. Following the model of gnostic revolutionaries throughout history, MacDara transforms the politically passive message of Christianity ('vision beautiful') into the activist desire to change *this* world.[52] As in the case of the prophets of Romantic millenarianism – Mazzini, Michelet and Mickiewicz – it necessarily gives rise to messianic imagery.

It seems that among the three great Romantic messianists, Mickiewicz remains the closest to Pearse's thinking, as he directly opposes Michelet and Mazzini, claiming that 'the essence of messianism points to a single man, Polish messianism ascribes to its nation a mission that is however represented by a single person'.[53] Even if the divine qualities are repeatedly ascribed by

49 Patrick Pearse, *Collected works of Padraic H. Pearse: political writings and speeches* (Dublin, 1922).　50 Cf. Pearse, *Political writings and speeches*, p. 169.　51 Pearse, *The singer* in Ní Ghairbhí and McNulty (eds), *Patrick Pearse: collected plays*, p. 219.　52 In the sense given to the term 'gnostic' by theorists of the modern mass political movements, such as Eric Voegelin or Alain Besancon, that is 'immanentization' of the eschatological message of Christianity, enclosing the Christian redemptive narrative in the limits of earthly history (see, for example, Eric Voegelin, *The new science of politics* [Chicago, 1951]).　53 Paweł Rojek,

Pearse to the people as a whole, his writings focus on charismatic individuals who perform the basic messianic functions (revealing and realizing, preaching and acting) and who receive their power simultaneously from above and from below. Both Pearse and Mickiewicz distinguish between the passive part of the nation, which undertakes suffering parallel to that of Golgotha, and the active process of redemption, whose agent is a single man. Such a leader is an individual lifted above the multitude: 'the Man-Word, the organ of God's revelation', whose mission is 'to lead the lesser and weaker brethren', as Talmon describes Mickiewicz's concept.[54] In a similar vein, the speaker of Pearse's poem 'The rebel' posits himself 'in between' the people and the divine, being the one who is 'of the people' and 'understand[s] the people', but who has at the same time been chosen to speak 'with God on the top of His holy hill'.[55]

Characteristically, in both Mickiewicz's and Pearse's thought, the identification of the elected one with the national community transcends a merely spiritual or emotional dimension. In the lengthy poetic monologue 'The great improvisation', Gustaw-Konrad, the protagonist of *Forefathers Eve*, claims his physical unity with the nation:

> Now my soul is incarnate in my country,
> My body has swallowed her soul,
> And I and my country are one.
> Million is my name, for I love
> And I suffer for millions.
> I look at my unfortunate fatherland
> As a son at his father on the rack,
> And I feel all the pain of my people
> Like a mother the child in her womb.[56]

He concludes then with a final demiurgical gesture:

> I love a whole nation! And I have embraced
> All its generations, past and to come;
> I pressed it to my breast
> Like a friend, a lover, a husband, a father [...][57]

'Mesjanizm integralny', *Pressje*, 28 (2012), 39.   **54** Jacob Talmon, *The political messianism: a romantic phase* (New York, 1961), p. 273.   **55** Patrick Pearse, *The literary writings of Patrick Pearse*, ed. Séamas Ó Buachalla (Cork, 1979), pp 25–6.   **56** Quoted in Adam Mickiewicz, 'Prophecies', in Balazs Trencsenyi and Michal Kopeček (eds), *National Romanticism: the formation of national movements* (Budapest, 2013), pp 408–20. **57** Quoted in Mickiewicz, 'Prophecies', pp 408–20.

In Pearse's 'The fool' the speaker wants to build in his heart 'a noble house' for all the members of the nation 'to dwell'. In *The singer* MacDara echoes also the 'physical' dimension of Konrad's attitude: 'My heart has been heavy with the sorrow of mothers, my eyes have been wet with the tears of the children.'[58] What is crucial is that MacDara (unlike Konrad) turns his verbal declarations into practice by facing the enemies of the tribe alone, in a redemptive act of sacrifice. The corporeal metaphors of both texts take us back to the image of Christ's body, at once tormented and glorified, as the guarantor of the unity and identity of the community of the church. In the final passages of the play, MacDara moulds himself into a 'lesser Christ', offering his own body[59] – at once earthly and temporary, and glorified by the act of sacrifice – as a similar guarantor that the community of the nation exists. The language used in MacDara's final speech ('one man can free a people as one Man redeemed the world'[60]) is the language of the Pauline theology of *corpus* that enables all humanity to participate both in the body of Adam and his sin and in the body of Christ and his sacrifice.[61]

To conclude, then, MacDara's journey – away from his *Heimat* and back again – forms a physical correlative to his spiritual evolution. The abandonment of the native village is concomitant with the gradual repulsion of the confinements of tradition and of the old, 'unformed' self, culminating in the establishment of the sovereign subject free of all social and spiritual bonds. There is an opposing movement of appropriation or absorption of the external reality – that is, the *corpus* of the *patria* now identified as MacDara's own – into the self. He returns to his native village to teach by his words and example both how to become a sovereign self and how to become a part of the community of the nation. Finally, MacDara transcends the boundaries of his earthly, temporal body, moulding it through the act of sacrifice into the mystical foundation of the national community. The *Bildungsdrama* of the Irish national consciousness turns in this final step into a dramatization of the narrative of the national messiah, comparable to other texts of Romantic national messianism.

---

58 The same motif is elaborated on in 'The rebel': 'I am sorrowful with their sorrow, I am hungry with their desire:/My heart has been heavy with the grief of mothers,/My eyes have been wet with the tears of children' (Pearse, *Literary writings and speeches*, pp 25–6).   59 We should notice the prominence of the motif of the body in the final lines of the play, from Máire's 'there will be many a noble corpse to be waked before the new moon' through the mention of Christ 'hung naked before men' to the scene of MacDara's exit, where we see him 'pulling off his clothes as he goes' (Pearse, *The singer* in Ní Ghairbhí and McNulty (eds), *Patrick Pearse: collected plays*, pp 227–8).   60 Ibid., p. 228.   61 1 Cor. 15:21–2. See also Daniel O'Neill, 'The cult of self-sacrifice: the Irish experience', *Éire-Ireland*, 24:4 (Winter 1989), 95.

7 / 'To right the wrong of the people': vulnerability and revolutionary desire in Patrick Pearse's drama

MICHAEL G. CRONIN

In 'Violence, mourning, politics', Judith Butler argues that, contrary to our common perception of mourning as privatizing and apolitical, grief can 'furnish a sense of political community of a complex order'.[1] Butler suggests that grieving does not follow the neatly linear stages identified by pop psychology, but washes over us in sudden and unexpected waves of emotion. We are undone and dispossessed by grief, and are thus made aware, affectively and viscerally, of our fundamental vulnerability and dependence on others. This perception of vulnerability can lead us to apprehend how thoroughly relational our subjectivity is. As Butler observes, it is not so much that 'I' grieve for 'you' as that 'I' grasp that there is no 'I' without, or prior to, that relationship with 'you'. Writing in the wake of the 2001 attacks on New York and Washington, and the subsequent invasions of Afghanistan and Iraq by US-led forces, Butler is aware that this perception of vulnerability can be politicized in very different ways. One is the transformation of grief into rage, the urge to deny one's vulnerability by violently imposing that condition on others. On the other hand, Butler is also hopeful that 'mindfulness of vulnerability' can become the basis for a different type of politics, through which 'we might critically evaluate and oppose the conditions under which certain human lives are more vulnerable than others, and thus certain human lives are more grievable than others'.[2]

In Patrick Pearse's *The singer* (1916), the male body is simultaneously erotic and vulnerable, and thus, I will argue, political. Indeed, as we will see, a variety of political desires adhere to this discursive body. Pearse wrote this one-act English-language play in early 1916. A production scheduled for the week before the planned Rising was cancelled and so the first public production was in Liverpool in 1918 (though some former pupils of Scoil Éanna staged

---

1 Judith Butler, *Precarious life: the powers of mourning and violence* (London, 2004), p. 22. Butler continued her exploration of the political potential of vulnerability in *Frames of war: when is life grievable?* (London, 2009).
2 Butler, *Precarious life*, p. 30.

a production in Dublin in December 1917). In 1932 Micheál Mac Liammóir and Hilton Edwards staged a production at the Gate Theatre and a radio version was broadcast the following year.[3] In contrast to the earlier realist productions, Mac Liammóir and Edwards staged the play in an expressionist style, and sought to create a theatrical space where, as Edwards put it, 'anything was possible and the imagination might soar'.[4]

The singer is set in Connemara, in an unspecified historical period, on the eve of an armed uprising against 'the Gall' that is to be led by a young man named Colm. Pearse is reasonably successful at conveying a mood of tension and anxious foreboding about the approaching military confrontation. However, the play's dramatic and emotional interest is principally focused on the unexpected return of the titular character, Colm's brother MacDara, who had been banished from the locality by the authorities because of his subversive ballads. Dramaturgically, it is a weakness that none of 'Madara's songs' are performed, and so we depend on the actor playing MacDara to credibly convey the powerful charisma that the other characters ascribe to him. The most striking moment comes at the end, when MacDara's last speech concludes: 'one man can free a people as one Man redeemed the world. I will take no pike. I will go into battle with bare hands. I will stand up before the Gall as Christ hung naked before men on the tree!' This is followed by the stage direction: 'he moves through them, pulling off his clothes as he goes.'[5]

One need not search far for evidence to support a biographical reading of this work. A play about an armed insurrection penned while its author was helping to organize one; a production cancelled lest the play 'give too much away' about the planned events of Easter Week, as Margaret Pearse later recalled; another production staged by young men, Pearse's former pupils, who had actually participated in the Rising.[6] Most damning, for unsympathetic Pearse critics, is the character of MacDara who, in this view, is little more than a projection of Pearse's narcissistic self-image and another symptom of the 'messiah complex' diagnosed by Ruth Dudley Edwards. For Dudley Edwards, *The singer* was the culmination of Pearse's 'religious nationalism'. She dismisses its 'extravagances of language and messianic utterances' and notes that 'had Pearse not suffered MacDara's fate, the play would have failed'.[7] More sympathetically, Roy Forster identifies the play as a 'homoerotic

3 Róisín Ní Ghairbhí and Eugene McNulty (eds), *Patrick Pearse: collected plays/Drámaí an Phiarsaigh* (Dublin, 2013), pp 40–2.   4 Cited in Ní Ghairbhí and McNulty (eds), *Patrick Pearse: collected plays*, p. 41.   5 Ibid., p. 228.   6 Cited in ibid., p. 40.   7 Ruth Dudley Edwards, *Patrick Pearse: the triumph of failure* (Dublin, 2006), pp 246–7.

fable'.[8] In his discussion of Irish sexual culture in the revolutionary period he argues that 'homoeroticism is safely diverted into servitude and death' in Pearse's plays. He goes on to reiterate how Pearse 'supressed' and 'sublimated' his erotic desire for young men and boys into his writing, theatre and political work.[9]

In contrast to these biographical interpretations, this essay proposes a reading of the play that weaves together a consideration of Pearse's distinctive and unsettling aesthetic, the play's queering of gender and sexual identities and its critically utopian politics. Is this play just a crudely realist work of naive sentimentality, or do we need to search elsewhere in its cultural moment for an explanation of its strange effects? Máire Ní Fhlathúin argues that the 'saving grace' of Pearse's often flawed writing is 'its fantastic expression of the emotional and imaginative concerns of anti-colonialism and anti-realism'.[10] We might, for instance, reconsider Pearse's 'extravagances' as a deliberately stylized use of language, comparable to J.M. Synge's mode of writing English-language dialogue with the rhythm and syntax of the Irish language. In this regard, Ní Fhlathúin has noted the radical defamiliarization produced by Pearse's 'distinctly unEnglish English'.[11] We might also widen our attention out from the text of the play as Pearse wrote it to consider the emotional resonances we might expect from a performance of this play. This brings us to the character of MacDara, or more precisely the embodiment of that character by an actor on stage. Thinking about MacDara as a body moving through a theatrical space usefully shifts our attention from adjudicating between Pearse's desire to be MacDara and his desire for MacDara (or, more precisely, for the sexy, charismatic masculinity embodied by that character). Instead we might consider MacDara's body as the locus of the audience's desires – and in particular a complex amalgam of emotional, erotic and political desires. To do this we must first recalibrate that radical disjunction between sexuality and creativity, and between the sexual and the political, underpinning Forster's reading of the play. That disjunction, a staple of modern bourgeois ideology, assumes that while erotic desires, energies and identifications may be diverted into politics, the sexual and the political remain substantively different. This precludes another possibility; that all

8 R.F. Foster, *Vivid faces: the revolutionary generation in Ireland, 1890–1923* (London, 2014), p. 112.   9 Ibid., p. 116, 135–6.   10 Máire Ní Fhlathúin, 'The anti-colonial modernism of Patrick Pearse' in Howard J. Booth and Nigel Rigby (eds), *Modernism and empire* (Manchester, 2000), p. 176.   11 Ní Fhlathúin, 'The anti-colonial modernism of Patrick Pearse', p. 163. For a very useful discussion of Pearse's Irish-language prose style in his stories, and Joseph Campbell's distinctive translation of this, see Anne Markey, 'Introduction' in Patrick Pearse, *Short Stories*, ed. Ann Markey, trans. Joseph Campbell (Dublin, 2009), pp xvii–xliv.

politics is inherently sexual and that desire, like hope, is the ambient state of all transformative political mobilizations.

In a recognizable scenario from revivalist drama, recalling the opening of Yeats and Gregory's *Cathleen Ni Houlihan* (1902) or Synge's *Riders to the sea* (1904), the play opens on an older woman and a younger woman in a cottage kitchen. Máire is the mother of Colm and MacDara, while Sighle is their foster-sister. In the opening scene Sighle makes the following speech:

> I shiver when I think of them all going out to fight. They will go out laughing: I see them with their cheeks flushed and their red lips apart. And then they will lie very still on the hillside – so still and white, with no red on their cheeks, but maybe a red wound in their white breasts or their white foreheads. Colm's hair will be dabbled with blood.

> MÁIRE: Whist, daughter. That is not talk for one that was raised in this house. I am his mother, and I do not grudge him.

> SIGHLE: Forgive me. You have known more sorrow than I, and I think only of my own sorrow. *(She rises and kisses her.)* I am proud other times to think of so many young men, young men with straight strong limbs and white smooth flesh, going out into great peril because a voice has called to them to right the wrong of the people. Oh, I would like to see the man that has set their hearts on fire with the breath of his voice! They say that he is very young. They say that he is one of ourselves, a mountainy man that speaks our speech, and has known hunger and sorrow.

> MÁIRE: The strength and sweetness he has comes maybe out of his sorrow.[12]

This exchange crystallizes a significant structure of feeling in Pearse's writing. Firstly, there is a palpable tension between terror and fascination. We hear this tension in Sighle's 'shiver', which might be of excitement or of fear, and in the startling juxtaposition of the sound of laughter and the sight of corpses on the hillside. We also hear it in the recurring, sensual colour imagery: the red of the flushed cheeks and full lips; the red of spilled blood;

12 Ní Ghairbhí and McNulty (eds), *Patrick Pearse: collected plays*, p. 206.

the red of the blood and the white of pale, lifeless bodies. Secondly, erotic desire is interwoven with a desire that is political. The longing that is evoked, or called forth, by bodies (specifically male bodies) merges with that longing that is evoked, or called forth, by utopian visions of a transformed future. As she describes her vision of revolutionary action, men going forth to 'right the wrong of the people', Sighle's description dwells on how physically desirable these men are, with their 'straight strong limbs and white smooth flesh', and there is an insistent, discordant erotic undertone to that description – 'their cheeks flushed and their red lips apart'.

This structure of feeling takes a distinctive shape in Pearse's writing, but it is also emblematic of his epoch. Surveying European history in the decades before the First World War, Eric Hobsbawm identified a fundamental structural contradiction: 'the era of peace, of confident bourgeois civilisation, growing wealth and Western empires inevitably carried within itself the embryo of the era of war, revolution and crisis which put an end to it'.[13] During those decades at the turn of the twentieth century, capitalist modernity promised the exhilaration of technological innovation and rapid social change, while simultaneously generating 'hunger and sorrow' (or 'the homeless and the breadless', as MacDara describes it later in the play) on an unprecedented scale in Europe and its colonies. Writing about Yeats' 'Nineteen hundred and nineteen', Michael Wood observes that the poem 'dramatises frightful violence and suggests that violence may alter the world … the promise of violence was inseparable from everything that made you afraid of it'.[14] Thus, while Pearse's drama lacks the signature aesthetic self-consciousness of modernism, it nevertheless exhibits the same deeply ambivalent relationship to modernity – as well as the same fascination with the primitive. To explore this aspect of Pearse's style further we might usefully contrast it with Igor Stravinsky's score, written for Nijinsky's ballet *The rite of spring*, which was first produced by Sergei Diaghilev's Ballet Russe a few years before Pearse wrote this play. This is not to argue for any equivalence of aesthetic achievement or cultural historical significance between *The rite of spring* and Pearse's dramaturgy; *The singer* is, and will remain, a minor work in the Irish canon. It is merely to acknowledge that poor workmanship only partially explains the unsettling oddness of Pearse's drama, and that any rigorously political interpretation of his style must be alert to epochal energies at work in disparate locations and texts.

13 Eric Hobsbawm, *The age of empire, 1875–1914* (London, 1994), p. 327.   14 Michael Wood, *Yeats and violence* (Oxford, 2010), p. 15.

When we listen to Stravinsky's score we experience that same tension between terror and exhilaration that, I am arguing, we can detect in Pearse's play. We experience this kinaesthetically rather than rationally. As we listen, the percussive diction, jarring rhythms and jagged tempo (sweeping sharply from urgent to lyrical) work together on our nervous system rather than our rational mind, and this leaves us in a state of nervous tension. At the same time, we are exhilarated by these strangely beautiful sounds, and also excited as, even from this distance, we can still detect the echo of that original moment of excitement about this innovative pushing against the possibilities offered by musical composition.

Moreover, when listening to this music we are tuning into frequencies that are at once aesthetic and historical. The aestheticized sensation of shock delivered to the ballet's audience in May 1913 eerily foreshadowed the horrifically brutal shock inflicted on the bodies of soldiers by technological warfare less than two years later. In *Touch and intimacy in First World War literature*, Santanu Das describes what he terms the 'haptic geography' of the trenches.[15] This was a zone of horror in which the human body was not only destroyed by the *matériel* of war – bullets, shells, gas – but also endlessly assaulted through each of the senses. This was a space where the fragility and vulnerability of the body was painfully apparent, and where the mind was powerfully confronted with the horror of abjection – the threatened collapse of the boundary between the human and the non-human. Describing the alteration of human experience in the wake of the war, Walter Benjamin wrote that:

> a generation that had gone to school on a horse-drawn streetcar now stood under the open sky in a countryside in which nothing remained unchanged but the clouds, and beneath these clouds, in a field of force of destructive torrents and explosions, was the tiny, fragile human body.[16]

Thus, the crisis of faith in the progressive narrative of modernity that we associate with modernism was initially experienced physically rather than intellectually by the majority of soldiers, and the women who nursed them, at the front. As Das puts it:

15 Das, *Touch and intimacy* (Cambridge, 2005), p. 77.   16 Walter Benjamin, 'The storyteller', *Illuminations*, trans. Harry Zohn, ed. Hannah Arendt (New York, 2007), p. 84.

if the First World War is described as the end of illusion for a whole generation of young men, mud can be said to be the beginning of that end. The process of disillusionment began at a daily intimate level, often in the attempt to find one's footing or one's boots.[17]

    This not only reminds us of the obvious historical fact that we cannot begin to comprehend the 1916 Rising in Dublin outside of the context of the war, but acts as useful corrective to the biographical reading that interprets Pearse's play as a sort of dress rehearsal for the Rising, in which he egotistically gives himself the starring role of the doomed, sacrificial hero. To be sure, the Rising had a theatrical element to it. More interesting, however, is Pearse's (unevenly successful) attempt to develop a theatrical form that would give expression to the epochal pressures and anxieties – the contradictions of modernity at the beginning of the twentieth century, and the unsustainable political, intellectual and psychic pressures generated by those contradictions – that would make revolution appear not so much strategic as necessary. Since the form he chose was a style of theatrical performance that depends on the audience's affective response rather than narrative coherence, he emphasized above all how those pressures were experienced affectively on the human body.

    There are other interesting similarities between *The rite of spring* and Pearse's theatre. The ballet tells, in its highly stylized and plotless form, the story of a ritual sacrifice. A virginal young woman is sacrificed to ensure the fertility of the earth as part of a hectic, bacchanalian ritual to welcome the return of spring.[18] This juxtaposition of destruction and creation, of Eros and Thanatos, is an equally productive lens for approaching Pearse's theatre, where an act of destruction in the present that is oriented towards the future (towards ensuring a better future) is a recurring and central motif. We might also note that the emphasis on the purity and innocence of the sacrificial victim is a common trope. In *The singer*, for instance, MacDara has 'tried to keep my heart virginal'.[19] However, the most obvious comparison here is with the young boy, Giolla na Naomh, in Pearse's earlier Irish-language play, *An rí/The king*. In that play, which is set in a version of an early Christian monastery, it is precisely the boy's innocence that makes him the necessary sacrificial victim to set right the social and cosmic order.

    An rí/The king also bears the most obvious similarity with the ballet because

---

17 Das, *Touch and intimacy*, p. 42. 18 See the translation of Stravinsky's libretto in Modris Eksteins, *Rites of spring: the Great War and the birth of the modern age* (New York, 2000), pp 9–10. 19 Ní Ghairbhí and McNulty (eds), *Patrick Pearse: collected plays*, p. 217.

of its archaic idiom. In each we have the creation of a highly stylized version of the primitive or pre-modern past: pre-Christian Russia and early Christian Ireland, respectively. Arguably, the Connemara setting of *The singer* (and of Pearse's short stories) functions as a similar geo-temporal marker of the Gaelic archaic or pre-modern.[20] We also have the fascinating use of archaic narrative materials (folklore and myth) to create proleptically modern artistic forms, which was so distinctive of modernism and its characteristic 'mythic method'.[21] What is really interesting about Stravinsky, Diaghilev and Pearse (as well as Joyce) is that the recourse to these archaic materials is never a retreat from the modern but about making the modern more intelligible. It is never an argument for recreating traditional artistic forms or restoring some traditional social or political order. The turn to the past is not a retreat but a gesture towards the future; it is a distinctive style of advancing into the future. It is an instance of what Linda Dowling describes as 'those ceaseless recombinations of cultural materials in which the new or contemporary or modern most often comes to birth through some transmutation, under the pressure of history and ideology, of the old or ancient, or even the archaic'.[22] Moreover, the juxtaposition of past and future is key to the revolutionary act, artistically and politically. It is a gesture of refusal and resistance against the linear temporality of capitalist modernity and its ideological commitment to a narrow, instrumental and alienating model of 'progress'. What Modris Eksteins wrote about Diaghilev is equally true of Pearse:

he wished to fuse the double image of contemporary life – an age of transition – into a vision of wholeness, with emphasis, however, on the

---

20 For a useful discussion of the Connemara setting of the stories, see Anne Markey, 'Introduction' in Patrick Pearse, *Short stories*. Markey argues that, despite Pearse's emphasis on the authenticity of the Connemara setting, the earlier stories, in *Íosagán agus sgéalta eile* (1907), reflect his view of the region as an idealised, pastoral paradise. Pearse ignores the desperate poverty of its inhabitants and 'not only aestheticises deprivation but also allows the political and social causes and effects of that destitution to pass unchallenged' (p. xxii). In the later stories, in *An mháthair agus sgéalta eile* (1916), she argues that Pearse developed a more realistic portrayal of the region. By contrast, Angela Bourke argues that we should read Pearse's stories less as he intends us to – as a transparent, unself-conscious, unmediated view in to the 'real' Connemara – but as part of an ongoing debate among largely urban-based intellectuals about a discursive 'Connemara'. In the stories Pearse was actively creating an imagined community in response to the prevailing stereotypes about the region. See Angela Bourke, 'The imagined community of Pearse's short stories' in Roisín Higgins and Regina Uí Chollatáin (eds), *The life and after-life of P.H. Pearse* (Dublin, 2009), pp 141–55.   21 The phrase was coined by T.S. Eliot in a review of *Ulysses*. T.S. Eliot, '*Ulysses*, order and myth' in Clive Hart and David Hayman (eds), *James Joyce's Ulysses: critical essays* (Berkeley, 1974). 22 Linda Dowling, *Hellenism and homosexuality in Victorian Oxford* (Ithaca, NY, 1994), pp 3–4.

vision rather than the wholeness, on the quest, the striving, the pursuit of wholeness, continuing and changing though this had to be.[23]

We can still listen to performances and recordings of Stravinsky's score, but we cannot return to the Théâtre des Champs-Elysées in Paris in May 1913 and see that first scandalous production of the ballet. In particular we cannot see Nijinsky's performance and witness that famous body in motion. This body enthralled and beguiled a generation of the avante-garde, and their patrons, defying the conventions of 'masculine' and 'feminine' beauty and merging fragility with an extraordinary physical prowess; as Cocteau put it, Nijinsky's performances combined 'grace and brutality'.[24]

In the extract from *The singer* above, it is Sighle who articulates a desire for the male body and this would, at first glance, appear to situate such desire in a reassuringly heterosexual matrix. However, on closer examination, there is a startling transposition of gender roles here. Sighle might be said to have appropriated two conventionally 'masculine' prerogatives to a female subject: the prerogative of creativity – she is the 'author' of this vision that she is calling up – and the prerogative of the male gaze. Moreover, while Sighle situates herself gazing on these young men, she also imagines the young men ostentatiously not gazing at her. Instead they are transfixed by the 'voice'; they have rapturously and deliriously abandoned themselves to this voice, as the visceral sensuality of the prose reiterates – it is not the sound of the voice that enthrals them but its 'breath'. As we soon learn, this 'voice' originates in the body of MacDara. Thus, if we were to translate Sighle's vision into the idiom of the Gaelic poetic tradition – and specifically where that poetic tradition overlaps with the Jacobite and republican political tradition – we might say that in this *aisling* MacDara is not the heroic young man conventionally roused to action by the apparitional woman. Instead, he appears to play the role of that woman; rather than being the young man roused to action by the *spéirbhean*, the sky woman, in this version MacDara *is* the *spéirbhean*.

The formation of heroic masculinity is an abiding preoccupation in Pearse's drama and pedagogical writing. 'Heroic' evokes the chivalric ideal of the warrior; the manly ideal most powerfully embodied symbolically by the mythological figure of Cúchulainn for Pearse, as well as for the other Irish writers of the revival.[25] Unquestionably, this heroic ideal was reactionary and

23 Eksteins, *Rites of spring*, p. 33.   24 Cited in Eksteins, *Rites of spring*, p. 35.   25 On Pearse's adaption of the Cúchulainn story for his pageant *Macghníomhartha Chúchulainn/The boyhood deeds of Cúchulainn*, see Elaine

derived from a patriarchal nineteenth-century bourgeois and colonial gender ideology. The Victorian ideal of 'manliness' – which, as Michael Kimmell alerts us, is something different from the twentieth-century concept of masculinity – depended on a set of familiar ideological constructs.[26] Chief among these were the distinctions between a masculine public sphere and a feminine domestic sphere and between masculine rationality and feminine emotion. The manly ideal took shape in a cluster of rhetorical and narratological figures, including the 'free-born Englishman', the ideal of muscular Christianity, the public-school ethic of schoolboy stories, heroes-of-empire adventure stories and Arthurian romance. As David Alderson outlines, this gendered structure of thought shaped the formation of English Protestant identity and British imperial identity in the nineteenth century, and took as its defining opposites not only womanhood but also Catholicism and Irishness.[27]

Joe Valente argues that as a 'metrocolonial' people – simultaneously participants in the project of overseas empire and colonial subjects in their own land – the Irish experienced the cultural production of manliness as a 'double-bind'.[28] For an Irishman to practice the self-restraint demanded by the manly ideal was to appear acquiescent to colonial subjugation, and thereby to fail to achieve the self-possession demanded by that ideal – and thus to confirm his lack of readiness for the freedom licensed by the ideal. What appeared as manly self-restraint in the Englishman looked like the dreamy femininity of the Arnoldian Celt in an Irishman. But for an Irishman to challenge his colonial subjugation showed him to be just as deficient in manliness and unfit for liberty; it demonstrated his failure to exercise control over those inherently violent passions to which the Irish were, in the British imperial imagination, peculiarly prone. This leads Valente into an innovative

Sisson, *Pearse's patriots: St Enda's and the cult of boyhood* (Cork, 2004), pp 78–98.   26 Michael Kimmel, *Manhood in America: a cultural history* (New York, 1996), pp 19–22. For a useful discussion of the historical transition from 'manliness' to 'masculinity' as a cultural dominant, see Kevin Floyd, *The reification of desire: towards a queer Marxism* (Minneapolis, 2009), pp 87–8.   27 David Alderson, *Mansex fine: religion, manliness and imperialism in nineteenth-century British culture* (Manchester, 1998), pp 15–70.   28 Joseph Valente, *The myth of manliness in Irish national culture, 1880–1922*, (Springfield, 2011), pp 22–5. Here we might pause to consider the interpretative and political utility of the 'metrocolonial' as a concept. While usefully capturing a significant historical phenomenon, it also threatens to divert our understanding of that phenomenon into the realm of reified identities and psychologies, while also reiterating that the Irish experience was in some way unique. This risks downplaying a more rigorously materialist and dialectical grasp of imperialism as a stage in the global expansion of capitalism in which all – coloniser, colonised, and 'metrocolonial' alike – lost and profited in complex ways. I am obliged to Abdulrazak Gurnah for raising this point in response to an earlier version of this chapter presented at the University of Kent (Canterbury).

reading of Charles Stewart Parnell's public image, for instance, but when it comes to Pearse's concern with heroic manliness Valente keeps with convention and emphasizes the conservative anti-colonial mimicry of the colonial master tropes.[29]

However, a closer examination of Pearse's writing reveals that something more complex may be at stake here. For Pearse the heroic, like the archaic, is less about resuscitating the past than about forming revolutionary subjects for the future. As an aesthetic and ethical project, the heroic is concerned with the formation of a more holistic, less alienated subjectivity. Thus, in his writings on education, Pearse argues that the fundamental fault of the colonial education system is the narrow, utilitarian stripping of individual distinctiveness to produce indistinguishable, interchangeable automatons for the labour market. As he argues in 'The murder machine', 'the system has aimed at the substitution for men and women of mere Things ... these Things have no allegiances. Like other Things they are for sale.' By contrast, Pearse's ideal educational system 'addresses itself to the most generous side of the child's nature, urging him to live to his finest self'.[30] In Pearse's imaginary, the heroic subject is never actually realized, but is that envisioned modern subject, that modern subject-to-be, who will be able to seize hold of history and transform it.

Lexically, manliness is everywhere in the pedagogical writings and in the drama. 'Manly', along with its variations and cognate terms, is scattered liberally throughout the writing. But if we pay attention to characterization, plot and performance in the drama it becomes very clear that the heroic figure embodies a quite different style of masculinity to that prescribed by the manly ideal. Most often the heroic ideal is embodied by boys, who are not yet men – but, crucially, will almost invariably never become men. It is notable how many of the boys in Pearse's writing are spectral figures associated with death, or die (or nearly die) in the course of the narrative. Thus, the eponymous Íosagán, who reconciles Matthias to religion before the old man dies, is in fact, we are led to assume, an apparition of Jesus in the guise of a peasant boy. Several of the plays turn on a boy dying, or nearly dying, violently to save the life of an adult (the eponymous *Owen*; Iollan Beag in *The master*) or to reconcile competing political forces (Giolla na Naomh in *An rí/The king*). The writing dwells unsettlingly on the vulnerability of these boys – invariably the boy hero is less physically robust than the other boys – and

29 Valente, *Myth of manliness*, pp 156–64.   30 Séamus Ó Buachalla (ed.), *A significant Irish educationalist: the educational writings of P.H. Pearse* (Cork, 1980), p. 381.

this is registered as a manifestation of his purity and innocence. While the boy's vulnerability is idealized as a marker of innocence, it is also troublingly eroticized. Invariably, the narrative dwells on the boy's physical beauty in some detail; Iollan Beag, we are told by the other boys, has 'a high, manly heart' and 'a beautiful white body'.[31] The boy's beauty is another physical manifestation of his innocence, and the attraction of both is intensified by the threat posed by the passage of time. The boy is an idealized and a tragic figure; that which makes the boy so special is fleeting and destined to be lost and this mood is intrinsic to the structure of feeling. From this perspective, the boy's death is not necessarily an unhappy outcome. As Vincent Quinn notes in relation to *An rí/The king,* 'death heightens the child's erotic pull by freezing him in a moment of perpetual innocence'.[32] Thus, the boy's perfection is preserved, but at the cost of the future, since the possibility of change or development is the price to be paid.

Pearse's vulnerable, threatened boys offer vivid symbols of that volatile fusion of the tragic and the heroic that characterized his epoch. They are at once symbols of futurity, luminous with the promise and potential of a transformed future, and symbols of catastrophe – doomed figures suggesting the impossibility of any future.[33] This conjunction of youth and death was a recurring trope in European culture in those decades: Wilde's *The picture of Dorian Gray* (1891) and Mann's *Death in Venice* (1913) are just two notable instances. In his study of the modernist *Bildungsroman,* Jed Esty argues that this motif of stalled youth was central to the emergence of modernist fiction. The literary figure of the 'frozen youth', which recurs throughout the literature of those decades, symbolized, as Esty observes, 'an era in which the time of modernisation seemed both *hyper* and *retro,* futurist and barbaric'.[34]

As an adult man MacDara, the heroic figure in *The singer,* appears to be the exception here. But, as we have seen, in the play he is symbolically transposed onto the allegorical figuration of Ireland as a woman. He is the leader of the planned rising, but not in any military or strategic sense. Instead he inspires

31 Ní Ghairbhí and McNulty (eds), *Patrick Pearse: collected plays,* p. 178.   32 Vincent Quinn, 'Fostering the nation: Patrick Pearse and pedagogy', *New Formations,* 42 (2001), 71–84 at 74.   33 My analysis here overlaps with, and is indebted to, that of Elaine Sisson. She emphasises that the ambivalent figure of the boy 'serves as an ideal national form' and notes that Pearse's nationalist contemporaries encouraged 'the production and consumption of the eroticised sacrificial male ideal' (by Pearse, but also by other figures, such as Joseph Campbell and Beatrice Elvery). By contrast I wish to emphasise the degree to which a range of fluid and contradictory symbolic referents, not wholly reducible to a positive cultural nationalist hermeneutic, also adhered to this figure. See Sisson, *Pearse's patriots,* pp 146–50.   34 Jed Esty, *Unseasonable youth: modernism, colonialism and the fiction of development* (Oxford, 2012), p. 37.

and mobilizes young men through his songs, just as Yeats and Gregory's Cathleen does through her rhetoric (and as Maud Gonne did through her performance of the role in 1902). Later in the play, he is also symbolically transposed onto that other important female figure in Pearse's writing: the mother. As MacDara tells Maoilsheachlainn about his time exiled in the city he dwells particularly on his time as tutor to a young boy, 'a winsome child' who 'grew into my heart'.[35] MacDara's language infuses the educational project with an unusually high pitch of emotional intensity that is obliquely erotic while also connecting education with the emotional sustenance and nurturing of motherhood. This sets up the teacher and the mother as like each other – so alike indeed that they must invariably become rivals. MacDara had to leave his post, he tells us, because the boy's mother 'grew jealous of me. A good mother and a good teacher are always jealous of each other.'[36] This opposition between teacher and mother clearly confirms what critics such as C.L. Innes and Elizabeth Cullingford have argued. Pearse's writings offer women a single role – motherhood. Moreover, if this was not sufficiently limiting, his use of the old Irish practice of fosterage as a paradigm for education suggests that foster-fathers, such as the abbot in *The king* and Ciarán in *The master*, are even better than women at that mothering role anyway.[37]

Yet in MacDara's narrative we also see that this idea of mother and teacher occupying opposing roles sits alongside a series of images and associations in which the body of the male teacher and the maternal body merge. In the most striking of these images the act of teaching the young is figuratively aligned with that uniquely female bodily experience of breastfeeding a child, and pedagogy, a distinctively male practice in Pearse's writing, is figuratively aligned with parturition:

> sometimes I think that to be a woman and to serve and suffer as women do is to be the highest thing. Perhaps that is why I felt it proud and wondrous to be a teacher, for a teacher does that. I gave to the little lad

35 Ní Ghairbhí and McNulty (eds), *Patrick Pearse: collected plays*, p. 219. Strikingly, McDara's narrative offers a synoptic précis of Henry James' *The pupil* (1892). That novella also turns on the emotional struggle over a young boy that takes place between the boy's mother and a male teacher. Again, as with *The rite of spring*, this narrative coincidence does not suggest influence – it would be difficult to imagine two more different writers – but the traces of an epochal structure of feeling.   36 Ní Ghairbhí and McNulty (eds), *Patrick Pearse: collected plays*, p. 220.   37 Elizabeth Butler Cullingford, 'Thinking of her ... as ... Ireland: Yeats, Pearse and Heaney', *Textual Practice*, 4:1 (1990), 1–21; C.L. Innes, *Women and nation in Irish literature and society, 1880–1915* (London, 1993), pp 23–5, 57–60.

> I taught the very flesh and blood and breath that were my life. I fed him on the milk of my kindness. I breathed into him my spirit.[38]

In *The gender of modernity*, Rita Felski explores how 'mobile and shifting meanings of the modern as a category of cultural consciousness' were expressed through figures of femininity in *fin-de-siècle* European culture.[39] Through such figures as the archaic mother, the female prostitute and the female shopper, writers contended with the dialectic of modernity as a phenomenon that held both oppressive and emancipatory possibilities for men and women. Among these figures Felski numbers the 'feminised male' so prominent in late nineteenth-century aestheticism and exemplified by Wilde's Dorian. Through an imaginary identification with an aestheticized femininity – and in particular the increasingly powerful association in capitalist society between women, conspicuous consumption, adornment and display – male writers reiterated their alienation from traditional models of heterosexual masculinity, and rejected the prevailing conventions of realist representation by turning to a decadent style of surface and parody that was explicitly coded as 'feminine' and 'modern'. This appropriation of the cultural markers of femininity signalled 'a formal as well as a thematic refusal of an entire cluster of values associated with the ideology of bourgeois masculinity: the narrative of history as progress, the valorisation of function over form, the sovereignty of the reality principle'.[40] Moreover, the feminized male was both aestheticized and eroticized. Thus, the intense and ultimately tragic passions Dorian arouses in Basil Hallward provided a cultural space for the coded and indirect expression of same-sex desires. (But, ironically, the definitive alignment of the dandy with the newly minted figure of the homosexual was achieved in 'life' rather than 'art' and took shape on the media image of Wilde's own body in the wake of his trial and imprisonment.) As Felski warns us, this artistic appropriation of femininity was ambivalent in its political effects, most especially in its relationship with the contemporary feminist movements and the dandy's feminist counterpart – the new woman; as Felski observes, 'the resistive power of feminine artifice is predicated upon a radical disavowal of and dissociation from the "natural" body of woman'.[41]

Can we usefully read Pearse's MacDara as such a feminized male figure? To be sure, his earnest asceticism bears little obvious resemblance to the stylized, glamorous artifice of the dandy. In this respect, Pearse is working in an older

---

38 Ní Ghairbhí and McNulty (eds), *Patrick Pearse: collected plays*, p. 220.   39 Rita Felski, *The gender of modernity* (Cambridge, MA, 1995), p. 8.   40 Ibid., p. 101.   41 Ibid., p. 92.

Romantic tradition, with its idealized male artist as an androgynous figure endowed with the 'feminine' attributes of sensitivity and intuition and thus in contact with a source of authenticity that stands in contrast to the alienation of modernity.[42] Nevertheless Pearse's figuration of heroic masculinity, as embodied by MacDara, involves an anxious and uneasy fusion of the masculine and the feminine; a figure that invokes, and seemingly reinforces, inherited serotypes about female nurturing and passivity – 'to serve and suffer as women do' – while simultaneously undermining the gender ideology of complementary opposites by detaching those stereotypical attributes from the female body. In other words, this figure took its coordinates from modern bourgeois ideology and simultaneously attempted to scramble those coordinates, and thus it provided a provocative emblem of a historical epoch where there stirred everywhere, in Fredric Jameson's phrase, 'an apocalyptic dissatisfaction with subjectivity itself and the older forms of the self'.[43]

At the end of Pearse's play, the conventionally manly heroic act – Colm and the other men taking up arms and going out to fight the British – appears, in Pearse's telling, rather futile and inadequate to the times. It is a misjudged response to the demands of history and the urgency of revolutionary action. The heroic act – the revolutionary act – is represented very differently. MacDara walks alone and unarmed to his death, and submits passively to his sacrifice. Invariably, a Pearse audience is reminded of those doomed, sacrificial young boys – those symbols of a 'manliness' and a future that will never be. MacDara not only walks out unarmed but strips away his clothing as he does so. In this way, the actor's performance reiterates the gesture of self-sacrifice, while also emphasizing the fragility and vulnerability of the human body. As Butler reminds us, our confrontation with human vulnerability can create radical possibilities for reimagining community, ethical responsibility and political commitment. But MacDara's exposed body is not only vulnerable. We are reminded by the gesture of undressing that this now exposed, doomed body was also that virile body from which the entrancing voice issued forth in Sighle's vision earlier in the play; that desirable male body that set the hearts of the men on fire, spurring them on to 'right the wrongs of the people'. In this way, the revolutionary act, as it is imagined in Pearse's drama, fuses the heroic and the erotic and weaves together desires that are sexual and political. But to complicate this further, for those of us committed to a more secular and Marxist hermeneutic, Pearse

42 Ibid., p. 94.   43 Fredric Jameson, *A singular modernity* (London, 2002), p. 124.

also figures the revolutionary act in a religious, specifically Christian, idiom: 'one man can free a people as one Man redeemed the world'. However, it is notable that the imagery Pearse takes from Christianity in this ending is not that of a messiah returning in glory, nor even that of Christ's body emerging from the tomb after three days restored and made whole again. As Marx observed, 'religious suffering is, at one and the same time, the expression of real suffering and a protest against real suffering'.[44] And so it is striking that the Christian image Pearse adapts at the end of his play is that image with which those of us raised as Christian become so familiar that we no longer register its strange and unsettling affective, symbolic and political charge: the naked body of a young man battered, brutalized and broken.

[44] Karl Marx, *Critique of Hegel's 'Philosophy of right'*, trans. Annette Jolin, ed. Joseph O'Malley (Cambridge, 1970), p. 5.

8 / Pádraig Mac Piarais agus forbairt na drámaíochta dúchais

RÓISÍN NÍ GHAIRBHÍ

Agus é ag scríobh sa *Claidheamh Soluis* i mBealtaine na bliana 1906, dhearbhaigh Pádraig Mac Piarais go raibh gá le téamaí nua a chur dá gcíoradh i bprós na Gaeilge agus mhaígh go raibh sé in am 'bogadh amach ón gcruach mhóna agus ón gcarn aolaigh.'[1] Bliain chinniúnach don Phiarsach ab ea 1906 ar an-chuid slite. Ba léir go raibh smaointe chuige ina rabharta agus sraith alt ar ghnéithe éagsúla den chultúr á fhoilsiú aige sa *Claidheamh*. Lag go maith a bhí drámaíocht na Gaeilge um an dtaca seo agus gan í ach i dtús a ré. San alt 'The Irish stage' a foilsíodh ar an 16 Meitheamh 1906 d'fhógair an Piarsach nárbh ann fós do dhráma Gaeilge. Agus idirdhealú á dhéanamh aige idir 'play' agus 'drama', d'aithin sé gurbh ann do chluichí ('plays') i ngluaiseacht na Gaeilge ach nárbh ann fós, dar leis, do 'dhráma'. Thug sé ansin sainmhíniú ar dhráma:

> A drama is a picture of human life intended and suitable for represen-
> tation by means of action. 'A picture of human life': a study of men and
> women; an effort on the part of the dramatist to induce you to see the
> march of lives and fates as he sees it.[2]

Níorbh ionann dráma de réir shainmhíniú an Phiarsaigh agus 'a mere piece of philosophising' nó 'the mere telling of a tale'; b'ionann é agus 'a picture so treated that, however well it may read as a piece of prose or verse, it imperi-ously demands *viva voce* representation in order that it may yield up its full message.'[3] Ba ar na féidearthachtaí a bhain le *léiriú* drámaí seachas le *cumadh* téacsanna a bhí an Piarsach ag díriú san alt tábhachtach seo. Dhá mhí ina dhiaidh sin, san alt 'Irish acting', ba ar chúrsaí léirithe a bhí a bhéim arís agus dhá mholadh ar leith aige do lucht léirithe (an dream atá i gceist de réir dealraimh le 'stage managers') agus aisteoirí:

> Two things we would recommend to Irish actors and stage managers:
> first to study the art of the Irish traditional reciter; and secondly to pay

---

1 'Nua-litridheacht', *An Claidheamh Soluis*, 19 Bealtaine 1906.   2 'The Irish stage', *An Claidheamh Soluis*, 16 Meitheamh 1906.   3 Ibid.

an occasional visit to the Abbey Theatre. Not that the traditional reciter
is a model to be religiously copied (for – other considerations apart –
acting is essentially different from recitation), or that the Abbey Theatre
has said the last word on the drama; but that the one puts the student in
touch with Ireland, whilst the other puts him in touch with the best
contemporary ideals.[4]

Theastaigh ón bPiarsach go mbeadh gnéithe traidisiúnta agus gnéithe nua-
aimseartha araon i gceist leis an drámaíocht Ghaelach a bhí le forbairt agus le
léiriú; is é sin le rá go mbeadh dhá mhianach sa drámaíocht nua, an nua-aimsir
agus an dúchas. Ach cén bua a bhain le healaín agus le *repertoire* na scéalaithe
traidisiúnta? Agus cad a bhí i gceist ag an bPiarsach le 'the best contemporary
ideals'? An mbeadh saintionchar eile fós le brath ar an saothar drámata a
léireodh sé féin sna blianta beaga a lean? Chun freagra cuimsitheach a
sholáthar ar na ceisteanna seo ní mór mionléamh a dhéanamh ar shaothar
drámata an Phiarsaigh agus ar na cuntais iomadúla atá againn ar a chuid
léirithe.[5] Ach anuas air sin is gá na drámaí a mheas agus iad suite ina
mbunchomhthéacsanna féin agus i gcomhthéacsanna oiriúnacha eile.

Seachas díriú ar na téacsanna féin, pléifidh an aiste seo cuid de na fearainn
a bhain le cumadh agus le léiriú dhrámaí an Phiarsaigh. Tuigtear anois níos
fearr an idirghabháil a bhí ag pearsana uile na hAthbheochana Cultúrtha le
chéile.[6] Cuireadh smaointe faoin drámaíocht Éireannach chun cinn in ailt
nuachtáin, in irisí agus i gcainteanna poiblí agus na cainteoirí éagsúla seo go
léir i mbun díospóireachta paiseanta le chéile maidir leis an bhfoirm a
ghlacfadh an drámaíocht nua.[7] Bhí teagmháil phearsanta agus cairdeas idir na
rannpháirtithe éagsula. Scríobh Mary Colum, ar chara leis an bPiarsach í, faoi
shainchairdeamh lucht freastail na drámaíochta nua lena chéile: 'the habitués,
or nearly all of them, knew one another and the audience was a sort of social
gathering. Between acts one drank tea, chatted to one's friends, discussed their
work with the authors'.[8] Mar bharr air seo bhí aithne ag lucht drámaíochta ar
rannpháirtithe eile na mórghluaiseachta: lucht ealaíne, eití Béarla agus Gaeilge
na hAthbheochana, lucht ghluaiseacht na teanga agus gníomhairí polaitiúla.

4 'Irish acting', *An Claidheamh Soluis*, 7 Iúil 1906. 5 Philip O'Leary, *The prose literature of the Gaelic revival,
1881–1921* (University Park, PA, 2008); Róisín Ní Ghairbhí and Eugene McNulty (eds), *Drámaí an
Phiarsaigh* (Dublin, 2013) 6 Féach mar shampla, R.F. Foster, *Vivid faces: the revolutionary generation in Ireland,
1890–1923* (London, 2014); Róisín Ní Ghairbhí, *Willie Pearse* (Dublin, 2015) agus beathaisnéisí lucht
Athbheochana ar an mbunachar www.ainm.ie atá bunaithe ar an tsraith mháistriúil *Beathaisnéis*. 7 Féach
O'Leary, *The prose literature of the Gaelic revival, 1881–1921*. 8 Mary Colum, *Life and the dream* (London, 1947),
p. 153.

Tabharfar aghaidh anseo ar chúig shampla den idirphlé dinimiciúil seo, snáithe a thugann léargais éagsúla ar shaothar drámaíochta an Phiarsaigh.

- saol ealaíne Bhaile Átha Cliath agus a thionchar
- baint an Phiarsaigh le saol na drámaíochta Angla-Éireannaí.
- an mianach drámata a bhraith an Piarsach i litríocht na Gaeilge
- léiriú an dráma dúchais *Dúnlaing Óg agus an Leannán Sidhe* sa bhliain 1915
- 'In my garden'– fianaise an Phiarsaigh ar an ionad a bheadh ag an drámaíocht in Éirinn san aonú aois is fiche.

Solathrófar *inter alia* léargais ar chuid de na pleananna praiticiúla a bhí ag Mac Piarais maidir le forbairt na drámaíochta dúchais.

SAOL EALAÍNE BHAILE ÁTHA CLIATH AGUS A THIONCHAR

Ní taobh le lucht seanchais agus le hAmharclann na Mainistreach amháin a bhí an Piarsach agus a shainléamh féin ar mhianach drámata na litríochta dúchais á fhorbairt aige (rud a shonraigh sé féin níos déanaí san alt 'Irish acting'). Sa sainmhíniú a bhí deanta aige ar dhráma ('a picture so treated [...] it imperiously demands *viva voce* representation') bhí an Piarsach tar éis béim a chur ar léiriú agus ar fhísiúlacht. Léirithe físiúla iad drámaí uile an Phiarsaigh, fiú na drámaí a raibh script ag baint leo. Thóg léirmheastóirí na linne ceann ar leith den atmaisféar a bhain leo, de na feistis ealaíonta agus de na prapanna taibhsiúla. Ní hiontas an ghné fhísiúil seo a bheith chomh suntasach: bhí súil ealaíontóra ag Pádraig. Dealbhadóir aitheanta ab ea a athair, agus bhí a leasdeartháir James ina dhealbhadóir/mhaisitheoir eaglasta chomh maith. Bhí deartháir óg an Phiarsaigh, Uilliam, rannpháirteach i saol ealaíne na hardchathrach agus é cúig bliana déag ar fad ag plé leis an Metropolitan School of Art. Tá an ceart ar fad ag an scoláire ealaíne John Turpin nuair a deir sé gur gá plé a dhéanamh ar an ngaol idir an scoláireacht Ghaeilge, an ghluaiseacht ealaíne, an scríbhneoireacht chruthaitheach agus fás an náisiúnachais. Tá rianadh déanta cheana ar an mórthionchar cinniúnach a bhí ag gluaiseacht ealaíne na hAthbheochana ar an bPiarsach.[9]

9 John Turpin i gcomhrá leis an údar, 2014; John Turpin, *A school of Art in Dublin since the eighteenth century: a history of the National College of Art and Design* (Dublin, 1995); John Turpin, *Oliver Sheppard: symbolist sculptor of the Irish revival, 1865–1941* (Dublin, 2000); Elaine Sisson, *Pearse's patriots: St Enda's and the cult of boyhood* (Cork, 2004). Féach chomh maith Ní Ghairbhí, *Willie Pearse*.

Ar an 5 Bealtaine 1906 scríobh an Piarsach alt dar teideal 'The art revival' sa *Claidheamh* mar ar mhaígh sé go bhféadfaí a rá go raibh ghluaiseacht ealaíne Éireannach ar an bhfód. Tá na béimeanna a bheadh i gceist ina chuid drámaí féin le sonrú sa tuar a dhein an Piarsach faoin treo a ghabhfadh an athbheochan ealaíne nua: 'It will be an open air art and not an esoteric thing';

> It will bear to English art and to recent Anglo-Irish art respectively the same relation that a Middle Irish nature poem bears on the one hand to a story in the Family Herald and on the other to one of the sicklier plays in the Abbey Theatre.[10]

Thug 'The art revival' aitheantas ar leith do Oliver Sheppard mar dhuine a bhí lárnach sa ghluaiseacht nua ealáine. Na heocharíomhánna a fhaighimid i ndrámaí an Phiarsaigh, go háirithe íomhá an duine óig agus údarás a shinsear aige le dul chun troda, agus an uaisleacht agus an chuirtéis a bhain le dualgas troda na laochra, bhíodar le rianadh chomh maith i saothar Sheppard. Tá fianaise againn ó pheann an Phiarsaigh féin maidir le tionchar Sheppard air. Ar an 11 Lúnasa 1906 scríobh sé léirmheas ar shaothar dealbhadóireachta 'Inis Fáil' Sheppard, saothar a bhí ar taispeáint ag Oireachtas na bliana sin. Léiriú ar bhanlaoch óg neamheaglach agus leanbh a bhí oilte chun troda aici á sheoladh amach a bhí sa saothar. Thíos fúthu bhí corpán agus scríobh Mac Piarais faoin mbean:

> Mark the form and above all the face of the Woman of Sorrows who stands erect before the prostrate shape of one who has died for her ... Though the world run red with blood, the cause of that Woman shall triumph. Mark next him who lies prone – the victorious vanquished, crowned in death. This is a generation that has fought and fallen – but the Woman of Destiny blanches not: 'I have my memories ... and I have my hopes.'[11]

D'aithin an Piarsach sa dealbh den bhuachaill 'the growing of a great resolve ... he will fight the fight – win it, it may be, or failing gloriously go serenely to his death'.[12] D'fhéadfaí a rá go raibh réamhphlota *The singer* (1916) aimsithe aige sa dealbh. An réalachas agus an fuinneamh dinimiciúil a d'aithin an Piarsach in 'Inis Fáil' bhain sé leis an athrú stíle a bhí tagtha i dtreis le

---

10 'The art revival', *An Claidheamh Soluis*, 5 Bealtaine 1906.   11 'Our national salon', *An Claidheamh Soluis*, 11 Lúnasa 1906. Turpin, *Oliver Sheppard: symbolist sculptor*, pp 70–1.   12 Ibid.

teacht chun cinn an 'New Sculpture'.[13] Bhí an laochas Gaelach (agus an fuinneamh) a bhí le sonrú i saothar Sheppard i gcodarsnacht ghlan le saothar dealbhadóireachta ollmhór den Bhanríon Victoria de chuid John Hughes a nochtadh díreach taobh amuigh den Scoil Ealaíne sa bhliain 1907, saothar a bhéimnigh dílseacht mhíleata don choróin. Frithdhíoscúrsa a bheadh i ndrámaí an Phiarsaigh chomh maith, lena stair mhalartach agus a dteach-taireacht cheannairceach.

Luaitear Alice Milligan go minic mar dhuine de cheannródaithe na drámaíochta dúchais nua-aimseartha in Éirinn mar gheall ar an dlúthbhaint a bhí aici le cur chun cinn *tableaux vivants* Inghinighe na hÉireann.[14] I mBealtaine na bliana 1908 scríobh Mac Piarais alt sa *Claidheamh* a liostaigh na buanna ar leith a bhain leis na *tableaux* a bhí i morshiúl bliantúil Chonradh na Gaeilge:

> Each tableau was a thing of beauty in itself, the whole series not only produced a fine artistic effect, but leant grace and dignity to the procession. They helped to recall stirring and eventful incidents in our history, they recalled the glories of the past, and conveyed a message of hope for the future.[15]

Tar éis oscailt Scoil Éanna an Fómhar sin thapaigh an Piarsach an deis drámaí a léiriú é féin: bheadh na buanna a bhí luaite aige maidir leis na *tableaux* i gceist iontu. I Márta na bliana 1909 thug sé léacht ar an 'Fionn saga' sa Metropolitan School of Art, roimh léiriú Aontas Mac Léinn na scoile ar *The last feast of the Fianna* le Milligan.[16] Is féidir dlús cheangal an Phiarsaigh le saol na healaíne a rianadh sna chéad léirithe drámaíochta a deineadh i Scoil Éanna coicís ina dhiaidh sin. Ba iad sin *An naomh ar iarraidh* le Dubhghlas de hÍde agus *The coming of Fionn* le Standish O'Grady. Dhein Uilliam Mac Piarais stáitse agus feistis a dhearadh agus chabhraigh a chara, an dealbhadóir Albert Power, leis an radharcra a phéinteáil. Ba é an dalta Pádraig Ó Tuathaigh, (a bhainfeadh cáil amach mar an t-ealaíontóir Patrick Tuohy) a dhear céad leathanach an chláir.[17] Nuair a thagair an Piarsach don bhfreastal ollmhór a bhí ar léiriú a ghlór-réime *Macghníomhartha Chúchulainn* i Meitheamh 1909 thug sé comhstádas don ealaíon agus don litríocht: 'We had over five hundred guests in our playing-field, including most of the people in Dublin who are

13 Ibid., pp 2, 70–1.   14 Catherine Morris, *Alice Milligan and the Irish cultural revival* (Dublin, 2012). 15 'Mórshiubhal na nGaedheal', *An Claidheamh Soluis*, 26 Meán Fómhair 1908.   16 'Annála na Sgoile', *An Macaomh* (Meánsamhradh 1909), 80–9.   17 Na cláir, *An naomh ar iarraidh* le Dubhghlas de hÍde agus *The coming of Fionn* le Standish O'Grady, LNÉ.

interested in art and literature.'[18] Bhí Milligan agus an Scoil Ealaíne ina ndroichead an-chinnte idir na Piarsaigh agus an drámaíocht nua fhísiúil seo. Bhí suim ag Oliver Sheppard i gCúchulainn chomh maith. Go deimhin féin chítear na téamaí céanna – nóisean na híobartha agus stair ársa uasal an náisiúin Ghaelaigh – ag teacht chun cinn i saothar an Phiarsaigh agus Sheppard timpeall an ama chéanna seo. Bhí na téamaí seo pléite chomh maith ag an scoláire George Sigerson, duine eile a d'imir mórthionchar ar an bPiarsach. Ba léir súil ealaíontóra an Phiarsaigh mar armlón aige ina cháilíocht mar chriticeoir drámaíochta agus é ag cur síos ar an tsollúntacht a bhain le léiriú *The destruction of the hostel* (cóiriú Phádraic Colum ar eagrán Whitley Stokes de 'Togáil bhruidne Da Derga') ag scoláirí Scoil Éanna i mí Feabhra 1910:

> in the mood of great antique art, the mood of Egyptian sculpture and dán díreach verse, solemn, uplifting, serenely sad, like the vision of those high ones who watch with pitying but unrelenting eyes the awful dooms and dolours of men.[19]

Ní miste gné fhísiúil seo dhrámaí an Phiarsaigh féin a mheabhrú de shíor: ba cheart breithiúnas a dhéanamh orthu ina gcáilíocht nó ina mianach mar léirithe agus ní mar théacsanna amháin.

AN DRÁMAÍOCHT ANGLA-ÉIREANNACH.

Cé go raibh difríochtaí béime agus teanga dhifriúil i gceist, fós féin bhí mórán i bpáirt ag an bPiarsach leis na drámadóirí Angla-Éireannacha a bhí meáite ar shnáithe dúchais a fhobairt i ndrámaíocht na hÉireann. Tá cáil ar litir a chuir an Piarsach óg chuig an *Claidheamh Soluis* ag clamhsán faoi bhagairt na drámaíochta Angla-Éireannaí agus ag caitheamh anuas ar fhiontar nua Yeats, an Irish Literary Theatre.[20] Ní ar an bPiarsach amháin a bhí an drochamhras. I 1906 bunaíodh Cluicheoirí na hÉireann/The Theatre of Ireland ag buíon aisteoirí agus lucht amharclainne a raibh olc orthu toisc Amharclann na Mainistreach a bheith á hiompó ina comhlacht agus amhras orthu, de réir dealraimh faoi shaoirse na n-aisteoirí agus faoi thiomantas náisiúnach na hamharclainne.[21] Labhair Mac Piarais ag cruinniú tionscnaimh an

18 'By way of comment', *An Macaomh* (Nollaig 1909), 17.   19 'By way of comment', *An Macaomh* (Nollaig 1910), 25.   20 Litir, *An Claidheamh Soluis*, 13 Bealtaine 1899.   21 Féach, *The splendid years* (Dublin, 1955).

chompántais nua agus toghadh ar an gcoiste ina dhiaidh sin é. I measc bhaill
an chéad choiste sin bhí Eoin Mac Néill, Pádraic Colum agus Countess
Markievicz. Ach ba mar thráchtaire sa *Claidheamh* is mó a ghlac Mac Piarais
páirt i gcúrsaí drámaíochta an chuid eile den bhliain sin. Ba í aidhm na
gCluicheoirí ná 'to carry on dramatic work in Ireland, to produce plays in
English and Irish and the masterpieces of foreign dramatic authors'.[22]
Chloígh na Cluicheoirí lena rún drámaíocht na Gaeilge a thabhairt san
áireamh ach ba dhrámaí Béarla is mó a léirigh siad. Faoi 1907, aimsir
chonspóid an *Playboy*, bhí an Piarsach fós ag caitheamh amhrais ar
Amharclann na Mainstreach cé go raibh a léamh ar an Playboy níos caolchúisí
ná a lán.[23] Ach faoin mbliain dár gcionn (agus ciall cheannaithe an té a raibh
a fhiontar nua scolaíochta ag brath ar dhea-thoil an phobail mhóir aige, seans)
bhí an Piarsach ag tacú le cuid de mhórphearsaí ghluaiseacht Bhéarla na
hAthbheochana agus é ag tabhairt daltaí a scoile nua chuig Amharclann na
Mainistreach. Bhí Yeats, Lady Gregory agus Edward Martyn báúil riamh le
hobair an Chonartha. Tháinig Yeats chuig céad léirithe Scoil Éanna. Ach go
fiú roimh an *entente* seo, bhain Mac Piarais leis an bhfearann céanna le cuid de
phearsana móraithnide Athbheochan cultúrtha an Bhéarla – a bhí chun
tosaigh ar lucht an Chonartha maidir le fís uaillmhianach do nuadhrámaíocht
Éireannach a nochtadh. Pléadh forbairt na drámaíochta Gaeilge in *Samhain*,
iris an Irish Literary Theatre, agus go deimhin féin d'fhoilsigh Yeats téacsanna
drámaí dúchais Gaeilge in *Samhain*. Orthu seo bhí *An naomh ar iarraidh*, a léirigh
Mac Piarais i bhFeabhra na bliana 1909. Is léir go raibh eolas ag an bPiarsach
ar dhíospóireachtaí *Samhain*. Dhein sé tagairt shonrach do phlé Yeats ar
sheasamh tosaigh Standish O'Grady maidir le mí-oiriúnacht litríocht eipiciúil
na Gaeilge don amharclannaíocht agus thagair sé do fhreagra AE ar O'Grady
sna nótaí cláir do 'The coming of Fionn'. Chuir Mac Piarais leis an
díospóireacht ina dhiaidh sin agus d'fhoilsigh sé ailt le Stephen McKenna
agus le Thomas MacDonagh maidir le forbairt glór-réimeanna agus an
amharclannaíocht Ghaeilge in *An Macaomh*.[24] Fearacht an Phiarsaigh, chum
Yeats agus Lady Gregory saothar a tharraing ar an Rúraíocht agus ar an
bhFiannaíocht. I Márta na bliana 1910 ba é an Piarsach a mhol rún buíochais
le Yeats tar éis dó siúd léacht a thabhairt ar 'The theatre and Ireland' agus bhí
an Piarsach an-bhuíoch de thacaíocht Yeats sa bhliain 1913 nuair a stáitsíodh
An rí i dteannta *The post office* le Rabindranrath Tagore in Amharclann na

---

22 Miontuairiscí Chluicheoirí na hÉireann (The Theatre of Ireland) 1906–7, LS 7388.　23 'The
passing of Anglo-Irish drama', *An Claidheamh Soluis*, 9 Bealtaine 1907.　24 Thomas MacDonagh, 'For
plays in Irish: a suggestion', *An Macaomh* (Nollaig 1910), 40–2; Stephen McKenna, 'Pageants', ibid., 36–8.

Mainstreach ar mhaithe le ciste Scoil Éanna. Tá cuntas fíorspéisiúil (agus cuntas an-ghreannmhar) ar fáil i ndialann Joseph Holloway maidir le fíorsmaointe an Phiarsaigh i leith Yeats agus Amharclann na Mainistreach. Má bhí blas an ghleáchais ar chuid dá ndúirt an Piarsach ar an ócáid seo, fós féin ba dhíol spéise a chuid tuairimí:

> I visited The Hermitage and was in town with P.H. Pearse. We spoke of the reception of the Irish Players in America. He is very tolerant of everyone's views and never hisses. The Abbey is a freak theatre and should be treated as such; if you don't like it, stop away [...] Pearse thought the Abbey was run too much on Ascendancy principles. He often saw Lady Gregory enjoying her own pieces and laughing at her own jokes. Yeats does the same. Truly they were both like little children in their ways. It would be fine for someone to burlesque the whole Abbey movement, and get the Abbey theatre and produce the burlesque with someone got up as Yeats to run up and down the stairs, etc. [...] Pearse did not rightly know whether Yeats was a man of self-consciousness or childlike simplicity. Much they thought artistic was eccentricity [...] Pearse did not believe all the Irish were as bad as the Abbey plays would have us believe. He maintained that those who did not hold with the Abbey and its doing should stay away: he believed in freedom for all.[25]

Mhair ceangal an Phiarsaigh leis na Cluicheoirí chomh maith. Chabhraíodh Máire Nic Shiubhlaigh agus a cairde leis na cleachtaí i Scoil Éanna, léirigh an Piarsach dráma le Pádraic Colum agus bhí lámh ag an ealaíontóir Jack Morrow ar choiste Fhleadh Mhór Mheitheamh 1913.[26] Chítear ar chlár do 'Fhéile na Bealtaine' 1913 sampla de chomhoibriú idir na Cluicheoirí agus Scoil Éanna, nuair a léiríodh *Mac na mná déirce* agus *Bairbre Ruadh* ag na Cluicheoirí i dteannta *Íosagán* agus *The destruction of the hostel* le haisteoirí óga Scoil Éanna.[27]

MIANACH DRÁMATA LITRÍOCHT NA GAEILGE

Thrácht an Piarsach go minic ar an mianach drámata a bhí go smior, dar leis, i luathlitríocht na Gaeilge. Agus aitheantas á thabhairt aige (ní den chéad uair

---

25 Dialann Joseph Holloway, 2 Eanáir 1912, LNÉ.　26 Tá cuntas ar na ceangail seo in Róisín Ní Ghairbhí, *Willie Pearse* (Dublin, 2015).　27 Clár, 'Na Cluicheoirí, Féile na Bealtaine', LNÉ.

nó den uair dheiridh) do thionchar George Sigerson, rianaigh an Piarsach an mianach tragóideach a bhain leis an Rúraíocht, dar leis:

> In that glorious anthology *The bards of the Gael and Gall* Dr Sigerson long ago pointed out that the story of Deirdre fell naturally into the five acts of a great tragic drama. Since then four dramatic poets, three in English, and one in Irish, have given us tragedies on the Deirdre story. But the whole Ulster epic falls just as naturally into a great trilogy of tragedies, with a prologue and an epilogue. The prologue tells of the primal sin and the curse of Macha; the three great tragedies are, in order, Deirdre, the Tain and the death of Cuchulainn; the epilogue is the death of Conor. Each of the great tragedies is complete in itself, yet through the whole cycle unrolls in inevitable sequence the doom of Ulster.[28]

Bhain corráiste leis an léirmheastóireacht chomparáideach a dhein an Piarsach ar luathlitríocht na Gaeilge. Phléigh sé an tsíceolaíocht a bhain le pearsana na litríochta. Ní raibh aon leisce air drámadóir comhaimseartha mar Ibsen a tharraingt isteach sa scéal agus é ag plé na Rúraíochta agus na Fiannaíochta. Chuir a eolas leathan ar litríochtaí eile agus an t-eolas scolártha a bhí aige ar litríocht na Gaeilge ar a chumas léamha dána a dhéanamh, fiú má chuaigh sé beagán thar fóir leis an argóint uaireanta. Scríobh sé in 'About literature':

> In Diarmuid and Gráinne we have the first patient and detailed analysis of the *mind* of a human being that was ever invented in Europe since the days of Greek drama. Has it ever occurred to anyone that Gráinne is a prototype of Hedda Gabler?[29]

Ba léir go raibh an smaoineamh seo maidir le léiriú shíceolaíocht Ghráinne éirithe chuige. Dhein sé cur síos ar Ghráinne ar ócáid eile mar 'the Hedda Gabler of Irish literature, the woman who craved to have her destinies interwoven with that of a strong silent man'.[30]

Bhí an Piarsach eolach chomh maith ar thraidisiún na ndaoine. Foilsíodh a chnuasach *Songs for an Irish anthology* (aistriúcháin maille le bunleaganacha amhrán) mar shraith san *Irish Review* sa bhliain 1913. Ba shuntasach ar fad an leas a bhain sé as amhráin thraidisiúnta ina shaothar drámaíochta. Uaireanta

---

28 'Some aspects of Gaelic literature' in *Collected works: songs of the Irish rebels*, n.d.   29 'About literature', *An Claidheamh Soluis*, 26 Bealtaine 1906.   30 'Some aspects of Gaelic literature' in Patrick Pearse, *Collected works: songs of the Irish rebels* (Dublin, n.d.).

ba ar mhaithe leis an bplota a chuir an Piarsach amhráin thraidisiúnta ina chuid drámaí, uaireanta eile ba ar mhaithe le deis a thapú an cultúr dúchais a chur ar taispeáint é. Seans gurbh é seo a bhí i gceist le hamhráin na leanaí in *Íosagán* agus le canadh 'Gráinne Mhaol' in *Eoghan Gabha*. Ach rud eile ar fad ab ea úsáid deasghnáthaíoch 'Ding dong didearó' in *Macghníomhartha* agus 'Caoineadh na dTrí Muire' in *An Pháis/The Passion play*.

AN DRÁMA DÚCHAIS *DÚNLAING ÓG AGUS AN LEANNÁN SIDHE*

I mBealtaine na bliana 1915 léiríodh *The master* and *Íosagán* san Irish Theatre, amharclann a bunaíodh samhradh na bliana 1914 ag Thomas MacDonagh, Joseph Plunkett agus Edward Martyn. Le linn an tsosa léiríodh mír ghairid as dráma 'dúchais'. Má bhí a cheangal leis na hÓglaigh ag treisiú, is léir ó nóta beag ar an gclár go raibh an Piarsach fós meáite ar fhoirmeacha dúchais drámaíochta a chur ag obair sa nuadhrámaíocht:

> During the interval Mr Pearse will give a short address on the Irish style of dramatic speaking. The address will be illustrated by the performance of the only surviving fragment of an Irish drama prior to the language revival. The fragment was taken down in Co. Kerry in 1898, and is part of a play that was enacted by the people up to sixty or seventy years ago. The subject is the hero Dúnlaing and his fairy lover, and the action takes place just before the battle of Clontarf.[31]

Bhailigh an scoláire Ciarraíoch James Fenton an téacs a luaitear sa nóta seo, 'Dúnlaing Óg agus an Leannán Sidhe', ó sheanchaí darbh ainm Seán Crochán Ó Beirne ón tSnaidhm i mí Lúnasa 1898. Chreid Seosamh Laoide go raibh an téacs ar a laghad trí chéad bliain d'aois.[32] Níorbh é an Piarsach a bhailigh 'Dúnlang Óg agus an Leannán Sidhe' agus níorbh é a chéadphléigh an mianach drámata a bhí ann ach mar is gnáth d'éirigh leis snáithe éagsúla scoláireachta a tharraingt le chéile i gcomhthéacs nua. Sa chás áirithe seo, scag sé taighde Uí Fhiannachta, a foilsíodh ar dtús sa *Kerry Sentinel* sa bhliain 1899 agus a luadh arís sa bhliain 1914 i leabhar Uí Fhiannachta *It all happened* agus ansin thug sé an fhianaise seo ar thraidisiún drámaíochta dúchais chun beochta do lucht éisteachta cathrach. Díol spéise an láthair léirithe a

---

31 Fógra/Clár, *Íosagán: a miracle play* and *The master*, LNÉ. 32 Féach Seán Ó Morónaigh, *Drámaíocht ó dhúchas: Ó bhéalaithris Thaidhg Uí Chonchubhair* (Camas, 2005), lch. 203.

roghnaíodh. Ba mhinic drámaíocht thurgnamhach ailtéarnach á stáitsiú ag an Irish Theatre.[33]

Ní mhaireann script na cainte a thug an Piarsach le linn an léirithe ar *Dúnlaing Óg* ach bhreac an dialannaí Joseph Holloway nótaí cuimsitheacha. Dar le Holloway, shéan an Piarsach gur feinimeán de chuid na fichiú aoise drámaíocht na Gaeilge agus dhearbhaigh nárbh fhíor gurbh é *Casadh an tSugáin* de hÍde an chéad dráma Gaeilge. Luaigh an Piarsach iarrachtaí ar dhrámaí Gaeilge a thit amach roimhe sin i nDún na nGall agus ar an gCarraig Dhubh. Bhí an ceart aige, cé gur iomaí tráchtaire ó shin a luaigh 'Casadh an tSúgáin' mar an chéad dráma Gaeilge. Ní go dtí foilsiú shaothar ceannródaíoch Sheáin Uí Mhorónaigh *Agallaimh na hÉigse* (2001) a rianaíodh mianach drámata na n-agallamh beirte ar bhealach cuimsitheach sa nua-ré (cé gur thagair scoláirí mar Fenton agus de hÍde don cheist).[34] Thrácht an Piarsach ar ghné thábhachtach eile de mhianach drámata na litríochta Gaeilge le linn a chainte: an drámatúlacht a bhain le hurlabhra na scéalaithe traidisiúnta. Arís eile níor leasc leis an bPiarsach comparáidí dána a dhéanamh idir gnéithe den traidisiún agus an cultúr comhaimseartha:

> He spoke of the old storytellers he knew in West Connaught and of their style of telling their stories and spoke of one old woman's method as as beautiful as the speech of Sarah Bernhardt in some of her passages of wonderful dignified musical utterance. [...] Irish storytellers rarely used any gesture, they got all the emotions out of the words as a part of varying about chant like sounds that couldn't be called singing, nor yet spoken words. He thought this was the real meaning of the word elocution which was speech – English elocutionists teach a lot of fantastical things [...] which he doesn't hold with [...][35]

Bhí suim riamh ag an bPiarsach i dtábhacht an ghutha, sa reacaireacht agus san aithriseoireacht.[36] Mhol sé 'stately elocution' Denis Gwynn agus Eamonn Bulfin agus 'passionate declamation' Desmond Ryan in *The coming of Fionn*: thógadh léirmheastóirí ceann ar leith d'urlabhra na n-aisteoirí óga ag Scoil Éanna.[37] Dealraíonn sé gur tugadh tuiscintí seo an Phiarsaigh maidir le stíl

---

33 Is fiú a lua *inter alia* go bhful trácht sa ghiota seo ó *Dúnlaing óg agus an Leannán Sidhe* ar dhoirteadh fola le linn catha, íomhá ar dóigh leis an bPiarsach í a bheith ar fáil go leanúnach i litríocht na Gaeilge. 34 Seán Ó Morónaigh, *Agallaimh na hÉigse, Cíoradh agus Cnuasach* (Camas, 2001). 35 Dialann Joseph Holloway, 20 May 1915, LNÉ. 36 Mary Brigid Pearse, *The home life of P.H. Pearse* (Dublin, 1934), pp 62–3. 37 Annála na Sgoile, *An Macaomh* (Meánsamhradh 1909), 86.

shainiúil urlabhraíochta a bheith ag na Gaeil san áireamh sa léiriú ar *Dúnlaing Óg*:

It was […] played by Michael O'Sullivan and Mary Bulfin who spoke the text as nearly as they could after the method of the old storytellers – using a chanting method for the immortal – almost a sort of singing and a less formal style for the [doléite] – the effect was impressive.[38]

Níor chadhan aonair an Piarsach. Bhí scríofa ag Yeats faoi chúrsaí ulabhraíochta san iris *Bealtaine* agus bhí cáil ar Willie Fay Amharclann na Mainistreach mar gheall ar an traenáil gutha a chuir sé ar fáil. B'fhada suim ag an bPiarsach i dtábhacht na reacaireachta agus laige teacht i láthair aisteoirí Éireannacha pléite aige ina alt 'Irish acting' chomh fada siar le 1906.[39]

'IN MY GARDEN': FIS AN PHIARSAIGH DON DRÁMAÍOCHT ÉIREANNACH

'O wise men riddle me this/ What if the dream came true' a scríobh Mac Piarais sa dán 'The rebel' sa bhliain 1916. Bhí fís ar leith ag Mac Piarais maidir leis an saghas sochaí a thógfaí in Éirinn tar éis na réabhlóide agus dhein sé cur síos ar an bhfís seo chomh luath leis an mbliain 1906. Foilsíodh 'In my garden' mar chuid d'fhorlíonadh Oireachtais a scaipeadh leis an *Claidheamh Soluis* i Lúnasa na bliana 1906. Sa scéal seo samhlaíonn reacaire an scéil (Mac Piarais) go bhfuil sé tar éis dúiseacht in Éirinn sa bhliain 2006. Tugann fear an phoist nuachtán – *The Daily Claidheamh* Lúnasa 2006 – chuig an reacaire atá tar éis dúiseacht tar éis codladh céad bliain. Tuigtear ón nuachtán samhlaithe seo gur bhain Éire stádas poblachta amach am éigin tar éis na bliana 1911. Is léir gur mhian leis an bPiarsach go mbeadh ionad lárnach ag an amharclannaíocht sa phoblacht nua mar go bhfuil scata tagairtí don amharclannaíocht agus don dramaíocht in ailt shamhlaitheacha an nuachtáin. Seans gur ar mhaithe le greann a luaitear go nglacfaidh ionad náisiúnta amharclannaíochta na tíre 15,000 duine ach mar sin féin léirítear anseo suim leanúnach an Phiarsaigh i bhforbairt fhearainn nua don amharclannaíocht. Ar ndóigh níor leasc leis féin Jones' Road – Páirc an Chrócaigh – a ghlacadh ar láimh mar ionad dá ghlór-réimeanna féin sa bhliain 1913. Déantar tagairt sa nuachtán chomh maith do

---

38 Dialann Joseph Holloway, 20 Bealtaine 1915.   39 'Irish acting', *An Claidheamh Soluis*, 7 Iúil 1906.

léirithe 'alfresco' drámaí a bheith tar éis titim amach i bPáirc an Fhionnuisce
ón mbliain 1921. Pléann ceann de dhá phríomhalt *An Daily Claidheamh* le
dramaíocht na hÉireann. Déantar tagairt do 'to the forthcoming performance
of a new play by the great psychological dramatist Aodh Ó hAodhagáin, at
the Oireachtas'. Luaitear mar scéal thairis gur bhain Ó hAodhagáin an duais
Nobel agus gur tugadh aitheantas do aistriúchán Fraincise dá dhráma, *Parnell*,
ag An Academie Française. Chítear mar sin, trí bliana sular léirigh sé féin
drámaí go raibh mórphlean ag an bPiarsach maidir le forbairt na drámaíochta
Éireannaí. Tá tuiscint an Phiarsaigh ar chumhacht na drámaíochta mar mheán
a achtaíonn brí soiléir agus é ag cur síos ar oscailt Fhéile (shamhlaithe) an
Oireachtais sa bhliain 2006:

> The Herald of Ireland will proclaim the Peace of the Gael, the Bard of
> Ireland will invoke the spirit of Gaelic thought and imagination and the
> Ard Rí will declare the one-hundred-and-tenth Oireachtas in session.
> The trumpets and cannon will then salute the Oireachtas and the
> National Hymn will be intoned.[40]

Insíonn tuairisceoir an *Daily Claidheamh* dúinn go mbeidh píobairí, mar aon le
hionadaithe ó Na Fianna Éireann and an Macraidhe and daoine eile ag
máirseáil. Chífí máirseálacha deasghnáthaíocha dá leithéid i nglór-réimeanna
an Phiarsaigh, i *Macghníomhartha Chúchulainn* sa bhliain 1909 agus arís i nglór-
réimeanna *The defence of the ford*, *The Fianna of Fionn* agus *Fionn: a dramatic spectacle*.
I gcuntas samhailtheach 'In my garden' bíonn fráma ilchultúrtha timpeall ar
an taispeántas dúchasach agus deirtear linn: 'Among the learned bodies which
will be represented are the French Academy, the Hungarian Academy, the
Norsk Theatre and the Japanese Society of Arts.'[41] Glacann an t-alt leis go
dtabharfaidh Éire neamhspleach tús áite don chultúr agus don éigse.

Má bhí fís an Phiarsaigh don drámaíocht nua dúchasach bhí sí dinimiciúil
iolrach chomh maith agus is tabhachtach go dtabharfaí an t-iolrachas seo san
áireamh agus a shaothar á mheas. Ba mhó ar fad tionchar na ndrámadóirí
Angla-Éireannacha, tionchar na gCluicheoirí, tionchar na *tableaux vivants* agus
tionchar na healaíne nua-aimseartha ar dhrámaí an Phiarsaigh seachas
iarrachtaí drámaíochta lucht na Gaeilge féin. Is fíor go raibh cuid mhaith de
na daoine a bhí luaite le drámaí an Phiarsaigh rannpháirteach sa Chonradh
agus go ndéanadh sé féin cúram léirmheastóireachta do dhrámaí an

---

40 'In my garden', Duilleachán an Oireachtais, *An Claidheamh Soluis*, 4 Lúnasa 1906.   41 Ibid.

Oireachtais sa *Claidheamh.* Níorbh é an Piarsach a chéadsmaoinigh ar dhrámaí a léiriú taobh amuigh faoin aer: bhí a leithéid ar bun ag na Feiseanna agus ins na *tableaux vivants.* Bhí na léirithe sin agus léirithe drámata an Phiarsaigh araon ina réamhtheachtaithe ag leagan amach a d'fhorbródh drámadóirí iarchoilíneacha mar Ngugi Wa Thiong'o agus an grúpa Siamsa Tíre anseo in Éirinn.[42] Bhain foirmeacha agus fearainn shamhailtheacha le léirithe an Phiarsaigh agus deineadh ceangal iontu idir an dúchas agus an nua-aimsir.[43] Bhí síol fhís an Phiarsaigh maidir le mianach fuascailteach na drámaíochta nua Éireannaí le fáil ina shainmhíniú féin ar dhráma, mar ar thrácht sé ar 'a study of men *and women*; an effort on the part of the dramatist to induce *you* to *see* the *march* of lives and fates as he sees it' (leis an údar seo na béimeanna). Bhí loighic an Éirí Amach féin le fáil i dtuiscint an Phiarsaigh ar an difríocht idir mianach 'play' (cluiche) agus dráma, 'a picture of human life intended and suitable for representation by means of action', scéal fear agus ban a éilíonn léiriú trí ghníomh:

> not a mere piece of philosophising (though it may enshrine a world of philosophy); and yet not the mere telling of a tale (though a tale of some sort it must almost of necessity tell); but a picture so treated that, however well it may read as a piece of prose or verse, it imperiously demands *viva voce* representation in order that it may yield up its full message. This is drama.[44]

Tá súil ag údar na haiste seo scoláirí agus léiritheoirí araon a spreagadh le hathbhreithniú a dhéanamh ar dhrámaí an Phiarsaigh mar mhír i scéal fhorbairt na drámaíochta trí chéile agus mar shnáithe ina bheatha féin. Ní leor Athbheochan na Gaeilge agus forbairt litríocht na Gaeilge a ghlacadh mar fhráma critice do litríocht na ré úd, mar a mbíodh lucht na Gaeilge agus lucht an Bhéarla ag comhrá agus ag comhoibriú le chéile agus le lucht éigse agus ealaíne trí chéile, leathshúil acu ar an dúchas agus leathshúil eile ar an domhan mór.

---

42 Féach Róisín Ní Ghairbhí, 'An cath atá romhainn anois is geall le briatharchath é: Pádraig Mac Piarais agus Léann an Iarchoilíneachais' in Roisín Higgins agus Regina Uí Chollatáin (eag.), *The life and after-life of P.H. Pearse* (Dublin, 2009), lgh. 168–78. 43 Ibid. 44 'The Irish stage', *An Claidheamh Soluis*, 16 Meitheamh 1906.

9 / *Caithréim: ceol agus amhráin ó dhrámaí an Phiarsaigh*

SÍLE DENVIR

RÉAMHFHOCAL

Tá ceol agus amhráin luaite i nach mór chuile dhráma a scríobh Pádraig Mac Piarais. Is léir go raibh an ceol fíorthábhachtach i gcur chuige cruthaitheach an Phiarsaigh agus é ag scríobh agus ag léiriú na ndrámaí seo. Mar chuid den siompóisiam ar an bPiarsach agus an Amharclann a reáchtáladh i mí na Samhna 2013 beartaíodh go láithreofaí cuid den cheol a bhí fite fuaite aige sna drámaí. D'iarr lucht eagraithe an tsiompóisiaim orm cur i láthair de shórt éigin a dhéanamh ar an an gceol agus ar na hamhráin a luaitear sna drámaí agus bheartaigh mé cuid de na píosaí seo a chóiriú agus a láithriú go cruthaitheach ag an ócáid. Cur síos ar an gceol agus ar na hamhráin sin, ar an bpróiseas cruthaitheach a bhain le cóiriú an cheoil agus ar an láithriú féin atá san aiste seo. I réamhrá *Drámaí an Phiarsaigh* deir na heagarthóirí, Róisín Ní Ghairbhí agus Eugene McNulty, an méid seo: 'In the build up to 2016 we hope that these plays will draw a new generation of readers and that interested theatre practitioners may find in them a source for innovative and imaginative new productions.'[1] Freagra ar an méid seo a bhí sa léiriú ar a tugadh *Caithréim*.[2]

Dá mairfeadh an Piarsach go mbeadh na ceithre scór bainte amach aige samhlaím go mbeadh sé i láthair ag chéadléiriú an scannáin *Mise Éire*, mar a bhí Éamon de Valera, agus gurbh é a bhainfeadh sult as scór ceoil Sheáin Uí Riada agus an fonn 'Róisín Dubh' á athmhúnlú aige mar aintiún an Éirí Amach agus é ag breathnú siar ar eachtraí cinniúnacha 1916.[3] Fearacht Uí Riada, ba nuálaí é an Piarsach a thuig cumhacht agus tábhacht thaibhiú an cheoil agus na hamhránaíochta i gcruthú na féiniúlachta. Go deimhin, bhí an bheirt acu fadradharcach, cruthaitheach agus aislingeach ina ndearcadh ar fhorbairt an chultúir Ghaelaigh agus iad beirt ag maireachtáil ar scaradh gabhail idir saol na cathrach agus saol na tuaithe. Ba iad glúin an Phiarsaigh

---

1 'Note from the editors' in Róisín Ní Ghairbhí agus Eugene McNulty (eag.), *Drámaí an Phiarsaigh* (Cill Dara, 2013), lgh. ix–x. 2 Tá mé go mór faoi chomaoin ag Róisín agus ag Eugene as cead a thabhairt dom an t-eolas ón leabhar a úsáid don cheolchoirm féin agus don aiste seo. 3 Féach Deirdre Ní Chonghaile, '*Róisín Dubh*: mar a chruthaigh Seán Ó Riada aintiún an Éirí Amach' in *COMHARTaighde 1* (2015), le mion chur síos a fháil ar úsáid an fhoinn 'Róisín Dubh' don scannán *Mise Éire*.

a leag amach an bealach do ghlúin an Riadaigh, agus bhí tionchar thar cuimse ag meon agus ag cur chuige lucht na hAthbheochana, idir mhaith agus olc, ar an gceol agus ar na hamhráin atá anois mar chuid bhuan de thírdhreach ceoil agus amhránaíochta na tíre seo. Céad bliain sular bunaíodh Conradh na Gaeilge rinneadh iarracht ceol na gcláirseoirí a chaomhnú agus sa bhfógra a foilsíodh i mBéal Feirste i 1791 leis na cláirseoirí a chomhchruinniú dúradh: 'When it is considered how intimately the *spirit* and *character* of a *people* are connected with their *national poetry* and *music*, it is presumed that the Irish patriot and politician will not deem it an object unworthy of his patronage and protection.'[4] Is léir, os cionn céad bliain ina dhiaidh sin, gur chreid Pádraig Mac Piarais an méid céanna agus tá seans láidir ann go ndeachaigh sé i muinín bhailiúcháin leithéidí Edward Bunting agus é ag roghnú ceoil agus amhrán dá chuid drámaí. Cé go ndeirtear faoin bPiarsach nach raibh bua an cheoil aige féin, tá sé ríshoiléir ón gcaoi a bhfuil ceol agus amhráin fite fuaite sna drámaí gur thuig sé cumhacht agus tionchar an cheoil ar lucht féachana.

Bhí dlúthbhaint ag an bPiarsach le Conradh na Gaeilge agus leis an Oireachtas. Bhí suim faoi leith aige sa mbéaloideas, agus go deimhin sna hamhráin Ghaeilge. Chuala sé a aintín Margaret ag gabháil fhoinn i nGaeilge agus i mBéarla ina óige.[5] Bhí suim aige i mbailiú agus i bhfoilsiú amhrán agus foilsíodh amhráin go rialta sa nuachtán *An Claidheamh Soluis* fad a bhí an Piarsach ina eagarthóir ar an nuachtán. Chnuasaigh sé amhráin agus d'fhoilsigh iad mar dhá shraith san iris *The Irish Review*. Tá na hamhráin sin anois le fáil sa leabhar *Collected works of Pádraic H. Pearse: songs of the Irish rebels and specimens from an Irish anthology: some aspects of Irish literature: three lectures on Gaelic topics* mar a bhfuil fáil chomh maith ar a aiste *The folk-songs of Ireland* (1898). Léiríonn an aiste sin an machnamh a bhí déanta ag an bPiarsach óg ar amhráin na ndaoine, tráth go raibh borradh faoin tsuim a bhí á cur ag scoláirí sa réimse sin go hidirnáisiúnta:

> It is in the highest degree probable that every form of literature which we have at the present day has sprung from the folk-tale and the folk-song. These two were, to a by-gone age, all that the press, the novel and the drama are to ours. Co-aeval with man himself, they are, so to speak, the two elemental forms of literature. It is impossible to conceive a state of society in which they did not exist: since man first trod this earth to

4 Edward Bunting, *The ancient music of Ireland* (Dublin, 1840), p. 63. 5 Róisín Ní Ghairbhí, 'A people that did not exist? Reflections of some sources and contexts for Patrick Pearse's militant nationalism' in Ruán O'Donnell (ed.), *The impact of the 1916 Rising* (Dublin, 2008), p. 167.

the present moment, he has loved to wander in the land of fancy opened up by the folk-tale, and to pour forth in song the emotions of his soul.[6]

CUR CHUIGE DON LÉIRIÚ 'CAITHRÉIM'

Ceann de na bunfhadhbanna a bhaineann leis na taibhealaíona ná go n-imíonn an taibhiú le gaoth. San anailís a déantar ar thaibhléirithe a tharla le linn ré nach ndéantaí taifead ach go hannamh ar léirithe lena linn, bíonn an taighdeoir ag brath go huile agus go hiomlán ar an bhfoinse scríofa. Cé go dtugann an Piarsach treoir áirithe don léiritheoir sna drámaí caithfear brath fós ar a leithéid seo sa dráma *Eoghan Gabha*: 'Séideann an píobaire; damhsann siad pas', nó an méid seo sa dráma *The master*: 'The voice of Iollann Beag is heard singing.' Ach céard a shéid an píobaire? Agus céard a chan Iollann Beag? An méid sin ráite, fágann sé seo saoirse agus solúbthacht ag an léiritheoir. Agus mé ag léamh na ndrámaí bhí sé an-soiléir go raibh an ceol agus na hamhráin mar dhlúthchuid de na léirithe a chuir an Piarsach ar stáitse agus theastaigh uaim beatha nua a thabhairt do na píosaí seo. Bhí cuid de na hamhráin daingnithe sa stór amhrán atá agam féin, 'Ding dong dideró', 'Óró mo bháidín', 'An draighneán donn' agus 'Caoineadh Mhuire', mar shampla, agus cuid eile nach raibh cloiste agam riamh, 'Gráinne Mhaol' agus 'An chaithréim', mar shampla. Mar fhreagra cruthaitheach ar ghné na hamhrá-naíochta i ndrámaí an Phiarsaigh, bheartaigh mé taighde a dhéanamh ar leaganacha éagsúla de na hamhráin, rogha a dhéanamh maidir le leagan, agus ansin iad a chóiriú agus a láithriú mar aon phíosa amháin. Mar gheall nach luaitear go minic ach ainm an amhráin sna drámaí, bhí orm cinntí a dhéanamh maidir le leaganacha de na foinn agus de na focail, mar atá leagtha amach sa gcuntas thíos.

Ó thaobh an ionstramaithe de bheartaigh mé go mbeadh an chláirseach, an phíb uilleann agus an fhidil lárnach sa gcóiriú mar mhacalla ar na huirlisí a bhí á gcur chun cinn agus á gcasadh ag cuid de lucht na hAthbheochana ag tús na haoise seo caite. Rogha an-soiléir a bhí ann an phíb uilleann a úsáid don chóiriú mar go luaitear an píobaire i gcuid de na drámaí. Músclaíodh suim sa bpíb uilleann ag tús an chéid seo caite mar chuid den Athbheochan agus bunaíodh Cumann na bPíobairí i 1900. Bhí roinnt de bhaill Chonradh na Gaeilge agus d'Óglaigh na hÉireann ina mbaill de Chumann na bPíobairí,

---

6 Patrick Pearse, *Collected works of Pádraic H. Pearse: songs of the Irish rebels*, pp 198–9.

mar a léiríonn miontuairiscí na gcruinnithe ó mbliain 1900 go dtí 1904. Bhí Éamonn Ceannt ina rúnaí ar an gCumann ar feadh tamaill agus taispeánann miontuairiscí ón 14 Deireadh Fómhair 1913 gur chuir Pádraig Mac Piarais iarratas chuig Cumann na bPíopairí píobairí a chur ar fáil leis an bpíb mhór a chasadh ag feis ar mhaithe le Scoil Éanna.[7] Bheartaigh mé go mbeadh sé tábhachtach go mbeadh uirlis náisiúnta na tíre, an chláirseach, lárnach sa láithriú freisin. Bhí deireadh tagtha le traidisiún ársa cláirseoireachta an tseanchórais Ghaelaigh faoi lár an 19ú haois in aineoinn roinnt iarrachtaí a rinneadh ag tús an chéid sin athbheochan a dhéanamh ar an traidisiún. Cé nach raibh cur chun cinn na cláirsí mar chuspóir tosaigh ag lucht na hAthbheochana, tharla go raibh an cláirseoir Eoghan Laoideach (Owen Lloyd) páirteach i gConradh na Gaeilge.[8] Mhúin 'cláirseoir na hAthbheochana' (mar a tugadh ar an Laoideach go neamhfhoirmeálta)[9] i Scoil Éanna ó 1908 ar aghaidh. Cheannaigh an Piarsach cláirseach dá dheirfiúr Mary Brigid agus bhí sí ina dalta ag an Laoideach. Mhúin Mary Brigid ceol i Scoil Éanna freisin ag baint úsáide as an gcláirseach.[10] Bhí aithne ag an bPiarsach chomh maith ar an gcláirseoir Carl Hardebeck, a mhaígh, más fíor, 'I believe in God, Beethoven and Patrick Pearse.'[11] Bhí an-tionchar ag múinteoir eile de chuid Scoil Éanna, Tomás Mac Domhnaill,[12] ar an gceol a luaitear le drámaí an Phiarsaigh agus chum sé cuid den cheol a casadh sna drámaí. Chas Mac Domhnaill an veidhlín agus ar an ábhar sin tugadh an veidhlín san áireamh sa láithriú freisin. Agus ar deireadh, sheinntí an phíb uilleann go minic ag léirithe drámaí Scoil Éanna.

Ag an gcéadléiriú de *Caithréim* i mí na Samhna 2013 chas Thomas Johnston (Co. Mhuineacháin) an phíb uilleann agus an fheadóg, chas Aoife Ní Argáin (Baile Átha Cliath) an chláirseach agus an consairtín, chas Síomha Mulligan (Baile Átha Cliath) agus Éadaoin Ní Mhaicín (Co. Mhaigh Eo) na fidil agus chas mé féin an chláirseach agus chan na hamhráin le fonnadóireacht taca ó Shíomha, ó Éadaoin agus ó Thomas. Chuir mé le chéile an ceol agus na hamhráin ar bhealach a rinne ciall ó thaobh meanma an phíosa ina iomláine agus ó thaobh gléasanna de chomh maith, mar atá leagtha amach thíos. Chun ceangal a chruthú leis na bundrámaí agus a gcéadléiriú beartaíodh

7 Mick O'Connor, comhfhreagras ríomhphoist ar an 12 Eanáir 2016. Tá taighde forleathan déanta ag Mick O'Connor ar stair Chumann na bPíobairí nach bhfuil foilsithe go fóill.　8 Tá plé cuimsitheach déanta ar shaol agus ar thionchar Eoghan Laoideach in Mary Louise O'Donnell, 'Owen Lloyd: de-anglicizing of the Irish harp', *Éire-Ireland*, 48:3–4 (Fall/Winter 2013), 155–75.　9 Ibid., p. 163.　10 Brendan Walsh, *The pedagogy of protest: the educational thought and work of Patrick H. Pearse* (Bern, 2007), p. 223.　11 Seán O'Boyle, 'Hardebeck', *The Capuchin Annual* (1948), 80–7, 85.　12 Rugadh Tomás Mac Domhnaill i mBoth Chomhla, Maigh Eo in 1885. Féach www.ainm.ie.

go mbeadh gné fhísiúil ag baint leis an léiriú agus teilgeadh pictiúir agus míreanna ó na drámaí chomh maith le lirící na n-amhrán ar scáileán. Is é an dearthóir grafaicí Ciarán Ó Súilleabháin (Ráth Chairn, Co. na Mí) a dhear an cur i láthair físiúil.

NÓTA FAOIN NODAIREACHT CHEOIL

Tugtar an leagan de na hamhráin agus na foinn a casadh don léiriú i nodaireacht cheoil thíos. Níor breacadh síos ornáidíocht ar bith agus níl sa nodaireacht chéanna ach treoir. Beartaíodh an nodaireacht a bhreacadh síos sa ngléas inar casadh na hamhráin nó na píosaí ceoil don léiriú féin. Shocraigh mé gan nodaireacht cheoil a chur ar fáil do 'An draighneán donn' agus 'Caoineadh Mhuire' mar gheall ar na deacrachtaí a bhaineann le tras-scríobh a dhéanamh ar shaor rithim. Tharla nach féidir a thabhairt ach láithriú amháin ar leith mar théacs ceoil, níl sna téacsanna céanna ach treoir agus ní mór éisteacht leis an amhrán i dteannta an téacs scríofa. Is féidir taifead fuaime den cheol agus de na hamhráin seo a chloisteáil ar an dlúthdhiosca *Caithréim: ceol agus amhráin ó dhrámaí an Phiarsaigh.*[13]

NA HAMHRÁIN

'An chaithréim'
Bunaíodh teideal an tionscnaimh seo ar an amhrán 'An chaithréim' ón dráma *Macghníomhartha Chúchulainn.* Chum Tomás Mac Domhnaill an ceol d'fhocail an Phiarsaigh don dráma agus foilsíodh é i gcéad imleabhar *An Macaomh.*[14] I dtreoir an Phiarsaigh ag tús an dráma deir sé 'Ceol do sheinm. An Cór do theacht ar an láthair agus do ghluaiseacht ar fud na páirce, ag gabháil an rann seo inár ndiaidh.'[15] Casann an cór an t-amhrán ansin 'go mall éirimeach' mar a threoraíonn an Piarsach. Macalla is ea línte tosaigh an dáin, 'Scéal linn dhaoibh, a uaisle Gael, a ghasra éachtach eolgach,' ar dhán cáiliúil a cumadh sa 9ú nó 10ú haois 'Scél lem dúibh: dordaid dam; snigid gaim; ro fáith sam.'[16] Castar cúig véarsa ag tús an dráma, cúig cinn eile sa dara roinn agus 5 cinn eile

13 Síle Denvir, CIC 202, 2016. 14 Ní Ghairbhí and McNulty (eag.), *Drámaí an Phiarsaigh*, lch. 25. 15 Ibid., lch. 66. 16 Gerard Murphy, *Early Irish lyrics: eighth to twelfth century* (Oxford, 1970), p. 160; féach Ciarán Ó Coigligh (eag.), *Filíocht Ghaeilge Phádraig Mhic Phiarais* (Baile Átha Cliath, 1981) le haghaidh anailís ar an úsáid a bhain an Piarsach as seanfhoirmeacha filíochta ina chuid filíochta féin.

sa tríú roinn. Casadh an píosa seo go sollúnta, mall, rithimiúil mar a bheadh
máirseáil ann. Seo iad na véarsaí a casadh ag an gceolchoirm, le tionlacan
drandáin ó na fidil agus ón gconsairtín:

> Scéal linn dhaoibh, a uaisle Gael
> A ghasra éachtach eolgach
> Scéal nachar fríoth a shárú
> In irisibh ársa Fódhla.

> Lá dar éirigh Mac Neasa
> Rí neartmhar ógbhaidhe Uladh
> Do tháinig chuige an macaomh
> Cú chalma cróga Chulainn.

> D'iarr air airm agus trealamh
> D'fhág beannacht ag na hógaibh
> Is d'imigh roimhe 'na charbad
> Do dhéanamh catha is comhraic.

> Níor staon sé dá stárthaibh
> Go ráinig boird an chúige
> Gur mharbhaigh triúr Mac Neachtain
> Cé fearúil na búraigh.

> Scéal linn dhaoibh, a uaisle Gael
> A ghasra éachtach eolgach
> Scéal nachar fríoth a shárú
> In irisibh ársa Fódhla.[17]

17 Ní Ghairbhí and McNulty (eag.), *Drámaí an Phiarsaigh*, lch. 75.

'The wearing of the green'
Sa chéad mhír den dráma *Owen* tugann an Piarsach an treoir seo:

> The voice of ballad singer singing 'The wearin o' the green' is heard. The
> master and the boys listen. The singer seems to be at a little distance at
> first. When he starts the second stanza, 'I met with Napper Tandy', he has
> apparently come up to the school door, and he sings clearly and loudly. As
> soon as the second stanza is finished a knock is heard at the door.[18]

Is iomaí leagan atá ann den bhailéad seo, idir fhoinn agus fhocail, a
dhéanann cur síos ar Éirí Amach 1798 agus is cinnte go raibh tóir air ag tús
an 20ú haois. Tá ceann de na leaganacha clóite is luaithe den amhrán atá
againn le fáil san alt 'The native music of Ireland' sa *Citizen Magazine* a
d'fhoilsigh Samuel J. Machen i mí Eanáir na bliana 1841. Tá cur síos maoith-
neach ann ar an amhrán 'The wearing of the green':

> In the years which followed '98, it was the solace of every peasant – of
> every heart, gentle or simple, which felt for the sorrows of this distracted
> country. It is still thought of and treasured amid the same classes. Shall
> it longer be buried? Are our tyrants stricken down, and shall we hesitate
> to circulate its numbers, far and wide, amongst the young generation
> which has sprung up in times, behind in date, but, praised be Heaven!
> *not* behind in the love and adoration of our darling Mother-Land![19]

Is é leagan Dion Boucicault, a scríobh sé don dráma *Arrah-na-Pogue*, a léiríodh
don chéad uair i mBaile Átha Cliath in 1864, an leagan is coitianta a chloistear
go fóill.[20] Máirseáil thar a bheith rithimiúil atá i gceist le fonn an amhráin. Go
deimhin, is fonn é a bhfuil go leor leaganacha de le fáil agus macallaí de le fáil
i roinnt cornphíopaí agus máirseálacha éagsúla. Don léiriú *Caithréim* shocraigh
mé go gcasfaí fonn an amhráin ar na huirlisí agus go ndéanfaí teilgean ar chuid
de na lirící ar an scáileán. Bunaíodh an leagan de na lirící a roghnaíodh ar leagan
a foilsíodh sa leabhar *The minstrelsy of Ireland* in 1897:

> Oh, Paddy dear, and did ye hear the news that's going 'round?
> The shamrock is by law forbid to grow on Irish ground,

---

18 Ibid., lch. 168.   19 Henry Hudson (ed.), *The Citizen or Dublin Monthly Magazine* (Jan.–Dec. 1841), p. 64.
20 Georges D. Zimmermann, *Songs of Irish rebellion: Irish political street ballads and rebel songs, 1780–1900*
(Dublin, 2002), p. 169.

Saint Patrick's Day no more we'll keep, his colours can't be seen,
For there's a cruel law against the wearing of the green.

I met with Napper Tandy, and he took me by the hand,
And he said, 'How's poor old Ireland, and how does she stand?'
'She's the most distressful country that ever yet was seen,
They are hanging men and women there for the wearing of the green.'

Then since the colour we must wear is England's cruel red,
Sure Ireland's sons will ne'er forget the blood that they have shed,
You may take the shamrock from your hat, and cast it on the sod,
But t'will take root and flourish there tho' underfoot 'tis trod.

When law can stop the blades of grass from growing as they grow,
And when the leaves in summer-time their verdure dare not show,
Then I will change the colour that I wear in my caubeen,
But till that day, please God, I'll stick to the wearing of the green.

But if at last our colour should be torn from Ireland's heart,
Her sons with shame and sorrow from her dear old isle will part,
I've heard a whisper of a country that lies beyond the sea,
Where rich and poor stand equal in the light of freedom's day.

Oh Erin must we leave you driven by a tyrant's hand?
Must we ask a mother's blessing from a strange and distant land?
Where the cruel cross of England shall never more be seen,
And where, please God, we'll live and die still wearing of the green.[21]

21 Alfred Moffat, *The minstrelsy of Ireland: 206 Irish songs* (London, 1897), p. 65.

'Ding dong dideró'

Luaitear an t-amhrán 'Ding dong dideró' sa dráma *Macghníomhartha Chúchulainn* agus deirtear i dtreoir an Phiarsaigh:

> Ceárta Chulainn. Toirt mhór thine inti. Cearda óga ag bualadh ar inneonacha os comhair an dorais. Iad ag tosú ar na ranna seo inár ndiaidh do ghabháil. Go mear croíúil. Tomás Mac Domhnaill do ghléas.[22]

Amhrán saothair é 'Ding dong dideró' a bhfuil ársaíocht faoi leith ag baint leis, mar a áitíonn Petrie: 'The song and tune of "Ding dong didilum, buail seo, séid seo", must be one of great antiquity.'[23] Díol suntais nach i léiriú drámatúil an Phiarsaigh i gcéaduair a baineadh úsáid as fonn an amhráin seo i gcúrsaí drámaíochta, mar a léiríonn Petrie sa gcur síos a dhéanann sé ar chluiche áirithe a chonaic sé:

> I have also heard the following verse sung to the same melody, at a rude play which was carried on in the winter evenings, both by men and boys. A man sat in a chair, and another man, or boy, came and laid his head in the seated man's lap, face downwards, and his hand, palm opened and turned up, across his own back. The individuals around were then named after the various implements in a smith's forge. The man in the chair sang this verse, and at the end of it one of the bystanders gave the palm of the hand on the back a slap with his own palm, as hard as he himself could bear. He answered, 'Big sledge', 'Hand-sledge', 'Hammer', or whatever else he pleased; and the striking continued – often by the same person – until the guesser named the right person at last. Then the striker knelt down, and went through the same course; and so on all round.

Buail seo, Seán Gabha	Strike this, Shane Gobha,
Íseal is éadtrom;	Lowly and lightly;
Buaileam go léir é,	Let us all strike it
Trí na chéile:	Through each other:
Buaileam arís é,	Let us strike it again,
Is buaileam le chéile;	And let us strike together;
'S buailimid cuaird air,	And let us strike all round,
Go luath is go h-éasgaidh.	Both quickly and smartly.[24]

---

22 Ní Ghairbhí and McNulty (eag.), *Drámaí an Phiarsaigh*, lch. 71.   23 George Petrie, *The ancient music of Ireland* (Dublin, 1855), i, p. 172.   24 Ibid., p. 173.

Scríobh P.W. Joyce síos an fonn do Petrie ó Mary Hackett as Ard Pádraig i gCo. Luimnigh in 1853 agus bunaíodh an fonn a casadh in *Caithréim* ar an bhfonn seo. (Cheadaigh an Piarsach féin Petrie mar fhoinse agus foilsíodh nodaireacht Mhic Dhomhnaill i dteannta script *Macghníomhartha* in *An Macaomh.*) Seo thíos na lirící a casadh ag *Caithréim* atá bunaithe ar an leagan atá le fáil sa leabhar *Cas amhrán*:

> Ding dong dideró buaileam, a óga,
> Ding dong dideró ar na hinneona,
> Buail sin, a ghabha óig, íseal is éadrom,
> Buaileam go léir é lena chéile.

> Ding dong dideró lúbam, a bhráithre,
> Ding dong dideró an crú tiubh láidir,
> Buail sin, a ghabha óig, íseal is éadrom,
> Buaileam go léir é lena chéile.

> Ding dong dideró casam an t-iarann,
> Ding dong dideró 'na chorrán géar cíorach,
> Buail sin, a ghabha óig, íseal is éadrom,
> Buaileam go léir é lena chéile.

> Ding dong dideró teannam le fórsa,
> Ding dong dideró an banda cruinn córach,
> Buail sin, a ghabha óig, íseal is éadrom,
> Buaileam go léir é lena chéile.[25]

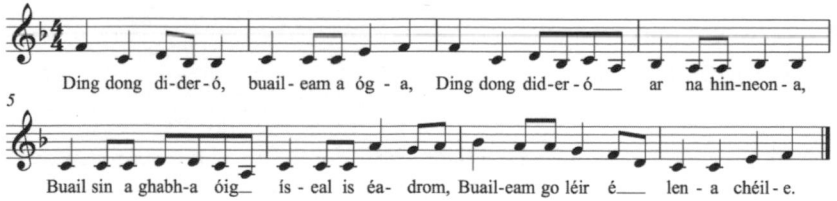

'Haigh didil dum'

Léiríonn an dráma *Íosagán* an chaoi ar shnigh an Piarsach na hamhráin trína chuid drámaí mar atá soiléir ón gcaoi ar bhain sé úsáid as an amhrán 'Haigh didil dum' sa gcomhrá idir Maitias agus na malraigh mar seo a leanas:

---

25 Mícheál Ó hEidhin, *Cas amhrán* (Indreabhán, 1975), lch. 18.

MAITIAS

Haigh didil dum, an cat is a mháthair
D'imigh go Gaillimh ag marcaíocht ar bhardal.

NA MALRAIGH

Is haigh didil dum!

MAITIAS

Haigh didil dum, do tháinig an bháisteach
Gur fliuchadh go craiceann an cat is a mháthair.

NA MALRAIGH

Is haigh didil dum!

MAITIAS

Haigh didil dum, ba dhóbair go mbáifí
An cat is a mháthair, mo chreach is mo chrá iad!

NA MALRAIGH

Is haigh didil dum!

MAITIAS

Do rug leis go Gaillimh

CÓILÍN

– Ar éigin –

MAITIAS

Maith thú, a Chóilín. Do rug leis go Gaillimh ar éigin sa tsnámh iad.

NA MALRAIGH

Is haigh didil dum![26]

Amhrán éadrom do pháistí é 'Haigh didil dum' agus is furasta focail nua a
chumadh don fhonn mar a dhéantaí sna hamhráin oibre. Foilsíodh leagan den
amhrán i nuachtán polaitiúil an Phiarsaigh, *An Barr Bua,* ar an 20 Aibreán 1912.
Chum Eoghan Ó Ceallaigh, mac feirmeora as Tír Eoghain a rugadh in 1897,[27]
na focail agus is léir go raibh a theanga in a phluic aige agus é ag cumadh cuid
de na véarsaí:

---

26 Ní Ghairbhí and McNulty (eag.), *Drámaí an Phiarsaigh,* lch. 97.   27 Aindrias Ó Cathasaigh (eag.), *An Barr Bua* (Baile Átha Cliath, 2012), lch. 102.

> Haigh didil dum, gráin linn an Niallach,
> 'S b'fhearr linn an donas ná Pádraig Mac Piarais!
> B'fhearr linn an donas ná Pádraig Mac Piarais,
> Haigh didil didil dó, haigh didil dum![28]

Casadh fonn an amhráin, atá le fáil sa leabhar *Cas amhrán*,[29] ar na fidil don léiriú *Caithréim*.

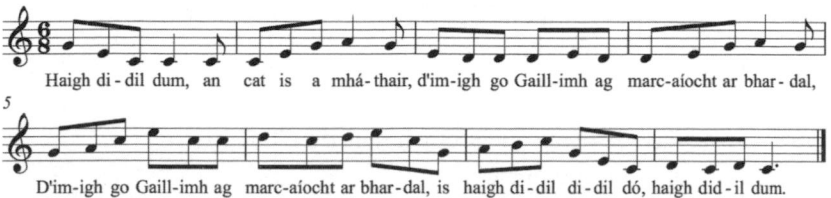

'Óró mo bháidín' / 'An curaichín'

Bhain an Piarsach an úsáid chéanna as an amhrán 'Óró mo bháidín' (nó 'An curaichín') sa dráma *Íosagán* agus bíonn Maitias agus na malraigh ag déanamh comhrá arís is iad ag baint úsáide as línte ón amhrán agus iad ag ligean orthu féin go bhfuil siad ag iomramh. Luaitear an t-amhrán leis an bPiarsach scaití agus deirtear sa leabhar *Amhránleabhar Ógra Éireann* 'Idir An Piarsach agus Colm Ó Lochlainn agus Tomás Ó Colmáin do ceapadh na véarsaí seo. Tomás Mac Domhnaill a rinne an ceol.'[30] Deir Peadar Ó hAnnracháin ina shaothar dírbheathaisnéiseach *Mar Mhaireas É* gurbh é Tomás Ó Colmáin[31] 'a gheibheann creidiúint mar údar don amhrán deas san, "Óró mo bháidín"'[32] agus áitítear ar an suíomh idirlín www.ainm.ie freisin gurbh é Tomás Ó Colmáin a chum an t-amhrán faoin teideal 'I Ióró mo bháidín ag snámh ar an gcuan'. D'fhoilsigh Colm Ó Lochlainn leagan den amhrán mar chuid den tsraith bileog *An Claisceadal* i 1930 agus seo é an leagan ar baineadh úsáid as don léiriú *Caithréim*:

> Crochfaidh mé mo sheolta is gabhfaidh mé siar,
> Óró, mo churaichín ó,
> 'S go hOíche Fhéile Eoin ní thiocfaidh mé aniar,
> Óró mo bháidín.

28 Ibid., lch. 142.   29 Ó hEidhin, *Cas amhrán*, lch. 47.   30 *Amhránleabhar Ógra Éireann* (Baile Átha Cliath, 1950), lch. 33.   31 Múinteoir bunscoile as Baile Átha Cliath ab ea Ó Colmáin a chaith tréimhse ag múineadh sna Forbacha i gConamara agus a bhí gníomhach i gConradh na Gaeilge sna 1920í. 32 Peadar Ó hAnnracháin, *Mar mhaireas é* (Baile Átha Cliath, 1955), lch. 252.

Curfá
Óró mo churaichín ó,
'S óró mo bháidín,
Óró mo churaichín ó,
Óró mo bháidín.

Nach breá í mo bháidín ag snámh ar an gcuan,
Óró, mo churaichín ó,
Na céaslaí á dtarraingt go láidir 's go buan,
Óró mo bháidín.
Curfá

Nach éachtach a léimneach thar thonnta ard',
Óró, mo churaichín ó,
'S nach éadrom í 'iompar aníos thar an trá,
Óró mo bháidín.
Curfá

Nach lúthmhar í ag iomramh soir agus siar,
Óró mo churaicín ó,
A sárú ní bhfaighidh tú ó Árainn go Cliar,
Óró mo bháidín.
Curfá

Foilsíodh an t-amhrán seo i gcnuasaigh éagsúla amhrán, rinneadh taifead ar
an amhrán go minic agus áirítear anois é mar chuid dhílis de thraidisiún
amhránaíochta na Gaeilge.

'An draighneán donn'

Tosaíonn an dráma *Eoghan Gabha* le hEoghan istigh sa gceárta agus é ag gabháil fhoinn agus leanann an nós seo síos tríd an dráma. Tá véarsaí ón amhrán 'An draighneán donn' luaite leis an gcarachtar Muircheartach. Tá an t-amhrán seo ar cheann d'amhráin mhóra ghrá na Gaeilge agus tá leaganacha de le fáil ó cheann ceann na tíre. Insíonn an t-amhrán scéal faoi fhear a bhíodh ag triail ar aonach i bhfad ó bhaile agus a bhí an-tógtha le cailín óg a bhíodh ag fanacht sa teach lóistín a mbíodh sé de nós aige féin fanacht ann. Tar éis tamaill stop sé ag dul ag an aonach agus rinne sé dearmad ar an gcailín. Rinneadh cleamhnas ansin idir é féin agus col ceathrar an chailín. Shocraigh an cailín dul ag an mbainis gléasta mar sheanbhean. Níor aithin an fear í go bhfaca sé an fáinne a thug sé di. D'éalaigh an bheirt lena chéile sa deireadh.[33]

Ní hiontas ar bith gur bhain an Piarsach úsáid as an amhrán seo sa dráma mar go gcuireann sé leis an scéal grá a tharlaíonn idir beirt de na carachtair, Máire agus Colm. Tá trí cinn de na véarsaí (véarsaí 1, 2 agus 4 thíos) focal ar fhocal leis an leagan a d'fhoilsigh Mícheál agus Tomás Ó Máille sa leabhar *Amhráin Chlainne Gael* i 1905.

Tá ról ag an bpíobaire sa dráma seo chomh maith, agus i dtreoir an Phiarsaigh deir sé:

> Séideann an píobaire; damhsann siad pas. Cruinníonn na seandaoine thar an tine ag cur agus ag cúiteamh. Glaotar 'Go neartaí Dia sibh!' 'Dia leat, a Phíobaire!' 'Thug sé amach í' agus araile agus iad ag damhsa. Tá Eoghan ag obair i gcónaí.[34]

Beartaíodh mar sin don léiriú *Caithréim* go gcasfaí fonn an amhráin ar an bpíb uilleann agus teilgeadh na lirící seo thíos a luaitear go sonrach sa dráma ar an scáileán:

> Dá mbeinn 'mo bhádóir is deas a shnámhfainn an fharraige anonn,
> Agus scríobhfainn cúpla líne ag mo ghrá faoi fhonn,
> Bheinn ag éalú le mo chéad searc is ag fáisceadh a coim,
> Is an lá nach bhféadaim bean a bhréagadh níl an báire liom.
>
> Tá ribín le mo chéad searc in mo phóca thíos,
> Agus feara Éireann ní fhéadfaidís an chumha a bhaint díom,

33 Tomás Ó Máille and Mícheál Ó Máille, *Amhráin Chlainne Gael* (Indreabhán, 1991), lch. 188; Douglas Hyde, *Love songs of Connacht* (Dublin, 1968), lch. 30.   34 Ní Ghairbhí and McNulty (eag.), *Drámaí an Phiarsaigh*, lch. 250.

Tá mé réidh leat go ndéantar dom cónra chaol,
Is go bhfásfaidh an féar ina dhiaidh sin trí mo lár aníos.

Bhéarfainn comhairle do na mná óga dá nglacfaidís uaim é,
Gan a bheith ag comhrá leis na hógfhir ná ag creidiúint a scéal,
Níl na gcomhrá ach mar dhoirtfeá braon uisce ar ghé,
Is a Dhia na Glóire, go gcuirtear comhairle mo leasa orm féin!

Tabhair mo mhallacht do t'athair agus do do mháithrín féin,
Nár thug scoil duit ag tús t'óige le mo láimh a léamh,
Is moch ar maidin a chuirfinn chughat brí mó scéil,
Is bíodh mo bheannacht leat go gcastar ort in uaigneas mé.[35]

'S ambó aera'
Castar amhránaí eile orainn, Iollann Beag, sa dráma *The master*. Baineann an Piarsach úsáid as na siollaí gaoithe ón amhrán cleamhnais "S Ambó Éara' agus luath go maith sa dráma cloistear Iollann Beag ag casadh na bhfocal seo:

We watch the wee ladybird fly far away,
With an óró and an iero and an úmbó éró.[36]

Agus níos deireanaí cloistear na véarsaí seo:

Young Íosa plays with me every day
(*With an óró and an iero*)
Tig and pookeen and hide-in-the-hay
(*With an óró and an iero*)

We race in the river with otters gray,
We climb the tall trees where red squirrels play,
We watch the wee ladybird far away,
(*With an óró and an iero and an imbó éro*).[37]

Don léiriú *Caithréim* casadh fonn an amhráin seo go héadrom, bog mar a bheadh cineál idircheoil ann. Bunaíodh an fonn ar an leagan atá le fáil sa leabhar *Cas amhrán*.[38]

35 Ibid., lch. 245–6.   36 Ibid., lch. 181.   37 Ibid., lch. 185.   38 Ó hEidhin, *Cas amhrán*, lch. 153.

'Caoineadh na dTrí Muire'

Cé nár mhair script an dráma *An Pháis*, tá sé soiléir go raibh ról lárnach ag an gceol sa léiriú seo de réir na dtuairiscí a scríobhadh ar an dráma. Chum Tomás Mac Domhnaill ceol don dráma agus luaitear 'Caoineadh Mhuire' ann chomh maith.[39] Thuairiscigh Desmond Ryan 'in the last act certain speeches taken from an old Irish hymn "Caoineadh Mhuire", were spoke by Jesus, Mary and Peter'.[40] Tá cumhacht faoi leith ag baint leis an gcaoineadh mar dheasghnáth amhránaíochta agus is léir gur thuig an Piarsach an méid seo ón gcur síos a rinne sé ar an gcaoineadh a bhailigh sé ó bhean as Maigh Cuilinn i gCo. na Gaillimhe darbh ainm Máire Nic Fhlannchadha:

> Ba greann leat bheith ag éisteacht léithi agus í ag canadh an chaointe go cumhach ceolmhar. Bhí de mhéid a truaighe do Mhuire agus dá mac gur shil sí na frasa deor agus í ag rádh na rann gurb fhliuch gruadha agus brollach di. Ná déantar iongantas de sin, óir is minic Páis Chríost dá caoineadh go deorach ag Gaedhealaibh.[41]

Casadh véarsaí ó leaganacha éagsúla den amhrán 'Caoineadh Mhuire' (nó 'Caoineadh na dTrí Muire', mar a thugtar air freisin) sa léiriú *Caithréim*. Tá simplíocht agus láidreacht faoi leith ag baint leis an gcomhrá atá san amhrán seo idir Íosa agus Muire a théann i bhfeidhm go smior ar an éisteoir. Seo an leagan a bhailigh an Piarsach ó Mháire Nic Fhlannchadha:[42]

> A Pheadair, a aspail, an bhfaca tú mo ghrá geal?
> (m'óchón, is m'óchón ó!)
> Chonaic mé ar ball é i lár a námhad.
> (m'óchón, is m'óchón ó!)

39 Ní Ghairbhí and McNulty (eag.), *Drámaí an Phiarsaigh*, lch. 46.   40 Ibid., lch. 287.   41 Pearse, *Collected works of Pádraic H. Pearse: songs of the Irish rebels*, p. 94.   42 Ibid., pp 90–5.

Gabh i leith, a dhá Mhuire, go gcaoine sibh mo ghrá geal,
(m'óchón, is m'óchón ó!)
Céard atá le caoineadh againn muna gcaoinimid a chnámha.
(m'óchón, is m'óchón ó!)

Cé hé an fear breá atá ar chrann na páise?
(m'óchón, is m'óchón ó!)
An é nach n-aithníonn tú do mhac, a mháthair?
(m'óchón, is m'óchón ó!)

'S an é sin an maicín a d'iompair mé trí ráithe?
(m'óchón, is m'óchón ó!)
Nó an é sin an maicín do rugadh san stábla?
(m'óchón, is m'óchón ó!)

Nó an é sin an maicín do hoileadh in ucht Mháire?
(m'óchón, is m'óchón ó!)
Éist, a Mháthair, is ná bí cráite.
(m'óchón, is m'óchón ó!)

'S an é sin an casúr do bhuail tríot na tairní?
(m'óchón, is m'óchón ó!)
Nó an í sin an tsleá do chuaigh trí do lár gheal?
(m'óchón, is m'óchón ó!)

Nó an í sin an choróin spíonta chuaigh ar do mhullach álainn?
(m'óchón, is m'óchón ó!)
Éist, a Mháthair, is ná bí cráite.
(m'óchón, is m'óchón ó!)

'Gus éist, a Mháthair, is ná bí cráite,
(m'óchón, is m'óchón ó!)
Tá mná mo chaointe le breith fós, a Mháithrín.
(m'óchón, is m'óchón ó!)

A bhean atá ag gol de bharr mo bháis-se,
(m'óchón, is m'óchón ó!)
Beidh na céadta inniu i ngairdín Phárthais!
(m'óchón, is m'óchón ó!)

'Gráinne Mhaol'

Sa dráma *Eoghan Gabha* iarrann Eoghan ar Chonchubhar 'amhrán a chuirfeas misneach 'nár gcroíthe' a chasadh.[43] 'Gráinne Mhaol' an t-amhrán a roghnaíonn sé agus ag deireadh an chéad ghnímh den dráma tugtar an treoir seo:

> Tá Eoghan in airde ar stól i lár an ardáin: tá na daoine eile cruinnithe ina thimpeall ag glaoch ar Rí Séamus, Pádraig Sáirséal agus Gráinne Mhaol. Druidtear an brat anuas agus iad ag gabháil 'Gráinne Mhaol'.[44]

Chum Seán Clárach Mac Domhnaill an t-amhrán 'Gráinne Mhaol' nó 'A shaoi ghlain den phríomhscoth' agus tá leagan den téacs le fáil in eagrán 1902 an Duinnínigh[45] agus i mbailiúchán Joyce a foilsíodh i 1901.[46] D'fhoilsigh Bunting (1840) leagan den fhonn faoin ainm 'Granu Weal' leis an nod 'Very ancient, author and date unknown.'[47] Tá an cóiriú atá déanta ag Bunting ar an bhfonn mífheiliúnach don ghlór agus déantar cáineadh ar an leagan seo san Irisleabhar *The Citizen* a foilsíodh dhá bhliain dár gcionn: 'The air is published in a very un-vocal shape in Bunting's third collection, No. 46.'[48] Tá an leagan den fhonn a foilsíodh in *The Citizen* níos feiliúnaí don ghuth, cé gur liricí Béarla atá ann, agus tá sé an-chosúil leis an leagan atá le fáil i mbailiúchán Joyce agus sa leabhrán *An chóisir cheoil* le Seán Óg Ó Tuama a foilsíodh i 1958.[49] Baineadh úsáid as leagan *An chóisir cheoil* don léiriú *Caithréim*:

> A shaoi ghlan de phríomhscoth na sáirfhear saor,
> Is binn snoite laoithe 'gus ráite séimh,
> An aoibhinn leat díbirt ár námhad go léir?
> 'S an Rí ceart arís bheith ag Gráinne Mhaol.
>
> Tá an Laoiseach go buíonmhar thar sáile 'teacht,
> Le díograis chun díoltais, le garda 's faobhar;
> Beidh saoithe ár gcríche go brách 'na réim,
> Ag díbirt a naimhde ó Ghráinne Mhaol.

---

43 Ní Ghairbhí and McNulty (eag.), *Drámaí an Phiarsaigh*, lch. 250. 44 Ibid., lch. 251. 45 Pádraig Ó Duinnín (eag.), *Amhráin Sheagháin Chláraigh Mhic Dhomhnaill* (Baile Átha Cliath, 1902). 46 P.W. Joyce, *Irish music and song: a collection of songs in the Irish language* (Dublin, 1901), p. 27. 47 Bunting, *The ancient music of Ireland*, p. 63. 48 Henry Hudson (ed.), *The Dublin Monthly Magazine: being a new series of the Citizen* (Dublin, Jan.–June 1842) p. 47. 49 Seán Óg Ó Tuama, *An chóisir cheoil* (Baile Átha Cliath, 1958), lch. 16. D'fhoilsigh P.W. Joyce leagan den amhrán i 1901.

Beidh soilse 'gus tinte geal cnámh ag Gaeil,
Is fíonta dá ndíogadh ar chlár le scléip,
Beidh aoibhneas is intinn ar dháimh 's ar chléir,
Ag guí leis an Rí ceart 's le Gráinne Mhaol.

Chífear na mílte ón Spáinn go tréan,
Fíor-scoth na tíre do crádh le plé,
Fillfid gan moill chugainn thar sáil' gan bhréig,
Ag coimhdeacht an rí chirt is Ghráinne Maol.

Spreag t'intinn, bíodh meidhir ort, go láidir léir,
Glac claidheamh chugat is éirí, a ghrá mo chléibh,
Scinnfid ó Highlands lucht bláth-bhoinéad,
Agus sínfidh an rí ceart le Gráinne Mhaol.

Beidh muidne go fíontach, 's go fáilteach saor,
Is ár muintir go haoibhinn, gan cháin san tsaol;
Beidh Gaeil bhocht' go hinntinneach lán do scléip,
'S an scaoinse clamh díbeartha ó Ghráinne Mhaol.

Beidh ceartas, beidh aiteas, beidh dáin, beidh scléip,
Ag flathaibh ag freastal don árd-rí thréan;
Beidh Gaill 'na gcéadta dá leagadh le pilléir,
Is beidh sealbh ag Carolus ar Ghráinne Mhaol.

Samhlaítear an t-amhrán 'Óró 'sé do bheatha abhaile' (nó 'An dord Féinne')
a chum an Piarsach le Gráinne Mhaol go minic mar gheall ar an véarsa a
thosaíonn le 'Tá Gráinne Mhaol ag teacht thar sáile [...]' Ba dhual don
Phiarsach seanamhráin a athscríobh agus bhain sé úsáid as an amhrán

Seacaibíteach 'Séarlas Óg' dá leagan féin de 'Óró 'sé do bheatha abhaile'.[50] Más é an fonn 'Róisín Dubh' aintiún an Éirí Amach, d'fhéadfaí a mhaíomh go bhfuil 'Óró 'sé do bheatha abhaile' sna sála air. Theastaigh uaim dá réir sin macalla den amhrán a bheith mar chuid den léiriú agus bhain mé úsáid as fonn 'Óró 'sé do bheatha abhaile' mar idircheol agus mar chonrtaphointe d'fhonn 'Gráinne Mhaol'.

CONCLÚID

Thug an tionscnamh seo deis dom díriú ar ghné an cheoil de dhrámaí an Phiarsaigh ó dhearcadh an taighdeora agus ó dhearcadh an chleachtóra araon. Nuair a léigh mé na drámaí ceann i ndiaidh a chéile fuair mé léargas ar an gceol agus ar na hamhráin a bhí in intinn an Phiarsaigh agus é ag scríobh na ndrámaí seo. Bhí go leor de na hamhráin seo agam féin ar chúiseanna éagsúla – d'fhoghlaim mé cuid acu ar scoil; chuala mé cuid eile acu sa mbaile; fuair mé cuid eile fós acu ó amhránaithe éagsúla ag ranganna sean-nóis i gConamara agus mé ag éirí aníos. Is léir gur theastaigh ón bPiarsach an traidisiún seo atá fós beo beathaíoch i gceantair éagsúla ar fud na tíre a aistriú ón suíomh áitiúil as ar eascair sé agus é a chur i láthair i bpobal cathrach Bhaile Átha Cliath le haitheantas agus stádas a thabhairt don chultúr dúchasach. Thuig sé cumhacht agus tábhacht an traidisiúin, agus go háirithe cumhacht na hamhránaíochta agus an amhránaí, a chruthúnas sin sa dráma *The singer* áit a bhfeictear an t-amhránaí mar theachtaire agus mar cheannaire sa bpobal. Ní de thaisme ach an oiread go bhfuil carachtar an 'Ballad Singer' sa dráma *Owen*, 'Conchubhar na nAmhrán', 'Bríd an phíobaire' agus 'MacDara Píobaire' sa dráma *Eoghan Gabha*, gan trácht ar na na mná caointe sa dráma *An Pháis*.

Bíonn a léamh féin ag chuile dhuine ar an bPiarsach mar fhear, mar scríbhneoir, mar réabhlóidí, mar pholaiteoir, mar oideachasóir, mar Ghael. Léiríonn an ceol agus na hamhráin a luaitear ina chuid drámaí go raibh cúinne dá aigne a thug spás ar leith don cheol agus a chreid go raibh fiúntas agus luach ag baint leis ceol agus amhránaíocht na ndaoine do phobal na hÉireann trí chéile. Trí thabhairt faoin gceol agus faoi na hamhráin seo le sprioc chruthaitheach ag a dheireadh, .i. an léiriú *Caithréim*, fuair mé deis mo léamh

50 Féach Ó Coigligh, *Filíocht Ghaeilge Phádraig Mhic Phiarais*, lch. 77.

féin a dhéanamh ar fhuaimrian saoil an Phiarsaigh, rud a spreag an tsamhlaíocht ionam féin agus go deimhin an tuiscint atá agam ar an tréimhse sin.

Ar an dara lá déag de mhí Eanáir 1916 scríobh Mac Piarais litir chuig Tomás Mac Domhnaill agus d'iarr sé an méid seo:

> A Thomáis na gCarad,
> Tá buachaillí Coláiste Mhaoilsheachlainn chun Íosagán do léiriughadh ag Feis Bhéil Feirste, agus badh mhaith leis an Athair S. Mac Leanacháin go mbeadh ceol an dá amhrán (.i. 'Haigh didil dum' agus 'Mo Churaichín Ó') aige. An mbeadh am agat an ceol do sgríobhadh agus a chur chugam? Ba mhaith liom é bheith agam féin freisin. Beir buaidh, Mise do bhuan-chara, Pádraig Mac Piarais.[51]

Ar an dara lá deag de mhí Eanáir 2016, céad bliain go dtí an lá tar éis don Phiarsach an t-iarratas sin dhéanamh, a críochnaíodh an aiste seo. Nach deas iad comhtharluithe ceolmhara an tsaoil.

51 Séamus Ó Buachalla (eag.), *The letters of P.H. Pearse* (London, 1980), p. 430.

10 / Appeasing Pearse's ghosts:
history, memory and theatre

ELAINE SISSON

In the preface to his essay 'Ghosts', published in 1915, Patrick Pearse acknowledges the influence of Henrik Ibsen's play of the same name, not only in his
choice of title, but on his choice of themes. Pearse argues that we must
acknowledge the past before we can begin to build a collective future.
'Ghosts', he argues, 'are troublesome things in a house or in a family, as we
knew even before Ibsen taught us.' Pearse's ghosts are those of the nationalist
past, 'of dead men that have bequeathed a trust to us living men.'[1] If we do
not acknowledge their presence and their significance to our own experience,
he suggests, we remain incomplete both spiritually and nationally.

If, as Pearse suggests, 'ghosts are troublesome things in a house or a family',
I would like to argue that they are troublesome things in the theatre also. For
what is the theatre but an intense engagement with the ghostly? The physical
realization of other worlds that theatre offers is, in some sense, a haunting of
the present by the past. Characters brought alive, embodied and inhabited by
actors, are threshold creatures who occupy the boundaries between the
physical and the imaginative world. For what is the actor but a revenant who
embodies another for a short period and then disappears? What is theatre
itself but a vivid engagement with other, temporal worlds that call us momen-
tarily out of the present?

In Micheál Mac Liammóir's episodic 1929 pageant *The Ford of the Hurdles*,
Pearse appears at the end of an epic retelling of one thousand years of
Dublin history. His presence consolidates all the events of the past, bringing
the pageant to a close, and suggests that in 1916 the culmination of history
had been arrived at. Pearse is not merely a catalyst for the action of 1916 but
the symbol of the realized present: in Pearse's material presence, the ghosts
have been appeased. Mac Liammóir's reenactment of history, which both
conjures up the ghosts in the house and our attempts to domesticate them, is
a point to which I'd like to return. The figure of Pearse, physically absent yet
imaginatively present, appearing at the climax of the historical pageant

---

1 Patrick Pearse, 'Ghosts', *Collected works of P.H. Pearse: political writings and speeches* (Dublin, 1924), pp 222–55.

suggests that history, through theatre, has been realized. I would like to examine here how this 'messianic moment' is grounded in Pearse's own writings for the theatre, which are full of 'returning bodies' or 'transformative bodies' that appear to offer redress for the wrongs of the past. I'd like to do this first by looking at the recurrence of the ghostly or otherworldly boy who appears in Pearse's plays and considering how the body of the child operates as a liminal figure. Secondly, I'd like to think about the body in performance and how this liminality is both embodied and displaced by the actor, and about Pearse as a revenant or ghostly figure in the emerging Irish state of the 1920s and 1930s.

PEARSE'S GHOSTLY CHILDREN

Pearse's writings are populated by ghostly children. Within romantic nationalism, literary and visual images of the child are often used to recall a common past. However, a child also represents the promise of the future, and therefore is always understood in some sense as a threshold or boundary figure: the boundary of the past and the present, and the threshold between childhood and adulthood. The child as an imaginative trope may work as a symbol of loss and disintegration as well as of the future and hope. Pearse's strange, redemptive children are complex constructions, despite the simplicity of his narratives. They can certainly be contextualized within the terrain of late Victorian culture, which idealized and sentimentalized the purity and innocence of children. Yet Pearse's otherworldly children are also constructed within narratives of Irishness and a national identity bound up within a Catholic religious ethos.

The work of Avery Gordon in her book *Haunting and the sociological imagination* contextualizes the image of the ghost in much the same way as we might think about the child as a trope. Gordon suggests 'the ghost is primarily a symptom of what is missing. It gives notice', she says, 'not only to itself but to what it represents.' And what does it represent? For Gordon this is 'usually a loss, sometimes of life, sometimes of a path not taken'. Further, she determines that 'from a certain vantage point the ghost also simultaneously represents a future possibility, a hope'.[2] We might argue, therefore, that the ghostly, otherworldly children we encounter in Pearse's writings are doubly

2 Avery Gordon, *Haunting and the sociological imagination* (Minneapolis, 1997), pp 63–4.

inscribed within discourses of loss and of hope, of the past and the future, of what is missing and what yet can be achieved. David Lloyd traces the emergence of two discourses of the ghostly revenant that have haunted Irish culture since the Famine: one he sees as a phantom of 'future possibility'; the other, more familiar, is the ghost who rises from destruction, seeking redress for injustice.[3] Consider Pearse's words in the pamphlet *Ghosts*:

> Here be ghosts that I have raised this Christmastide [...] There is only one way to appease a ghost. You must do the thing it asks you. The ghosts of a nation sometimes ask very big things; and they must be appeased, whatever the cost.[4]

These ghosts are the unappeased dead wandering through the house, and they fuel Pearse's political imagination and energy. But his writing, his literary imagination, is haunted by more benign ghosts; they are not exactly dead but they exist on both a physical and a metaphysical plane; they are those little phantoms of future possibility. Let's look a little more closely at three of them:[5] Íosagán (played by Eunan McGinley); Giolla na Naomh in *The king* (played by Desmond Carney); and Iollann Beag in *The master*. I choose these because they are plays authored by Pearse rather than adaptations or stagings of plays by, for example, Standish O'Grady, Douglas Hyde or Padraic Colum.[6]

ÍOSAGÁN

The figure of Íosagán was one of the central literary and visual images promoted by Pearse in the early years of St Enda's. *Íosagán*, a morality tale of the Christ Child in Connacht, had already appeared in a number of guises before Pearse wrote his play. It was originally published as a short story that appeared in *An Claidheamh Soluis*, then became the title of a series of short stories before being published in book form in 1907. Pearse adapted it for the

3 David Lloyd, *Irish Times: temporalities of modernity* (Dublin, 2008), p. 43.   4 Patrick Pearse, *Ghosts* (Dublin, 1915).   5 St Enda's produced a number of plays and pageants between 1908 and 1915 that focused on themes of boyhood. For the purposes of this paper I'd like to look at *Íosagán* (performed in 1910 and 1915), *The king* (performed in 1912 and 1913) and *The master* (performed in 1915). The others are adaptations – for example, *The Passion play* (1911) *The boy deeds of Cúchulainn* – or were never performed (*Eoghan Gabha*), or were not written by Pearse: for example, *The lost saint* (1909), *The destruction of the hostel* (1910) and *The coming of Fionn* (1909).   6 For more details on the staging of plays at St Enda's, see Elaine Sisson. *Pearse's patriots: the cult of boyhood at St Enda's* (Cork, 2004); and Brian Crowley's essay in this volume.

stage in 1910, when it was performed at Cullenswood House and at the Abbey Theatre, and in 1915 it was performed at the Irish Theatre in Hardwicke Street.

Pearse described *Íosagán* as being about the beauty of childhood and particularly about the beauty of boyhood. It tells the story of an old man, Matthias, isolated by the villagers because he has lost his faith, who prefers his own company and the company of the local children. One morning a strange, barefooted, golden-haired child appears, wearing an unusual white garment. His face is radiant and there is a peculiar light surrounding him. He appears to be visible only to the children and to old Matthias, suggesting that he is a conduit between two extremes of age and of human experience. The child Íosagán is associated with the natural world (in which is included the world of childhood and of faith): he spends his days 'travelling the roads and walking the hills and ploughing the waves'.[7] His interactions with Matthias restore the old man's faith just in time: Matthias dies after being given the last rites by the local priest. Íosagán is not of this world – this is easily understood – and he is the first of Pearse's dramatic figures who represents the permeable boundaries between the physical and metaphysical world, as well as between the world of children and of adults. However, the adults cannot cross the threshold and return: only the children may. Moreover, Íosagán does not die, nor is he sacrificed. He is there to save, not to redeem through his own death. In other plays, the male child figure is closely associated with the redemptive power of his own life.[8]

It is easy to see the appeal for Pearse of Tagore's 1912 *The post office* (a somewhat prescient title in an Irish context), which was one of the plays favoured at St Enda's. It features a young boy with a sunny disposition, Amal, who is terminally ill. It has much in common with the allegorical narratives of Pearse's dramas, but Amal is less sentimentalized than Pearse's boys. He is good-humoured and mischievous rather than otherworldly. Where Pearse's children long to be reconciled to nature, Amal is drawn to the social world of community and work; as he sits by the window – a threshold space – he interacts with the herdsman, the dairyman, the flower seller and other villagers who pass by. Amal's death at the end of the play offers reflection to

---

7 Pearse, *Íosagán* in Róisín Ní Ghairbhí and Eugene McNulty (eds), *Patrick Pearse: collected plays/Drámaí an Phiarsaigh* (Dublin, 2013), p. 123.   8 The boy who played Íosagán at St Enda's, Eunan McGinley, was killed during the War of Independence, which perhaps tightens our interpretive reading of the play as a national and spiritual allegory.

those around him rather than their salvation, although the play is easily read as a religious allegory.

The death of Giolla na Naomh in Pearse's play *The king* is the first child death. The play was first performed as a pageant before being reworked for the stage. Consequently, as a dramatic work, it straddles the divide between the outdoor spectacles and the formal staged plays produced by St Enda's. *The king* is a piece of writing, or a dramatic event, where the boy enters into adolescence through a masculine rite of passage, from the cloister to the battlefield. It opens in the grounds of a cloister. A group of boys discuss the rumour that the pagan king is going to battle and they fantasize, as the king's horsemen pass by, about being kings or warriors when they grow up. Suddenly, a beautiful, bloodstained young man stumbles out of the forest (the darkly treacherous landscape of manhood) onto the sunlit plain. He considers himself unworthy to wear the crown and feels that the battle will be lost if it is not worn by somebody pure. The youthful Giolla na Naomh ('servant of the saints') is chosen 'as the noblest jewel in the house'. We have already witnessed how he has stood apart from the childish banter of his friends. Obediently the child takes on the mantle of kingship, and his 'golden head' goes into battle 'like a torrent through a mountain gap'.[9]

Leaving the cloisters of childhood, he moves upwards, on horseback, into the dangerous, unknown territory of manhood, where the reality of battle is taking place. As he advances, the enemy retreats, but at a great cost. The child is killed at the moment of victory and his body is borne back to the monastery. The king kisses the dead child and pays homage to his 'white body' since, he says, 'it is [his] purity that hath redeemed my people'.[10] However, the child's body is not immediately returned to the monastery, but is laid instead in the interim space between the forest and the monastic home.

This space, which links two off-stage worlds, is the literal, visible space of the playing stage; but it is also the liminal space that theatre occupies in our world. This no man's land, suspended between the concrete (although imaginary) forest and cloister may be understood as a metaphor for the theatre as cultural event. It is a clearing that enables us to map layers of meanings on top of each other, according to the audience and the context in which it is being produced and seen. This clearing allows us to conflate history, fiction, memory and the contemporary as a type of alchemy that

9 Pearse, *The king* in Ní Ghairbhí and McNulty (eds), *Patrick Pearse: collected plays*, pp 160, 163. 10 Ibid., p. 164.

creates a world simultaneously tangible (actors, sets, costumes) and yet insubstantial and temporal.

   The return of the past and transition are also thematically central to *The
master*. Set in a cloister, the presence of two arches suggests two off-stage
spaces: one to a forest that characterizes the public world, and the other to a
chapel – a reflective, interiorized space. Young Iollann Beag is the by now
familiar ethereal child. He is an innocent who praises God by climbing trees
and watching birds. His friends understand him to be special. The parallels
with Íosagán are obvious. Set at a time when the new religion of Christianity
co-exists with an older, Druidic culture, these two oppositional philosophies
are represented by the figure of Ciarán, the master, and Daire, the pagan king.
The dialogue between them plays out personal conflicts in Pearse's own state
of mind: the tension between public service and private belief, between
thought and action.

   Once boyhood friends, Ciarán and Daire have chosen different paths.
Daire accuses Ciarán of spending his life 'pursuing shadows that fled before
you', 'ghosts over wide spaces', instead of being part of the world of action.[11]
In his defence, Ciarán remonstrates that he has sought what is 'remote and
holy and perilous', suggesting that 'truth' is insubstantial and cannot be
grasped. Daire responds 'Ghosts! Ghosts!' and accuses Ciarán of following a
'mocking phantom'.[12] Asking him for proof of this ghostly world, Daire
challenges Ciarán to 'Call upon [his] God to reveal Himself' and save young
Iollann Beag from being killed by his sword.[13] The child stands in for all of
them, as Daire says: 'for your soul … and mine … and the souls of all [of]
this nation, born and unborn'. Unlike Ciarán, Iollann's faith is unwavering
and he calls upon the Archangel Michael to protect him. Pearse's stage directions indicate that the figure of 'a mighty warrior, winged, and clothed in
light' *seems* to stand beside the boy.[14] Iollann is spared, but Ciarán, faith
restored, dies as Daire kneels before the symbol of the other world. Here, it
is the ghost-child, twinned with the angel, who enables this cathartic moment
– this messianic moment of death through faith, of surrender, of salvation
and ultimately of personal liberation.

   David Lloyd's observation that we look to the 'unexhausted possibilities
secreted in the past' to shape 'utopian hopes for a more just, less destructively
exploitative, order of things' resonates in Pearse's return to the child to seek
redemption for the past and salvation for the future.[15] The spritely and benign

11 Pearse, *The master* in Ní Ghairbhí and McNulty (eds), *Patrick Pearse: collected plays*, p. 192.   12 Ibid., p.
193.   13 Ibid., p. 195.   14 Ibid., p. 196.   15 Lloyd, *Irish times: temporalities of modernity*, p.43.

child-ghost, Lloyd's 'little phantom of possibility', in Pearse's dramas offers
an imaginative alternative to the vengeful and paralysing ghosts of history
who tread heavily across the nation's attic. Studies on liminality and ritual
suggest that in transitional periods (for example, adolescence) initiation rites
involve a seclusion or sequestering from society, and that, as a consequence,
the initiates achieve a type of invisibility, what Victor Turner calls 'betwixt and
between-ness'.[16] Without wishing to raid the anthropological closet without
due consideration, it does offer us some interesting insights about the space
that the transitional body occupies – this no man's land, this presence but
absence, this ghostly invisibility not only of the child – but also to consider
the transformative power of the performing space: the stage.

STAGING THE TEXT: THINKING ABOUT PERFORMANCE

Pearse's plays are not just literary texts – they are written for performance and
so we have to think about them as being embodied, staged and performed.
How do we do this? It is sometimes easier for all of us to deal with the clean
and stable certainty of the written word. It is much more difficult, messy and
complex to pin down the text in performance. However, dramatists anticipate
that their plays will mainly be seen and not read, and so we must consider the
literary text as only a *partial* invocation of the play. If we are to argue for
theatre as a boundary space, a liminal space of temporality, ghostly hauntings
and returns, then we must be able to consider the text in performance and to
think about performers and audiences. The importance of the audience and
performers is crucial to thinking about how a play is seen and understood. As
W.J.T. Mitchell says, representation is 'always *of* something or someone, *by*
something or someone, *to* someone',[17] confirming Jerzy Grotowski's assertion
that 'at least one spectator is needed to make [theatre] a performance'.[18]

Yet, without extensive documentary evidence, it is difficult to know what
audiences felt, thought and experienced in response to what they saw on the
stage, which to a certain extent explains why so much literary criticism
sidesteps the issue of live performance. There is then the difficulty of *which*
performance we examine, and how we account for different interpretative
environments, contexts and audiences. Andrew Gurr, for example, states that

---

16 Victor Turner, 'Betwixt and between: the liminal period in rites of passage', *Proceedings of the American
Ethnological Society* (1964), 4–20.   17 W.J.T. Mitchell, 'What is an image?', *New Literary History*, 15:3 (Spring
1984), 503.   18 Jerzy Grotowski, *Towards a poor theatre.* (New York, 1968), p. 32.

'the hermeneutics of the theatre [...] depend as much on the audience's state of mind as it does on the author's and the players' expectations of what, mentally, their audience will be prepared for', or more succinctly, 'because almost nobody bothers to put down in writing what they feel about a play while they experience it' – and certainly not the actors.[19]

The plays I have referred to so far were all staged within Pearse's lifetime, but I would like to turn our attention now to the performative context of a play not staged until after Pearse's death: that is, *The singer*, written in 1915. *The singer* is the play whose protagonist, MacDara, is most closely identified with Pearse himself. While Ciarán and Daire in *The master* represent different aspects of Pearse, MacDara is understood to *be* Pearse. Certainly this was the interpretation offered in one of its most public stagings in 1932 at the Gate Theatre. The Gate (founded four years previously by Micheál Mac Liammóir and Hilton Edwards) was still finding its place in Dublin and the play was an unusual choice for a theatre committed to European experimentalism. This allegiance to experiment was perhaps fulfilled by the fact that *The singer* appeared as part of a triple bill. Sandwiched between Pearse's play and an episodic piece called *Easter 1916* was Anatole France's *The man who married a dumb wife.*

The conjunction of the three dramas is a curious one; the *Irish Times* remarked that 'Irish tragedy and French comedy make a perfect blend with the topicality of the two patriotic plays being separated by a bit of French spice'.[20] Certainly, France's play was a curious choice: it features a judge who laments the fact that he has married a woman who cannot speak. When, due to surgical intervention, his wife's speech is restored he finds that although the doctors could make her speak, none could keep her silent. Its function seems comedic as *The singer* and *Easter 1916* are antiphonal pieces.[21]

The *Irish Times* definitely saw them within a continuum, noting that the Irish plays 'hang together as the introduction and climax of a beautiful story for which a line of Pearse's provides the theme: one man can save a nation, as one Man redeemed the world'. The main interest of *The singer*, according to the paper, lay in the restless, tormented MacDara, into whose personality Pearse has managed to breathe his complete soul.[22] Unsurprisingly, MacDara

---

19 Andrew Gurr, *Playgoing in Shakespeare's London* (Cambridge, 2004), pp 6, 95.   20 'Triple bill at the Gate', *Irish Times*, 29 Mar. 1932.   21 The choice of plays does, however, raise the question of 'voice': who is speaking, who they speak for, who cannot speak. It also suggests how types of speech are important to the reception and interpretation of what is being said: oratory, chorus, monologue and poetic speech. 22 'Triple bill at the Gate', *Irish Times*, 29 Mar. 1932.

was played by Mac Liammóir – it was far too good an acting opportunity to miss, especially as the eponymous singer is described in the play as having 'the voice of a silver trumpet' and as speaking 'words so beautiful they make people cry'.[23] Importantly, the role was understood by the audience (and reviewers) to be an autobiographical portrait of Pearse. Mac Liammoir's identification with Pearse was reinforced by Mac Liammóir's role in *Easter 1916*, where he appears as 'the Strange Voice', which speaks the words of Pearse.

In the theatre magazine *Motley*, Constantine Curran affirms that for a contemporary audience *The singer* was less of a play and more of 'a spiritual manifesto and curious presentiment', and that the sense that the protagonist 'will never be dissociated from the writer's personality' was proven by the close attention of the crowded audience to Pearse and Mac Liammóir.[24] *Easter 1916* is a powerful piece of symbolism, telling in impressionistic terms the tale of a week that began in bewilderment and anger and ended in tragedy. *Easter 1916* is strange and dislocating. It was first performed as the final episode in a longer historical pageant in 1929 but was received so successfully that Mac Liammóir decided to revive it as a stand-alone piece in 1932. The transcripts for the original suggest the desire to present a shadowy, dreamlike sequence with voices, shadows, choreography and lighting used for dramatic effect. Set before dawn, the drama is framed by the rise and fall of voices from the sides of the stage, cries of longing and despair phrased in biblical terms: 'Long have we waited in the darkness/Too long, too long have we waited.' As the voices fade, the stage directions indicate that 'the light of dawn gradually creeps over the stage and shows the modern city sleeping'.[25]

The symbolism is clear: the Irish people are awakening to a new dawn and a new future. Some voices protest: 'we are happier when we can sleep/why should we awake?' Against the silhouette of the city, a figure appears, his shadow looming over the backdrop; the people are exhorted to 'wake, wake from your sleep' and to listen to the stranger. The messianic figure, in bearing and dress, is Pearse, something made explicit when 'the Strange Voice' speaks. Fragmented phrases include: Irishmen and Irishwomen; In the name of god and of the dead generations; and, the beauty of this world hath made me sad. Meanwhile, the voices rise and fall in both harmony and cacophony, grouped and single voices speaking together and across each other, giving the

23 Pearse, *The singer* in Ní Ghairbhí and McNulty (eds), *Patrick Pearse: collected plays*, p. 211. 24 Constantine Curran, 'Review', *Motley*, 1:2 (Apr. 1932). 25 Hilton Edwards and Micheál Mac Liammóir, *The Ford of the Hurdles* (1929), NLI, MS 24, 562.

impression of confusion but also of growing will and determination, as the single voices begin to mingle and swell. It is a powerful dramatic device and one that Edwards, in particular, knew how to combine with choreographed movements and lighting effects. A gunshot rings out and the silhouette of 'the Strange Voice' falls, accompanied by the Greek chorus of all the voices: '16 men/16 men who were faithful/What will become of us, what will become of us now?' The call and response is patterned on the rhythm and pattern of Pearse's oratory and writing, which appeals to the unborn to redeem the present generation of 'your rags and your shame'; it is a redemptive, rousing message to the citizens of the new state that identifies them as the keepers of 'the newest dawn' and the 'flame of my message'.

Performed together, *The singer* and *Easter 1916* provide the prologue and epilogue of the revolutionary moment. The dramatic and emotive conclusion of the pageant, drawing on recent memory and appealing to everybody's higher nature, was bound to please. Maud Gonne MacBride praised the production as 'a worthy Easter commemoration'.[26] Her imprimatur was not to be underestimated; her disapproval of Sean O'Casey's *The plough and the stars*, in which the Pearse-like character appears off-stage as the Figure, had created enormous public controversy just a few years earlier. The performances of *The singer* and *Easter 1916* helped to maintain Pearse's elevated status within the new state. What then is the performative effect of Pearse appearing, sixteen years after his death, as a thinly disguised character in a play, and as himself, all within the same evening – and mediated through the same actor – Mac Liammóir?

Returning to an idea introduced at the beginning: I would like to consider the idea of the actor as a type of ghost. If, as Pearse suggests, one of things the spectres of the past do is to call us out of the banality of our lived experience, then we return to the metaphor of the ghost in the house to think about the work of the actor. To recall the questions: What is theatre but a site of memory? What is the actor but a type of ghost? The actor is physically present and yet is also, through the temporary displacement of his persona by another character, absent. Live actors (material bodies) appear on the stage as characters creating a particular kind of theatrical energy because they appear both as themselves and as other people. Freddie Rokem has drawn attention to what the actor 'does' rather than which character he plays; this is critical to

26 Maud Gonne MacBride, *An Phoblacht*, 27 Apr. 1933. As one newspaper reviewer noted: the death of Pearse 'marks the end of a wonderful pageant in which men and events pass in terrible procession across a sombre stage' ('Triple bill at the Gate', *Irish Times*, 29 Mar. 1932).

the credibility, emotion and energy of a performance, but, he argues, its communicative power is often overlooked. In theatre history and scholarship, he argues that the actor 'often simply appear[s] as the central ligament around which discourses of the theatre have ... been organized'.[27]

Sometimes acting is treated as if it is a more sophisticated form of 'pretending'. Acting works best when it is not merely impersonation or a representation; it is a particular form of embodiment, and, when it succeeds, an audience see ghosts: the dead and the living materialized in the same body. The cognitive dissonance involved in looking at a dead person and a live person as one (Mac Liammóir as Pearse) creates a flattening of time. By collapsing the past (the dead) into the present (the living), it presents a shared imaginative past but also an immediately accessible *now.* To the 1932 audience Pearse becomes more than a figure from the recent past, his death is prefigured in *The singer* and his place in history is secured in *Easter 1916*: he now transcends history. Raphael Samuel has written on how 'the controlled reconstruction of the past' shows neither respect for the historical record or for the historical event.[28] Pearse and Mac Liammóir shared an understanding of the power of history: Mac Liammóir, after all, was a man who had rewritten his own past, but, like Pearse, he understood the theatre as a conduit for the temporal. Incidentally, Mac Liammóir's identification with Pearse carried on into the 1950s, when he recorded a selection of 'greatest hits of the revolutionary movement' including Pearse's 'Oration over the grave of O'Donovan Rossa', 'The proclamation of the Irish Republic', and 'The fool'.[29]

CONCLUSION

Have the ghosts in the house been appeased? I hope I have shown how theatre's emphasis on the temporal, ghostly and mutable is the antithesis of the fixed and documented historical text and demands that we consider the importance of the experiential when thinking and writing about performance. Yet it also forces us to consider the importance of the theatre as a space for playing out fantasies and phantoms about the past; indeed David Lloyd argues that 'ghosts of the unlived and unworked-through past appear in oblique and unexpected ways' all the time in culture. Pearse no

27 Freddie Rokem. *Performing history* (Iowa City, 2002), p. 188.   28 Raphael Samuel, *Theatres of memory: past and present in contemporary culture* (London, 1994), p. 197.   29 Argo Records, *Revolutionary speeches and poems of Ireland* (London, 1959[?]).

longer appears as a spectral figure in Irish drama, either as demagogue or messiah, although his presence threw a long shadow over the early years of state formation. The ghosts that *now* haunt Irish theatre are not the unappeased nationalist dead: we are no longer revisited by Emmet, or Pearse or Tone. Instead, our co-habiting ghosts are the return of the psychically repressed, and the slow, painful surfacing of individual traumas and family secrets; we see this, for example, in the work of Marina Carr, of Martin MacDonagh, of Enda Walsh and of Conor McPherson. The ghosts are still in the house, despite Pearse's attempts to exorcize them; and these little 'ghosts of hope that are the afterlife of lost imaginary futures' continue to haunt and influence the Irish stage.[30]

30 David Lloyd, *Irish times: temporalities of modernity*, p. 44.

11 / Decisions at Easter: Pearse takes the stage

BARRY HOULIHAN

While most of the essays in this collection have focused their analytical energies either on Pearse the playwright, or more broadly on the correlations between Pearse's sense of the performative and his sense of the political, the focus in what follows is on the 'after-life' of Pearse as a character on stage. Most famously, and at the time controversially, we find Pearse haunting the action of Sean O'Casey's *The plough and the stars* (1926) – his off-stage absent presence given added political resonance, of course, by the fact that O'Casey presented his scathing critique of the Easter Rising's legacy in the year of its tenth anniversary. Pearse, though named within the Abbey's original prompt-book only as 'the Speaker',[1] haunts the action of the second act – set, rather provocatively for many in the audience, in a pub as Ireland's revolutionary history unfolds outside on the street – through his aural rather than physical presence. His oratory is heard (they have no choice) by Rosie Redmond and the Barman – both of whom continue with their daily life (which for Rosie includes discussing the problems of life as a prostitute in Dublin). The stage directions at either side of Pearse's speech indicate that: 'Through the window is silhouetted the figure of a tall man who is speaking to the crowd. The barman and Rosie look out the window and listen', and afterwards, 'The figure moves away to the right and is lost to sight and hearing.'[2] Physically, Pearse is a peripheral figure, with his words coming from off-stage – but the specificity of the heard speech ruptures any sense of anonymity for both the inhabitants of the pub and the audience sitting in the auditorium. After all, O'Casey put together a selection of Pearse's most intemperate language to provide the soundscape for the scene's action:

It is a glorious thing to see arms in the hands of Irishmen. We must accustom ourselves to the thought of arms, we must accustom ourselves to the sight of arms, we must accustom ourselves to the use of arms ... Bloodshed is a cleansing and sanctifying thing, and the nation that

---

1 This off-stage role is often designated as 'The Figure' in published versions of the play. 2 Sean O'Casey/Abbey Theatre, *The plough and the stars*, 8 Feb. 1926 [prompt script], Abbey Theatre Digital Archive at National University of Ireland, Galway, 3051_PS_0001, p. 30.

regards it as the final horror has lost its manhood [...] There are many things more horrible than bloodshed, and slavery is one of them.[3]

The scene is most famous for sparking outrage among many in the audience in 1926 – who received it as an attack on the sacred status not just of Pearse but of the Rising, the totemic figure of which he had now become. The ensuing disturbances during its first performances at the Abbey prompted Yeats to make one of his most famous defences of a fellow playwright, telling an unruly audience:

> You have disgraced yourselves again. Is this to be an ever-recurring celebration of the arrival of Irish genius? Synge first and then O'Casey? The news of the happenings of the last few minutes will go from country to country. Dublin has once more rocked the cradle of genius. From such a scene in this theatre went forth the fame of Synge. Equally the fame of O'Casey is born here tonight. This is his apotheosis.[4]

Given these reactions it is understandable that subsequent productions of the play kept the Pearse figure confined to an ethereal voice from beyond the scene (a 'shout in the street', as Joyce may have put it). Interestingly, a colour photograph by Alan Mac Innes,[5] retained within the production file of the 1964 production of *The plough and the stars* directed by Proinsias Mac Diarmada, depicts this bar scene but with a male character in a Volunteers uniform viewed from side profile and standing in the centre of the bar. The character is undoubtedly Pearse and this was one of the first instances – in what might well be a staged shot rather than a production image – of Pearse being brought on stage in a production of O'Casey's masterpiece. That this image occurred just two years short of the Easter Rising's fiftieth anniversary (and thirty-eight years after *The plough*'s premier) reveals much about the length of Pearse's hagiographical shadow in the first decades of the Irish state and the delicacies involved in culturally representing this icon of rebellion.

These tensions and cultural negotiations are very much in play in terms of the focus of this essay, a little-known play that premiered some five years before this fascinating production shot from *The plough and the stars* was taken.

3 Sean O'Casey, *The plough and the stars* in *Sean O'Casey: Plays*, vol. 2 (London, 1998), p. 96.   4 Robert Hogan and Richard Burnham (eds), *The years of O'Casey: 1921–1926* (Newark, Delaware, 1992), p. 281. 5 Abbey Theatre, *The plough and the stars*, 11 Feb. 1964 [photographs], Abbey Theatre Digital Archive at National University of Ireland, Galway 3872_PH_0004, p. 1.

Decision at Easter by the Limerick-born playwright Gerry Gallivan premiered at the Gate Theatre on St Patrick's Day 1959, and is notable for the realistic way in which it presents Pearse. Indeed, I argue that Gallivan's play is an important event in Irish theatre because of its realist approach in depicting Pearse and his fellow rebels on their journey from early 1916 through the turbulent days of rebellion and right up to the final decision to surrender. This significant play is valuable not least as it seems to record a process of reflective reassessment in the build-up to the commemorative energies that would surround 1966.

The play was first staged professionally (Gate Theatre, 1959) by the Globe Theatre Company and produced by Godfrey Quigley. It had been rejected by the Abbey Theatre some years previously. There had been an amateur run of the play in Gallivan's native Limerick city the previous year, and Quigley had travelled there especially to see it. It seems that Quigley was struck by the play's historical texture (its particular kind of fictionalized reality) and immediately committed to produce the play professionally in Dublin. Gallivan's archive reveals that the play went through a number of iterations in 1958,[6] and that it was originally titled *The earth shall rock* – this being a line from James Clarence Mangan's poem 'Dark Rosaleen' ('O, the Erne shall run red,/With redundance of blood,/The earth shall rock beneath our tread'). There is no record of Gallivan's rationale for changing the title of his play, but given that it was professionally produced as *Decision at Easter* in March 1959 it is fairly clear that the choice to deliberately reference Easter 1916 was made in the hope of raising its public profile. The change of title certainly did Gallivan no harm; *Decision at Easter* was well-received. In the year of the Easter Rising's fiftieth anniversary, for example, John B. Keane would write in the *Limerick Leader* that the play deserved to be part of wider national consciousness:

> In 1959, Gerry Gallivan of Limerick wrote a fine play called *Decision at Easter*. For some strange reason the Abbey Theatre turned it down. They turned down *Sive* around the same time. The Dublin critics hailed it as a fine effort and many people think the Abbey should change its spots and put on the play now ...[7]

---

6 Gallivan's archive is held within the special collections of Glucksman Library, University of Limerick.
7 John B. Keane, *Limerick Leader*, 2 Apr. 1966.

Keane's sense of the play's timeliness had already been rehearsed by the foreword, written by Ignatius Johns, to the play's publication in 1960. As Johns notes:

> Decision at Easter is not history. Obviously its main theme and happenings are based on the events leading to those terrible days of beauty as Yeats called them, the Rising of Easter 1916, but it is not history; it is not journalism; it is theatre.

The complexity of the political and cultural terrain on which Gallivan had chosen to tread is nicely summed up by Johns in the following terms:

> The problems confronting the author were of a peculiar delicacy and difficulty, for though the events are only just over forty years ago, and there are many alive today who took part, the mental pictures of the executed leaders are sacrosanct. They are regarded as heroes, as larger than life, as motivated only by the highest ideals, and even more important, as being sure of their destiny.

It is exactly because of this, Johns argues, that Gallivan's achievement seemed to him all the more remarkable:

> It is the author's triumph that in his treatment he does not adopt a 'debunking' technique, but rather humanises his characters, bringing before us people rather than the one-dimensional patriotic symbol. Here is the schoolmaster with a school to run, labour union officials who work in their union, and others who go about the ordinary business of life, while underneath they dream of freedom. They are not even fully united even in this dream, for they all see freedom as a different concept; Gaelic freedom, social freedom from want, political freedom. All these positive attributes and many that are negative meet in the play.

Perhaps with one eye on the approaching fiftieth anniversary, Johns makes the case that the piece may play its part in sweeping 'away the over-sentimental cobwebs from the statues of the 1916 leaders'. If this is the case, he concludes, Gallivan will have 'not only done service to the drama, but even to the thinking of the nation'.[8]

---

8 Ignatius Johns, 'Foreword' in G.P. Gallivan, *Decision at Easter* (Dublin, 1960), no page number.

Decision at Easter may not quite have had the radical effect predicted by Johns, but it is undoubtedly a fascinating piece in terms of the representational strategies it deploys in its depiction of Pearse in the (imaginatively reconstructed) build-up to, and aftermath of, the Easter rebellion. As partially signalled by the title, the key dramatic tension in *Decision at Easter* is provided by two major choices faced by the rebel leaders: when to launch their military action, and, in the aftermath of this action at Easter, when and how to surrender. The first two acts centre on the first of these decisions and are set in the family home of the Bradshaws – 'a comfortably furnished middle class house in a Dublin suburb'. The Bradshaws have ties to the Volunteers, and they allow their house to be used as a safe meeting venue for that organization's leaders. In a move that allows him to explore more fully the period's skein of ideological discourses, Gallivan complexifies this dramatic environment by the introduction of the family's younger son, Donal, who has rejected the Volunteers in favour of Redmond's vision. As preparations for the Easter Rising gather pace, Donal will sign up for the British army and prepare to go to France, telling his brother Mick (a fervent republican):

> My God but I'd hate to be as narrow-minded as you. Thousands of Irishmen, Irishmen are risking their lives in France, not for your Ireland alone but for the whole of Europe – but of course, they are all wrong because they don't speak Irish and shout 'To hell with the king.'[9]

These first two acts are dominated by a dramatization of the crisis talks putatively held in January 1916 between Pearse, James Connolly and other senior IRB and Volunteers members. Gallivan's subject is inspired by the contested disappearance of James Connolly and the play presents its audience with his alleged kidnapping by the Volunteers, led by Pearse, as they attempt to persuade Connolly to ease back on his openly revolutionary talk – for fear that their plans would be exposed to British intelligence.[10] Connolly, in

9 Gallivan, *Decision at Easter* (Dublin, 1960), pp 44–5.   10 The idea of a 'kidnap' was obviously dramatically fruitful territory for Gallivan, and had achieved a certain currency in the 1950s. A series of letters, for example, would play out in the *Irish Times* in May 1953, between Denis McCullagh, Geraldine Dillon Plunkett and Cathal O'Shannon, owing to O'Shannon's previous recent remarks regarding Pearse and some putative intentions to begin the Rising early in 1916. As in Gallivan's fictionalised depiction, the letters focus on the fabled meeting that was erroneously labelled as Connolly's kidnap on 19 Jan. 1916. Geraldine Dillon, sister of Joseph Plunkett, a close friend of Connolly, agrees with Cathal O'Shannon, as does McCullagh, that no 'kidnap' took place, but rather speculation got the better among some as to why James Connolly went missing for three days in January 1916.

Gallivan's version of events, is highly sceptical that the Volunteers have any real intention of moving from talk to action:

> CONNOLLY (*heavily sarcastic*): Don't tell me that you're actually working on a plan of rebellion? But this is interesting; quick, tell me; when is it to be … 1966? Of course, there's always the possibility that we mightn't be here by then … but sure, that will be all the better. And … er … oh yes, you mustn't forget to make provision in case of a wet weekend … we wouldn't want anyone catching a cold.

> PEARSE (*in a quiet but firm tone*): Connolly, the sooner you understand your position the better. You have been brought here, because you are a danger to us. (*Patiently*) You have been asked on several occasions to tone down your newspaper articles because they are likely to bring the authorities down on top of us, but you persist in being foolhardy […][11]

The mention of 1966 is just one of many meta-theatrical nods through which Gallivan signals to his audience that he is as much interested in how these characters have been represented to us in the cultural transmission of the Easter Rising as he is in the actual event itself. At a number of key moments, for example, Gallivan presents characters on stage discussing the idea of theatre as either a preparatory space for real-world rebellion or a distraction from it. The Redmondite Donal, for example, suggests that the Volunteers' 'game-playing' is performatively dangerous:

> take my word for it, all this drilling and play-acting can be dangerous. It doesn't even have to be planned. All that's needed is for one of your 'heroes' to over-act his part … and then the fat will really be in the fire.[12]

In the course of one of their more heated exchanges, Connolly dismisses Pearse as more interested in the world of make-believe than in real-world action:

> PEARSE (*quietly*): I shouldn't be too contemptuous if I were you. Theatricals when properly handled can be quite effective.

11 Gallivan, *Decision at Easter* (Dublin, 1960), p. 21.   12 Ibid., p. 12.

CONNOLLY (*mockingly*): But of course I'd forgotten! You're an old hand at the game ... St Enda's ... school plays and all the rest of it. They stimulate the imagination ... develop situations ... and, I'll admit that as situations go this one promises to be interesting ...[13]

Tellingly, the meta-theatrical conceit is given a more tragic resonance as Éamonn Ceannt and Mrs Bradshaw discuss the lack of clarity engulfing the decision to launch military action:

CEANNT (*bitterly*): Must we always be damned by this indecision. Everything set for the final match but no-one to strike it. Even at this late stage we don't know whether we are musical comedy soldiers or the genuine article.

MRS BRADSHAW (*soberly*): Don't fret yourself on that, you'll be the real thing all right when the time comes ... musical comedy soldiers don't have to die.[14]

The debates around the timing of any proposed rebellion are largely between Thomas Clarke, Seán McDermott, Pearse and Connolly. Gallivan's presentation of Pearse in these heated discussions is particularly interesting. Intent, it would seem, on distancing Pearse from those images of him as a blinkered fanatic, Gallivan presents us with a man who is always open to other perspectives, other possible courses of action. Indeed Gallivan presents Pearse's fellow rebels attacking him for just this tendency towards equivocation:

McDERMOTT: Ah, you're too tolerant for your own peace of mind. Take my word for it Pat, there are only two ways to look at anything ... God's for the good of the soul and your own for the comfort of your body.

CLARKE: He's right in a way, P.H., you cause yourself a lot of trouble by seeing the other point of view too clearly. You've got to be a good hater to be a really effective leader.[15]

No original manuscript of the play survives. The text of the play was published in 1960. A later script, which has been heavily annotated and edited

13 Ibid., p. 19. 14 Ibid., p. 58. 15 Ibid., p. 8.

by Gallivan, also survives. This is presumably a working script linked to a later production, probably that of 1966. The changes made to the original published text in this typewritten script reveal some really useful insights into Gallivan's sense of Pearse's interior life. In particular, the annotations made to the typewritten script record a series of fascinating changes of tack as the playwright clearly struggled with the version of Pearse he sought to present to his audience. In the typed script, for example, Pearse openly admits that the rebellion could only really have had one outcome: 'We always knew there could only have been one ending for us. Anyway, we're in no position to dictate terms.'[16] Tellingly, these lines, which reveal a resignation to fate, are in turn completely crossed out by Gallivan. Some proposed lines for Pearse concerning England's possible weakness in the midst of the Great War also undergo revision. While in the original text Pearse simply states, 'We'll not argue any further on that', this is later adjusted to read, 'We'll argue that another day. The first thing is to ask for a meeting to discuss terms.'[17] Interestingly, Gallivan seems intent on depicting Pearse as actively thinking about participating in the consequences of the Rising, something that would involve prolonged face-to-face meetings and focused deliberations with the British. This nuanced re-presentation of Pearse positions him as someone who saw military action as just a necessary first step on the road to more democratic systems for delivering change.

These exchanges towards the end of the play take place on 29 April in the 'top room of a house in Moore Street'. At their heart stands the second 'decision at Easter' for the rebel leaders – whether or not to lay down their arms and surrender to the British forces. Having established Pearse as someone prone to equivocation and 'fuzzy logic', in these final moments Gallivan seems impelled to leave his audience with an image of Pearse that is much closer to the object of nationalist hagiographical desire. Pearse, while noting that there 'comes a time in every battle when the easiest thing left is to fight on', nevertheless demonstrates absolute clarity in the need to surrender in order to save the city from more bloodshed and physical damage.[18] Once again, in the play's final moment, the stage is enveloped in a kind of meta-theatrical haze as the imagined action from 1916 blurs with its reception in the contemporary moment occupied by the piece's audience. As Gallivan's version of Pearse puts it: 'I wish all the same that we could see forward a few years. If anything should happen to me I'll never know the result of this Rising ...

16 Gallivan Archive, Glucksman Library, University of Limerick, P30/356. 17 Ibid. 18 Gallivan, *Decision at Easter* (Dublin, 1960), p. 65.

and that will be the hardest part of it.'[19] The very final lines of the play indeed seem directly aimed at the audience – they also partially return Pearse to a space of hesitancy and historical apprehension: 'these days of Easter will be remembered … if only we could be sure of that'.[20]

I believe the decision by Gallivan to write *Decision at Easter* in the period immediately preceding the fiftieth anniversary of the 1916 Rising was a conscious effort to re-engage national thought and empathy with the Rising's major cultural figure. Where O'Casey deliberately separated the body and voice of Pearse and framed his voice to break through into a Dublin pub from its exterior streetscape, Gallivan succeeds in a role reversal. He made the courageous decision to formulate a drama that would, as Gallivan himself described, show the leaders of 1916, and especially Pearse, not just as figures of recent history, but as 'human beings'.[21] I would argue that this play adds an important facet to the study of Patrick Pearse, not just to the understanding of how he is featured in dramatic representation but also to wider historical and social criticism. Gallivan presents a version of Pearse who was deeply complex, nuanced but also at times equivocal about the desired outcomes and potential achievements of the Rising.

19 Ibid., p. 73. 20 Ibid., p. 74. 21 *Evening Herald*, 18 Mar. 1959.

Bibliography/*Leabharliosta*

Adamson, Walter L., *Embattled avant-gardes: modernism's resistance to commodity culture in Europe* (Berkeley, 2007).

Agamben, Giorgio, *Homo sacer: sovereign power and bare life* (Stanford, CA, 1998).

Agamben, Giorgio, *State of exception* (Chicago, 2005).

Alderson, David, *Mansex fine: religion, manliness and imperialism in nineteenth-century British culture* (Manchester, 1998).

Anderson, Benedict, *Imagined communities: reflections on the origins and spread of nationalism* (London, 1991).

Augusteijn, Joost, *Patrick Pearse: the making of a revolutionary* (Basingstoke, 2010).

Augusteijn, Joost, 'The road to rebellion: the development of Patrick Pearse's political thought, 1879–1914' in Roisín Higgins and Regina Uí Chollatáin (eds), *The life and after-life of P.H. Pearse* (Dublin, 2009).

Bell, Sam Hanna, *The theatre in Ulster* (Dublin, 1972).

Benjamin, Walter, *Illuminations*, trans. Harry Zohn, ed. Hannah Arendt (New York, 2007).

Berlin, Isaiah, *The roots of Romanticism* (Princeton, 2001).

Bourke, Angela, 'The imagined community of Pearse's short stories' in Roisín Higgins and Regina Uí Chollatáin (eds), *The life and after-life of P.H. Pearse* (Dublin, 2009).

Breatnach, Caoimhín, 'Exploiting the past: Pearse as editor and interpreter of *fiannaíocht* literature', in Roisín Higgins and Regina Uí Chollatáin (eds), *The life and after-life of P.H. Pearse* (Dublin, 2009).

Brecht, Bertolt, 'A short organum for the theatre' (1948) in John Willet (ed.), *Brecht on theatre* (London, 1964).

Brecht, Bertolt, 'The modern theatre is the epic theatre' (1930) in John Willet (ed.), *Brecht on theatre* (London, 1964).

Buhlmann, Otto, *Yeats and Nietzsche: an exploration of major Nietzschean echoes in the writings of W.B. Yeats* (Totowa, NJ, 1982).

Bunting, Edward, *The ancient music of Ireland* (Dublin, 1840).

Butler, Judith, *Frames of war: when is life grievable?* (London, 2009).

Butler, Judith, *Precarious life: the powers of mourning and violence* (London, 2006).

Cairns, David and Shaun Richards, *Writing Ireland: colonialism, nationalism, and culture* (Manchester, 1988).

Carty, Xavier, *In bloody protest: the tragedy of Patrick Pearse* (Dublin, 1978).

Clancy, W.F., *The Suburban Groove*, National Library of Ireland, MS 29, 123.

Clarke, Austin, 'A centenary celebration', *Massachusetts Review*, 5:2 (1964), 307–10.

Cleary, Arthur, 'Patrick Pearse's only case' in Louis Walsh, *Old friends: being memories of men and places* (Dundalk, 1934).

Colum, Mary, *Life and the dream* (London, 1947).

Colum, Padraic, 'Padraic Pearse' in Maurice Joy (ed.), *The Irish rebellion of 1916 and its martyrs: Erin's tragic Easter* (New York, 1916).

Crowley, Brian, '"His father's son": James and Pádraic Pearse', *Folk Life: Journal of Ethnological Studies*, 43 (2004–5), 71–88.

Cullingford, Elizabeth Butler, 'Thinking of her ... as ... Ireland: Yeats, Pearse and Heaney', *Textual Practice* 4:1 (1990), 1–21.

Curran, Constantine, 'Review', *Motley*, 1:2 (April 1932).

Czira, Sydney, *The years flew by* (Dublin, 1974).

Das, Santanu, *Touch and intimacy in First World War literature* (Cambridge, 2005).

Dean, Joan Fitzpatrick, *All dressed up: modern Irish historical pageantry* (Syracuse, NY, 2014).

Deane, Seamus, *Celtic revivals: essays in modern Irish literature* (Winston-Salem, NC, 1987).

Denvir, Síle, *Caithréim: ceol agus amhráin ó dhrámaí an Phiarsaigh* (CICD 202, 2016).

Derrida, Jacques, 'Before the law' in Derek Attridge (ed.), *Jacques Derrida: acts of literature* (London, 1992).

Dowling, Linda, *Hellenism and homosexuality in Victorian Oxford* (Ithaca, NY, 1994).

Dunn, James D.G., *The theology of Paul the Apostle* (Grand Rapids, MI, 2006).

Edwards, Hilton and Micheál Mac Liammóir, *The Ford of the Hurdles* (1929), National Library of Ireland, MS 24, 562.

Edwards, Ruth Dudley, *Patrick Pearse: the triumph of failure* (Dublin, 2006).

Eksteins, Modris, *Rites of spring: the Great War and the birth of the modern age* (New York, 2000).

Eliot, T.S., '*Ulysses*, order and myth' in Clive Hart and David Hayman (eds), *James Joyce's Ulysses: critical essays* (Berkeley, 1974).

Esty, Jed, *Unseasonable youth: modernism, colonialism and the fiction of development* (Oxford, 2012).

Fairhall, James, *James Joyce and the question of history* (Cambridge, 1995).

Faraday, L. Winifred (trans.), *The cattle raid of Cualnge* (London, 1904).

Feeney, William, *Drama in Hardwicke Street: a history of the Irish Theatre Company* (Rutherford, NJ, 1984).

Felski, Rita, *The gender of modernity* (Cambridge, MA, 1995).

Floyd, Kevin, *The reification of desire: towards a queer Marxism* (Minneapolis, 2009).

Foster, R.F., *Vivid faces: the revolutionary generation in Ireland, 1890–1923* (London, 2014).

Foster, R.F., *W.B. Yeats: a life, i: The apprentice mage, 1865–1914* (Oxford, 1998).

Gallivan, G.P., *Decision at Easter* (Dublin, 1960).

Gerson, Gal, 'Cultural subversion and the background of the Irish "Easter poets"', *Journal of Contemporary History*, 30:2 (1995), 333–47.

Girard, René, *The scapegoat* (Baltimore, MD, 1986).

Gordon, Avery, *Haunting and the sociological imagination* (Minneapolis, 1997).

Griffin, Roger, *Modernism and fascism: the sense of a beginning under Mussolini and Hitler* (London, 2007).

Grotowski, Jerzy, *Towards a poor theatre* (New York, 1968).

Gurr, Andrew, *Playgoing in Shakespeare's London* (Cambridge, 2004).

Hauptmann, Gerhart, *Hannele*, trans. Charles Henry Meltzer (New York, 1908).

Hauptmann, Gerhart, *The dramatic works of Gerhart Hauptmann, iii: Domestic dramas*, ed. Ludwig Lewisohn (New York, 1914).

Hay, Marnie, 'An Irish nationalist adolescence: Na Fianna Éireann, 1909–23' in Catherine Cox and Susannah Riordan (eds), *Adolescence in modern Irish history* (Basingstoke, 2015).

Hay, Marnie, *Bulmer Hobson and the nationalist movement in twentieth-century Ireland* (Manchester, 2009).

Hay, Marnie, 'Explaining *Uladh*: cultural nationalism in Ulster' in Betsey Taylor FitzSimon and James H. Murphy (eds), *The Irish revival reappraised* (Dublin, 2004).

Hay, Marnie, 'From rogue revolutionary to rogue civil servant: the resurrection of Bulmer Hobson' in Diarmaid Ferriter and Susannah Riordan (eds), *Years of turbulence: the Irish revolution and its aftermath* (Dublin, 2015).

Hay, Marnie, 'Kidnapped: Bulmer Hobson, the IRB and the 1916 Easter Rising', *Canadian Journal of Irish Studies*, 35:1 (Spring 2009), 55–6.

Hay, Marnie, 'The foundation and development of Na Fianna Éireann, 1909–16', *Irish Historical Studies*, 36:141 (May 2008), 53–71.

Hay, Marnie, 'The propaganda of Na Fianna Éireann, 1909–1926' in Mary Shine Thompson (ed.), *Young Irelands* (Dublin, 2011).

Hill, Rosemary, *God's architect: Pugin and the building of Romantic Britain* (London, 2007).

Hobbes, Thomas, *Leviathan* (Oxford, 2008 [1651]).

Hobsbawm, Eric, *The age of empire: 1875–1914* (London, 1994).

Hobson, Bulmer, *Ireland yesterday and tomorrow* (Tralee, 1968).

Hobson, Bulmer (ed.), *The Gate Theatre* (Dublin, 1934).

Hobson, Mary, *Memoirs of six generations* (Belfast, 1947).

Hogan, Robert and Richard Burnham (eds), *The years of O'Casey: 1921–1926* (Newark, Delaware, 1992), p. 281.

Hudson, Henry (ed.), *The Citizen or Dublin Monthly Magazine* (Dublin, Jan.–Dec. 1841).

Hudson, Henry (ed.), *The Dublin Monthly Magazine: being a new series of the Citizen: and including the native music of Ireland* (Dublin, Jan.–June 1842).

Hyde, Douglas, *Love songs of Connacht* (Dublin, 1968).

Innes, C.L., *Women and nation in Irish literature and society, 1880–1915* (London, 1993).

Jameson, Fredric, *A singular modernity* (London, 2002).

Jaspers, Karl, *Philosophy, ii: Existential Elucidation* (Chicago, 1969).

Joyce, James, 'Ireland at the Bar' in Ellmann and Mason (eds), *The critical writings of James Joyce* (London, 1959).

Joyce, P.W., *Irish music and song: a collection of songs in the Irish language, set to music/edited for the Society for the Preservation of the Irish Language* (Dublin, 1901).

Kafka, Franz, 'At the door of the law' in *Franz Kafka: stories, 1904–1924* (London, 1995).

Kafka, Franz, 'Reflections on sin, pain, hope and the true way' in *The Great Wall of China: stories and reflections* (New York, 1970).

Kantorowicz, Ernst H., *The king's two bodies: a study in medieval political theology* (Princeton, 1957).

Kennedy, David, 'Ulster unionism and the new nationalism' in Kevin B. Nowlan (ed.), *The making of 1916* (Dublin, 1969).

Kiberd, Declan, 'Patrick Pearse: Irish modernist' in Roisín Higgins and Regina Uí Chollatáin (eds), *The life and after-life of P.H. Pearse* (Dublin, 2009).

Kimmel, Michael, *Manhood in America: a cultural history* (New York, 1996).

Lee, J.J., 'Pearse, Patrick Henry' in James McGuire and James Quinn (eds), *Dictionary of Irish biography* (Cambridge, 2009).

Leerssen, Joep, *Remembrance and imagination: patterns in the historical and literary representation of Ireland in the nineteenth century* (Cork, 1996).

Le Roux, Louis, *Patrick H. Pearse*, trans. Desmond Ryan (Dublin, 1932).

Levitas, Ben, *The theatre of nation: Irish drama and cultural nationalism, 1890–1916* (Oxford, 2002).

Lloyd, David, *Irish times: temporalities of modernity* (Dublin, 2008).

Mac Congáil, Nollaig and Eadaoin Ní Mhuircheartaigh, *Drámaí Thús na hAthbheochana*, (Galway, 2008).

Mac Liammóir, Micheál, *All for Hecuba* (Dublin, 1961).

Marinetti, Filippo Tommaso, 'The founding and manifesto of Futurism' in *Marinetti: selected writings*, ed. R.W. Flint (London, 1972).

Marinetti, Filippo Tommaso, 'The pleasure of being booed' in *Marinetti: selected writings*, ed. R.W. Flint (London, 1972).

Marx, Karl, *Critique of Hegel's 'Philosophy of right'*, ed. Joseph O'Malley (Cambridge, 1970).

Mathews, P.J. and Declan Kiberd (eds), *Handbook of the Irish revival: an anthology of Irish cultural and political writings, 1891–1921* (Dublin, 2015).

Mays, Michael, *Nation states: the cultures of Irish nationalism* (Lanham, MD, 2007).

McCormack, Barbara, 'Patrick Pearse: The master' in David Bracken (ed.), *The end of all things earthly* (Dublin, 2016), pp 81–3.

McGarry, Fearghal, *The Abbey rebels of 1916: a lost revolution* (London, 2015).

McNulty, Eugene, '"Draw it not too rigidly": *Ulad* and the cultural partition debate' in Alison O'Malley-Younger and Frank Beardow (eds), *Representing Ireland: past, present and future* (Sunderland, 2005).

McNulty, Eugene, *The Ulster Literary Theatre and the Northern revival* (Cork, 2008).

Michelet, Jules, 'On the unity of fatherland, from historical view of the French

Revolution from its earliest indications to the flight of the king in 1791' in Hans Kohn (ed.), *Nationalism: its meaning and history* (Princeton, 1955).

Mitchell, W.J.T., 'What is an image?', *New Literary History*, 15:3 (Spring 1984).

Moffat, Alfred, *The minstrelsy of Ireland: 206 Irish songs adapted to their traditional airs, arranged for voice with pianoforte accompaniment, and supplemented with historical notes* (London, 1897).

Moran, James (ed.), *Four Irish rebel plays* (Dublin, 2007).

Moran, James, '"He calls his dada still": nineteenth-century English radicalism and the drama of Pádraic Pearse', *Kritika Kultura*, 14 (2010), 53–74.

Moran, James, *Staging the Easter Rising: 1916 as theatre* (Cork, 2005).

Morash, Christopher, *A history of Irish theatre, 1601–2000* (Cambridge, 2002).

Morris, Catherine, *Alice Milligan and the Irish cultural revival* (Dublin, 2012).

Murphy, Gerard, *Early Irish lyrics: eighth to twelfth century* (Oxford, 1970).

Ní Chonghaile, Deirdre, 'Róisín Dubh: mar a chruthaigh Seán Ó Riada aintiún an Éirí Amach', *COMHARTaighde* 1 [Idirlíon]. Ar fáil ag: *www.comhartaighde.com/eagrain/ 1/nichonghaile/*.

Ní Fhlathúin, Máire, 'The anti-colonial modernism of Patrick Pearse' in Howard J. Booth and Nigel Rigby (eds), *Modernism and empire* (Manchester, 2000).

Ní Ghairbhí, Róisín, 'A people that did not exist? Reflections on some sources and contexts for Patrick Pearse's militant nationalism' in Ruán O'Donnell (ed.), *The impact of the 1916 Rising* (Dublin, 2008).

Ní Ghairbhí, Róisín, '"The battle before us now is a battle of words": Pearse and postcolonial theory' in Roisín Higgins and Regina Uí Chollatáin (eds), *The life and after-life of P.H. Pearse* (Dublin, 2009).

Ní Ghairbhí, Róisín, *Willie Pearse*, 16 Lives (Dublin, 2015).

Ní Ghairbhí, Róisín and Eugene McNulty (eds), *Patrick Pearse: collected plays/Drámaí an Phiarsaigh* (Dublin, 2013).

Nic Congáil, Ríona, '"Some of you will curse her": women's writing during the Irish-language revival', *Proceedings of the Harvard Celtic Colloquium*, 29 (2009).

Nic Shiubhlaigh, Máire, *The splendid years* (Dublin, 1955).

Nicholson, David, 'Hauptmann's Hannele: naturalistic fairy tale and dream play', *Modern Drama*, 24:3 (Fall 1981), 282–91.

O'Boyle, Seán, 'Hardebeck', *Capuchin Annual* (1948).

Ó Buachalla, Séamas, *A significant Irish educationalist: the educational writings of P.H. Pearse* (Cork, 1980).

Ó Buachalla, Séamas (ed.), *The letters of P.H. Pearse* (Dublin, 1980).

Ó Buachalla, Séamas (ed.), *The literary writings of Patrick Pearse* (Dublin, 1979).

O'Casey, Sean, *Drums under the window* (London, 1945).

O'Casey, Sean, *The plough and the stars* in *Sean O'Casey: Plays*, vol. 2 (London, 1998).

Ó Cathasaigh, Aindrias (eag.), *An Barr Bua* (Baile Átha Cliath, 2012).

Ó Coigligh, Ciarán (eag.), *Filíocht Ghaeilge Phádraig Mhic Phiarais* (Baile Átha Cliath, 1981).

O'Donnell, Mary Louise, 'Owen Lloyd: de-anglicizing of the Irish harp', *Éire-Ireland*, 48: 3–4 (Fall/Winter 2013), 155–75.

Ó Duinnín, Pádraig (eag.), *Amhráin Sheagháin Chláraigh Mhic Dhomhnaill* (Baile Átha Cliath, 1902).

Ó hAnnracháin, Peadar, *Mar Mhaireas É* (Baile Átha Cliath, 1955).

Ó hEidhin, Mícheál (eag.), *Cas amhrán* (Indreabhán, Conamara, 1975).

O'Leary, Philip, 'The Irish renaissance, 1880–1940: literature in Irish' in Margaret Kelleher and Philip O'Leary (eds), *The Cambridge history of Irish literature*, 2 vols (Cambridge, 2006).

O'Leary, Philip, *The prose literature of the Gaelic revival, 1881–1921: ideology and innovation* (University Park, PA, 1994).

Ó Lochlainn, Colm (eag.), *An claisceadal* (Baile Átha Cliath, 1930).

Ó Máille, Micheál and Tomás Ó Máille (eag.), *Amhráin Chlainne Gael* (Indreabhán, 1991).

Ó Maoil Íosa, Liam (Liam Mellows), 'Boy Scouts organising notes', *Irish Volunteer*, 7 Feb. 1914.

Ó Morónaigh, Seán, *Agallaimh na hÉigse, Cíoradh agus Cnuasach* (Camas, 2001).

O'Neill, Daniel, 'The cult of self-sacrifice: the Irish experience', *Éire-Ireland*, 24:4 (Winter 1989).

Ó Siadhail, Pádraig, *Stair dhrámaíocht na Gaeilge, 1900–1970* (Indreabhán, Conamara, 1993).

Óg Ó Tuama, Seán (eag.), *An chóisir cheoil* (Baile Átha Cliath, 1958).

Ógra Éireann, *Amhránleabhar Ógra Éireann* (Dublin, 1950).

Pearse, James, 'England's duty to Ireland', National Library of Ireland, MS 21,079, f.16.

Pearse, Mary Brigid, *The home life of P.H. Pearse* (Dublin, 1934).

Pearse, Patrick, 'An ideal in education', *Irish Review*, 4:41 (June 1914), 170–3.

Pearse, Patrick, *Collected works of Pádraic H. Pearse: songs of the Irish rebels and specimens from an Irish anthology* (Dublin, n.d.).

Pearse, Patrick, *Collected works of Pádraic H. Pearse: plays, stories, poems* (New York, 1917).

Pearse, Patrick, *Collected works of Pádraic H. Pearse: political writings and speeches* (Dublin, 1924).

Pearse, Patrick, *Ghosts* (Dublin, 1915).

Pearse, Patrick, *Maingín scéal* (Dublin, 1936).

Pearse, Patrick, *Short stories*, ed. Anne Markey, trans. Joseph Campbell (Dublin, 2009).

Pearse, Patrick, 'The keening woman' in Joseph Campbell (ed.), *Plays, stories, poems* (Dublin, 1980).

Pearse, Patrick, *The murder machine* (Dublin, 1916).

Pearse, Patrick, 'The sovereign people', Tracts for the Times 13, (Dublin, 1916).

Petrie, George, *The ancient music of Ireland*, vol. 1 (Dublin, 1855).

Phelan, Mark, 'The rise and fall of the Ulster Literary Theatre' (MPhil, Trinity College Dublin, 1998).

Porter, Raymond J., *P.H. Pearse* (New York, 1973).

Pound, Ezra, *The selected letters of Ezra Pound to John Quinn, 1915–1924*, ed. Timothy Materer (Durham, NC, 1991).

Prozorov, Sergei, *Agamben and politics: a critical introduction* (Edinburgh, 2014).

Quinn, Vincent, 'Fostering the nation: Patrick Pearse and pedagogy', *New Formations*, 42 (2001), 71–84.

Ricoeur, Paul, 'Myth as the bearer of possible worlds' in Mark Patrick Hederman and Richard Kearney (eds), *Crane Bag book of Irish studies* (Dublin, 1982).

Rojek, Paweł, 'Mesjanizm integralny', *Pressje*, 28 (2012).

Rokem, Freddie, *Performing history* (Iowa City, 2002).

Rubin, Miri, *Corpus Christi: the Eucharist in late medieval culture* (Cambridge, 1991).

Rutherford, Jonathan, *Forever England: reflections on masculinity and empire* (London, 1997).

Ryan, Desmond, *Remembering Sion: a chronicle of storm and quiet* (London, 1934).

Ryan, Desmond, *The man called Pearse* (Dublin, 1919).

Ryan, Desmond, *The story of a success: being a record of St Enda's College, September 1908 to Easter 1916*, (Dublin, 1919).

Ryan, Phyllis, *The company I kept* (Dublin, 1996).

Samuel, Raphael, *Theatres of memory: past and present in contemporary culture* (London, 1994).

Schmitt, Carl, *Political theology: four chapters on the concept of sovereignty* (Chicago, 2006).

Schrag, Oswald O., *Existence, existenz, and transcendence: an introduction to the philosophy of Karl Jaspers* (Pittsburgh, 1971).

Shaw, Leroy R., *The playwright and historical change: dramatic strategies in Brecht, Hauptmann, Kaiser and Wedekind* (Madison, 1970).

Sisson, Elaine, *Pearse's patriots: St Enda's and the cult of boyhood* (Cork, 2004).

Spivak, Gayatri Chakravorty, 'Can the subaltern speak?' in Patrick Williams and Laura Chrisman (eds), *Colonial discourse and post-colonial theory: a reader* (Harlow, 1994).

Sweeney, Joseph A., 'In the G.P.O.: the fighting men' in F.X. Martin (ed.), *The Easter Rising, 1916 and University College, Dublin* (Dublin, 1966).

Szondi, Peter, *Theory of the modern drama*, ed. and trans. Michael Hays (Cambridge, 1987 [1956]).

Tagore, Rabindranath, *The post office*, trans. Devabrata Mukerjea (Dundrum, 1914).

Talmon, Jacob, *The political messianism: a romantic phase* (New York, 1961).

Tomaszewski, Nikodem Bończa, *Źródła narodowości: powstanie i rozwój polskiej świadomości narodowej w II połowie XIX i na początku XX wieku* (Wrocław, 2006). [*Sources of nationalities: the emergence and development of the Polish consciousness in the second half of the nineteenth and early twentieth century.*]

Tone, William Theobald Wolfe, 'A last effort; Tone's death' in Theobald Wolfe Tone, *The autobiography of Theobald Wolfe Tone, 1763–1798*, vol. 3, ed. R. Barry O'Brien (London, 1893).

Trencsenyi, Balazs and Michal Kopeček (eds), *National romanticism: the formation of national movements* (Budapest, 2013).

Trotter, Mary, *Ireland's national theaters: political performance and the origins of the Irish dramatic movement* (Syracuse, NY, 2001).

Trotter, Mary, *Modern Irish theatre* (Cambridge, MA, 2008).

Turner, Victor, 'Betwixt and between: the liminal period in rites of passage', *Proceedings of the American Ethnological Society* (1964).

Turpin, John, *A school of art in Dublin since the eighteenth century: a history of the National College of Art and Design* (Dublin, 1995).

Turpin, John, *Oliver Sheppard: symbolist sculptor of the Irish revival, 1865–1941* (Dublin, 2000).

Uther, Hans-Jörg, *The types of the international folktale: a classification and bibliography* (Helsinki, 2004).

Valente, Joseph, *The myth of manliness in Irish national culture, 1880–1922* (Springfield, MA, 2011).

Vandevelde, Karen, *The alternative dramatic revival in Ireland* (Dublin, 2005).

Voegelin, Eric, *The new science of politics* (Chicago, 1951).

Walsh, Brendan, 'Radicalising the classroom: Pearse, pedagogy of progressivism' in Roisín Higgins and Regina Uí Chollatáin (eds), *The life and after-life of P.H. Pearse* (Dublin, 2009).

Walsh, Brendan, *The pedagogy of protest: the educational thought and work of Patrick H. Pearse* (Oxford, 2007).

Walsh, Brendan J., 'The progressive credentials of Patrick Henry Pearse: a response to David Limond', *History of Education Review*, 35:2 (2006).

Welch, Robert (ed.), *The concise Oxford companion to Irish literature* (Oxford, 2000).

Wood, Michael, *Yeats and violence* (Oxford, 2010).

Yeats, W.B., 'Preface' in Rabindranath Tagore, *The post office* (London, 1914).

Yeats, W.B., *The collected poems of W.B. Yeats* (London, 2000).

Zimmermann, Georges D., *Songs of Irish rebellion: Irish political street ballads and rebel songs, 1780–1900* (Dublin, 2002).

Contributors

MICHAEL G. CRONIN is a lecturer in the Department of English at Maynooth University. His monograph *Impure thoughts: sexuality, Catholicism and literature in twentieth-century Ireland* was published by Manchester UP in 2012, and he is the author of essays on twentieth-century Irish fiction and on contemporary Irish sexual and gender politics.

BRIAN CROWLEY is the curator of the Pearse Museum in Rathfarnham. He is the author of *Patrick Pearse: a life in pictures* and has contributed articles to *The life and after-life of P.H. Pearse* and *Making 1916: material and visual culture of the 1916 Rising*. He is also the current chairperson of the Irish Museums Association.

SÍLE DENVIR is a lecturer in Fiontar & Scoil na Gaeilge, Dublin City University. She has a particular interest in newly composed Irish-language song and in 2008 Cló Iar-Chonnacht published her book *Dearcadh an tSaoil: Amhráin Chiaráin Uí Fhátharta*, an edition of songs composed by the Connemara songwriter Ciarán Ó Fátharta, including a critical analysis of the songs and their context. The CD/booklet *Caithréim: ceol agus amhráin ó dhrámaí an Phiarsaigh*, based on her current research project on music and song from the plays of Patrick Pearse, was published by Cló Iar-Chonnacht in 2016.

Is léachtóir Gaeilge í Síle Denvir in Ollscoil Chathair Bhaile Átha Cliath. Tá suim faoi leith aici in amhránaíocht nuachumtha na Gaeilge agus d'fhoilsigh Cló Iar-Chonnacht a leabhar *Dearcadh an tSaoil: Amhráin Chiaráin Uí Fhátharta*, eagrán criticiúil d'amhráin a chum an t-amhránaí Ciarán Ó Fátharta, maille le réamhaiste chomhthéacsúil i 2008. Tá dlúthdhiosca agus leabhrán darb ainm *Caithréim: ceol agus amhráin ó dhrámaí an Phiarsaigh* (CIC, 2016) curtha i dtoll a chéile aici bunaithe ar an ábhar atá faoi thrácht sa leabhar seo.

MARNIE HAY is a lecturer in history at the St Patrick's Campus of Dublin City University. She is the author of *Bulmer Hobson and the nationalist movement in twentieth-century Ireland* (Manchester, 2009). Her current research focuses on Irish nationalist youth culture in the early twentieth century.

BARRY HOULIHAN is an archivist at the James Hardiman Library, NUI Galway, and a PhD candidate in the School of English, researching theatre, politics and society in modernising Ireland.

ANNE MARKEY is president of the Irish Society for the Study of Children's Literature and a literature tutor with the Open Education unit of Dublin City University. Her research focuses on Oscar Wilde; Patrick Pearse; uses of folklore in Irish writing in English; literary representations of childhood from the seventeenth century to the present day; and early children's fiction. Among other publications, she is the author of *Oscar Wilde's fairy tales: origins and contexts* (2011); editor of *Children's fiction, 1765–1808* (2011); and co-editor of *Folklore and modern Irish writing* (2014).

EUGENE McNULTY is a member of the School of English, Dublin City University. His research mainly focuses on the various social and political contexts that have helped shape Irish literature and drama from the late nineteenth century to the present. His publications include: *The Ulster Literary Theatre and the Northern revival*; *Patrick Pearse: complete plays/Drámaí an Phiarsaigh* (co-edited with Róisín Ní Ghairbhí); and *Hearing Heaney* (co-edited with Ciarán Mac Murchaidh).

JAMES MORAN is a professor of modern English literature and drama at the University of Nottingham. His research has often focused on twentieth-century theatre in Ireland and Britain, and his books include *Staging the Easter Rising*; *Irish Birmingham*, *The theatre of Seán O'Casey* and *The theatre of D.H. Lawrence*. He is also co-editor (with Neal Alexander) of *Regional modernisms*.

RÓISÍN NÍ GHAIRBHÍ is a lecturer in Roinn na Gaeilge in Mary Immaculate College, Limerick. She has published widely on Irish-language literature and is the author of *Willie Pearse* (2015), in the O'Brien Press 16 Lives series, and co-editor with Eugene McNulty of *Patrick Pearse: collected plays/Drámaí an Phiarsaigh* with Irish Academic Press (2013). She is a member of the board of Imram, the Irish Language Festival of Literature and Culture, and active in Conradh na Gaeilge.

Tá an Dr Róisín Ní Ghairbhí ina léachtóir i Roinn na Gaeilge i gColáiste Mhuire gan Smal. Tá ailt iomadúla foilsithe aici ar ghnéithe éagsúla den litríocht. Foilsíodh a beathaisnéis ar *Willie Pearse* mar chuid den tsraith 16 Lives ag O'Brien Press sa bhliain 2015 agus bhí sí mar cho-eagarthóir ar an leabhar

Patrick Pearse: collected plays/Drámaí an Phiarsaigh (Irish Academic Press, 2013). Tá sí mar bhall de Bhord na Féile Imram agus tá sí gníomhach i gConradh na Gaeilge.

MACIEJ RUCZAJ is a graduate from the Department of Anglophone Literatures and Cultures and the Institute of Political Science at Charles University in Prague. He has recently completed his PhD on Patrick Pearse's 'political theology' at the Prague Centre for Irish Studies. He has published several articles on Patrick Pearse's writings, with a special attention to its religious dimension. He is also the author of several books on the contemporary political thought and modern history of his native Poland.

ELAINE SISSON is a senior lecturer in visual culture in the Department of Design and Visual Arts at IADT, specializing in Irish modernism, theatre and costume-design history and Irish cultural history. She is the author of *Pearse's patriots: the cult of boyhood at St Enda's*, and, with Linda King, *Ireland, design and visual culture: negotiating modernity, 1922–1992*. She has been an historical commentator for radio and television documentaries on the Irish revolutionary period and a podcast of her research on Pearse may be heard on the UCD Scholarcast website. She was a co-founder of the Graduate School of Creative Arts and Media (GradCAM), providing doctoral training for creative-arts practitioners, and was recently awarded a Moore Institute Fellowship in NUI Galway as part of her new research on theatre, culture and experiment in the Irish Free State.

Index